ROME

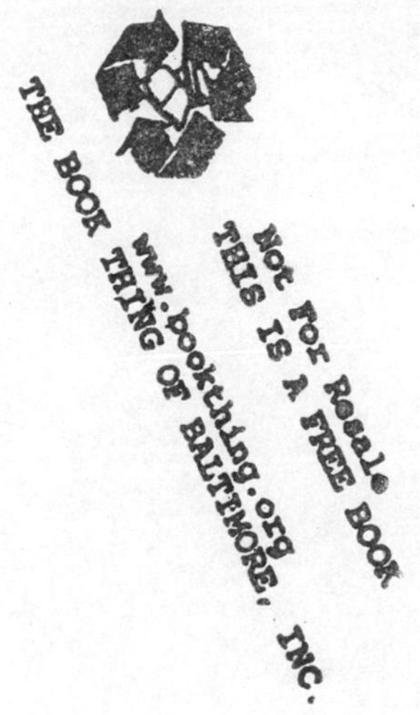
Not For Resale
THIS IS A FREE BOOK
www.bookthing.org
THE BOOK THING OF BALTIMORE, INC.

The Buildings of Europe

ROME

Christopher Woodward

Manchester University Press
Manchester and New York
Distributed exclusively in the USA and Canada by St. Martin's Press

The she-wolf, Romulus and Remus, Campidoglio

Published by
Manchester University Press
Oxford Road, Manchester M13 9NR, UK
and
Room 400, 175 Fifth Avenue,
New York, NY 10010, USA

Distributed exclusively in the USA and Canada by
St. Martin's Press, Inc., 175 Fifth Avenue,
New York, NY 10010, USA

British Library Cataloguing-in-Publication data
A catalogue record for this book is available from the British Library

Library of Congress-Cataloging-in-Publication data
Woodward, Christopher.
The buildings of Europe: Rome / Christopher Woodward.
p. cm,
Includes index.
ISBN 0-7190-4031-0, — ISBN 0-7190-4032-9 (alk. paper)
1. Architecture—Italy—Rome. 2. Rome (Italy)—Buildings, structures, etc. I. Title
NA1120.W66 1995
720'.945'632—dc20 95–22749
CIP

ISBN 0 7190 4031 0 *hardback*
ISBN 0 7190 4032 9 *paperback*

First published 1995

99 98 97 96 95 10 9 8 7 6 5 4 3 2 1

Typography by Nick Loat

Layout by the author

Printed in Great Britain by
Redwood Books, Trowbridge, Wiltshire

How to use this guide

There are 217 *entries*—buildings, squares, parks, engineering structures—arranged chronologically. Each entry has a *reference number.* This is followed by an uppercase letter which is the key to one of the five maps at the end of the book. The four maps A to D, each representing a 2.5 kilometre square, cover the area of Rome inside the Aurelian Wall. Map E covers the 15 kilometre square area which includes most of present-day Rome. A lowercase letter follows the map letter: this indicates the smaller square on the map in which the entry is to be found. Where appropriate, the nearest Metropolitana station 'M', and its line 'A' or 'B', are given for each entry.

Some entries are followed by the symbol ☞. This means 'nearby' and the text following gives the reference number of entries which are nearby, and may mention other buildings which, while of some interest, do not warrant a fuller description. The symbol is also used on the maps to point to nearby entries on neighbouring maps.

The inclusion of a building in this guide does not mean that its grounds or interior are accessible. Please respect the privacy of those living or working in the buildings mentioned.

Author's acknowledgements

I should like to thank the following people who offered valuable advice, help and criticism: Francesco Cascio, James Cummins, Christoph Grafe, Miles Lanham, Susan Newte, Andrew Martindale, Graham Southgate and Susan Ware.

Contents

Introduction

Republic and Empire 753 BC–AD 315

Later Romans told themselves that their city had perhaps been founded on 21 April 753 BC by the twins reared by a she-wolf: Romulus, who became the first of its seven kings, and Remus. The earliest evidence of the settlement of the hilly land to the east of the Tiber covered by present-day Rome can, however, be found on the Palatine hill where there are the remains of an early Iron Age village of huts. Later, two tribes, the Latins and Sabines, occupied two further hills, the Capitoline and Quirinal, and used the flat land between as their joint burial ground. The first city of Rome, 'Roma Quadrata', was probably established in the ninth century BC when the Palatine was enclosed with a rectangular wall of tufa blocks. The city commanded the first convenient crossing of the Tiber, north of its swampy estuary and where the Isola Tiberina reduced its width.

In 510 BC, Rome's last king, Tarquinius Superbus, was overthrown, and a Republic established. Its earliest temple, that of Saturn, was begun shortly afterwards, although evidence of this has been obscured by later rebuildings. By the fifth century when the emerging city state had started to expand, extending its hinterland and colonising territory formerly occupied by the Etruscans to the north, Rome had covered at least scantily the Septimontium ('seven hills'): the three eminences of the Palatine and the four of the Esquiline. This new territory had to be defended from attacks from the north, and at the beginning of the fourth century the city wall later attributed to Servius was started, to enclose the Septimontium. Stretches of this still remain and one of them can be seen in the forecourt of the Stazione Termini **1**. Between the building of this wall and the middle of the second century, Rome fought and conquered her powerful north African enemy, Carthage, and extended her European territory to include the whole Italian peninsular and, to the east, Macedonia and Greece. By the middle of the first century, Romans had crossed the Hellespont and occupied Asia Minor and much of the Near East.

In the middle of the first century BC, the great general Julius Caesar extended Roman rule northwards to Gaul and southern Britain. In Rome, he built the first of what was to become the series of Imperial Fora, establishing a type taken up and developed by subsequent rulers. The forum consisted of a walled enclosure with a temple at one of its ends, and it provided public outdoor space for commercial and social transactions, and for ceremonies. Julius Caesar's assassination in 44 BC provoked the ferocious civil war dramatised by Shakespeare. Octavian emerged as victor of this war.

In 27 BC Octavian, re-named Augustus, was established as emperor of the lands occupied by the Romans, and during his long and stable reign of forty-one years he rebuilt much of Rome. The expanding city was divided into the fourteen administrative districts (*regiones*) still used today, and the water supply and drainage systems were modernised. Augustus instituted a building programme in which Julius Caesar's unfinished projects were completed, and others started. Under the artistic influence of Greece, and probably using Greek masons and sculptors, Augustus introduced the widespread use of marble from the newly opened quarries at Carrara to the earlier city of travertine and tufa, brick and stucco.

While many of the ceremonial buildings started during Augustus' reign have been modified or destroyed, the Theatre of Marcellus **9**, and the Ara Pacis **10** have been rebuilt or excavated from later accretions; and the remains of the temples of Saturn and Mars Ultor are visible in the Imperial Fora. The hulk of Augustus' great Mausoleum is now stranded in an uncomfortable setting from the 1930s.

Ara Pacis Augustae: detail of frieze showing dedication ceremony of 4 July 13 BC

Augustus' successors, Tiberius (AD 14–37), Caligula (AD 37–41) and Claudius (AD 41–54), built little, although the walls of Tiberius' camp for the Praetorian Guard built from AD 21 to 23 on the north-east of the city survive under later additions; and Caligula began new aqueducts including the Aqua Virgo over the Via Lata. Claudius instigated few ceremonial buildings, concentrating instead on engineering work such as building a new harbour at Ostia, and finishing or repairing three of the city's aqueducts, the Aqua Claudia, Aqua Anio Novus and Aqua Virgo.

Claudius' step-son Nero reigned for fourteen years, during which he presided over the great fire of AD 64 which destroyed much of Rome, leaving only three of its fourteen districts untouched. He set about two major building programmes, the first being the reconstruction of the damaged areas of the city to a more orderly plan, with wide streets and a height limit of twenty-one metres. The second was that of his huge palace, the Domus Aurea ('Golden House') which occupied a site of between 125 and 145 hectares on the Oppian hill and overlooked an artificial lake on the site now occupied by the Colosseum. While the spatial sophistication of its interiors marked a turning point in Roman architectural design, and its rediscovery in the sixteenth century influenced the architects of the Roman Renaissance, very little of it now remains, and that is inaccessible.

Nero was the last emperor of the Claudian dynasty, and after a civil war he was succeeded by Vespasian, the first of the Flavians. His building programme included two public buildings of which one, the Temple of the Deified Claudius, exists only in ruins. The second, however, the Amphitheatre **13**, better known as the Colosseum, begun in AD 72, continues to dominate central Rome. Vespasian's successor, Titus, reigned for only two years (AD 79–81), built little and is remembered now for the Arch in the Fora which bears his name. Domitian, Vespasian's second son who succeeded Titus, completed the Colosseum and the Arch of Titus, and started the stadium in the Campus Martius (now the piazza Navona), the Forum Transitorium with its Temple of Peace, the remains of which are known as the Colonnacce, and the Flavian Palace on the Palatine hill.

Under Trajan (98–117), the first emperor to come from one of Rome's provinces, Spain, and who founded a dynasty which was to last for the next hundred years, the territory ruled by the Empire was at its greatest. He left as monuments of his reign the Baths on the Esquiline, the Forum **14** with its column and the associated commercial buildings bearing his name. Trajan's death in 117 marked the end of the century of essentially Roman building tradition begun by Augustus. The interests of his successor lay to the exotic east.

Hadrian reigned for twenty-one years, from 117 to 138, and his building programme is conspicuous for its extent and novelty. The Pantheon **16**, one of the few Roman buildings whose interior we can still see in something like its original state, and the first in which the interior is more important than the exterior, is breathtaking in the singularity of its idea, and in the engineering skill required to sustain it. The Villa at Tivoli **15** remains, even in its present fragmentary and partly reconstructed state, an extraordinary and exotic architectural reverie summoning up new forms and importing others from Asia Minor and the Near East. Little now remains of Hadrian's enormous Temple of Venus and Rome, a Greek building in the heart of Rome, but the well-preserved streets and blocks of flats at Ostia south of EUR, part of his non-monumental building programme, are largely from his time. Hadrian left his most bulky building on the far bank of the Tiber, the Mausoleum, now the Castel Sant'Angelo **17**, for himself and his successors. Roman architecture never again achieved the élan of Hadrian's programme, and the following two centuries were, with the exception of a flourish at the beginning of the fourth century, generally conspicuous for their consolidation, conservatism and a gradual decline in taste and craft.

The middle of the second century was marked by little building and fewer remains. The column of Marcus Aurelius (the 'Antonine Column') **19** still stands in the modern piazza Colonna, and the Temple of Antoninus and Faustina (now the church of San Lorenzo in Miranda) **7**, begun in 141, is preserved because it was converted into a church. With the death of Marcus Aurelius in 180, the Empire was thrown into one of its periods of turmoil. In the following century and a quarter until the accession of Constantine, forty-seven emperors ruled, like presidents of the United States or British prime ministers, for an average reign of four years each, scarcely time to launch or complete even a modern building programme.

At the end of the second century, a new dynasty, the Severans, from Rome's African colonies, established themselves. The first, Septimus, restored many of the existing monuments and parts of the city damaged by a fire of 191, commissioning to aid this task the plan carved in marble, fragments of which are now housed in the Capitoline Museum. This plan provides a picture of those areas of Imperial Rome which consisted of lower- and middle-class tenements of four or five storeys very like those preserved at Ostia. The smaller streets and alleys were often spanned by arches, as shown by a surviving example which can be seen in the Clivius Scauri near the church of Santi Giovanni e Paolo **44**. The upper classes, then as now, lived at suburban densities in detached villas. The most conspicuous monuments of the Severan dynasty are the Arch of 193–211 **7**, and the later Baths of Caracalla **20**, until then the most extensive single building ever constructed in Imperial Rome. Alexander, last of the Severans, left no buildings, and the anarchy following his murder in 235 was only suppressed by the accession of Aurelian in 270. He and his successor, Probus, were responsible for establishing the great eighteen-kilometre defensive wall **22** around Rome. In 284 Diocletian consolidated the power of the state and initiated the building programme which continued until 330 when Constantine moved the capital to the east. In about 298 the Baths of Diocletian (now the church of Santa Maria degli Angeli **84**) which were even larger than those of Caracalla, were started.

During what became the final phase of the history of Imperial Rome, Maxentius, the last emperor of the undivided Empire, started the Basilica Nova (now of Maxentius) **23**, built the palace which is still being excavated next to the Appian Way and doubled the height of Aurelian's walls. After reigning only six years, Maxentius was defeated in 312 in a civil war with Constantine, who then became ruler of the western half of the Empire.

Christian and medieval Rome 316–1474

The earliest evidence for the presence of Christians in Rome has been found in small tombs from about 160 near the shrine of St Peter. Constantine brought to Rome an oriental court and a highly centralising state. With the Edict of Milan of 313, he institutionalised Christianity, setting up the Church with bishops who became court officials, and who acquired land and needed buildings. Earlier, private, Christian buildings had been simple meeting halls; now public representation was required. Constantine established the Bishop of Rome at a new basilica at the Lateran, just within the walls but well away from existing centres of power. The arrangement of the first public churches was developed from the Roman basilica, a hall which could be approached from all directions through a continuous peripheral ambulatory. The Christian adaptation of this form emphasised the long axis of the rectangular plan, providing an approach to the building from one direction through a courtyard and porch or narthex, and terminating the processional route thus established with a semi-circular apse at its far end. Unlike their secular counterparts, none of the early Christian basilicas had vaulted ceilings: the simple roof trusses were either left exposed or were covered with a flat wooden ceiling. The architectural style and detail of these early churches was improvised and rarely of high quality. Except for the Baptistery at St John Lateran **112**, none of Constantine's establishments survive in anything like their original form: but Santa Sabina **32** on the Esquiline, though built later and since considerably restored, now offers a clear suggestion of the type.

In 326, the first Basilica of St Peter was inaugurated. The tomb of Constantine's daughter Constantia later became church of Santa Costanza **27**, while in his secular building programme, Constantine completed the Basilica of Maxentius, renaming it and installing a colossal statue of himself, parts of which are now in the Capitoline Museum. He also erected the last great example of Roman architecture, his Arch **24**, which stands outside the Colosseum. In 330, Constantine formally divided the Empire into western and eastern halves, and transferred the capital to Byzantium where he died in 337. No subsequent emperor ruled from Rome, which for the next millennium and a half was left in the control of an emperor with a mobile court, the Senate, the emerging Church and periodic invaders. In 346 non-Christian worship was suppressed, and the majority of pagan temples closed or put to other uses. By 395 the population of Rome which may have been about 800,000 at its highest began to decline.

The beginning of the fifth century saw the first of the invasions of the former capital from the north: the city was sacked in 410 by the army of Alaric the Goth, and while it offered little resistance and the physical damage was slight, the occasion allowed the papacy as successor to Saints Peter and Paul to begin to assume the secular and military power of the absent emperor. Pope Leo I, the Great (440–61), promoted Rome as *Caput Orbis*, the 'Head of the World', and instituted the programme in which were built the first basilica of Santa Maria Maggiore **31**, and the extraordinary circular church Santo Stefano Rotondo **34**. Further invasions and sackings during Leo's reign, and later in the fifth century, finally brought the Western Empire to an end. In 568, the Lombards occupied much of the northern half of the peninsular, and the last of Rome's aristocracy left for Ravenna or Byzantium.

As what remained of Rome's political power was snuffed out, the papacy found new leadership in Pope Gregory the Great (590–604). The city had become a small town (its population had shrunk to about 100,000) of no political significance. Gregory successfully relaunched it as a diplomatic and missionary centre under his protection, reaching understandings with the Lombards and Byzantium, and dispatching missionaries to much of north-western Europe. This activity conversely brought tourists and pilgrims to Rome, and the predecessors of this book, pilgrim guidebooks, were first written for them in the early seventh century. Gregory, though, was not a great builder, and the few buildings from his time have been overwhelmed by later activity.

The rise of Muslim power and its domination of the Mediterranean in the mid seventh century threatened Byzantium, and Rome's population swelled with refugees from the east. A century later, the Lombards, who had taken Ravenna from Byzantium and were threatening Rome, were defeated by Pepin the Frank. He then established the first of what were to become the Papal States by ceding part of Lombardy to the pope. In 800, Charlemagne was crowned in St Peter's as Augustus and Emperor, establishing the Holy Roman Empire which lasted in name until the abdication of Francis II of Austria in 1806. The first built consequences of this Empire in Rome were the four churches commissioned by Pope Pascal I (817–24) – San Prassede **40**, Santa Maria in Domnica nearby **34** (subsequently rebuilt), Santa Cecilia **39** and the since rebuilt Quattro Coronati **46** – and the first Leonine Wall surrounding the area of St Peter's. The authority of the Holy Roman Empire in Italy was maintained for nearly three centuries, but in 1084 Rome was sacked by Robert Guiscard the Norman. Recovery from this devastation only began at the end of the eleventh century when a new wave of church building was undertaken. The standard type for both parish and monastic churches was the basilica, of which San Giovanni a Porta Latina **43** is one of the few remaining unaltered representatives.

As the states and cities of northern Europe became more firmly established and trade between them developed, the papacy grew in importance. Rome became the acknowledged spiritual and administrative capital of the Christian world, the popes perceived as the equals of its emperors. New churches built in Rome in the twelfth century included Santa Maria in Trastevere **47**, San Clemente **42** and the Quattro Coronati **46**. These were basilican in type and sumptuously decorated with mosaics and fine marble pavements, but though contemporary with the beginnings of the Gothic in northern Europe they looked back conservatively to the early period of Christianity.

The Renaissance and Mannerism in Rome 1490–1590

1490 | 1500 | 1510 | 1520 | 1530 | 1540 | 1550 | 1560 | 1570 | 1580 | 1590 | 1600 | 1610

1486–98 **Palazzo della Cancelleria 58**
1527 Sack of Rome
1545– Council of Trent
1571 Battle of Lepanto

1444 Donato BRAMANTE 1514
born Urbino
1499 to Rome † Rome
1500–02 **Tempietto, S. Pietro in Montorio 62**
1504 **Cloister, S. Maria della Pace 122**
1506 **Plan for St Peter's 63**

1475 MICHELANGELO Buonarroti 1564
born Caprese
1534 left Florence for Rome † Rome
1546–64 **St Peter's 63**
1546–64 **Campidoglio 76**
1548 **Palazzo Farnese 73**
1561–64 **Porta Pia 83**
Sforza Chapel, Santa Maria Maggiore 31
1563–66 **S. Maria degli Angeli (Baths of Diocletian) 84**

1481 Baldassarre PERUZZI 1537
born Siena
1508–11 **Villa Farnesina 65**
1520–37 **Work on St Peters' 63**
1532–36 **Palazzo Massimi 72**

1483 Antonio da SANGALLO the younger 1546
born Florence
1503 moved to Rome † Rome
1510–15 Palazzo Baldasin
1517– **Palazzo Farnese 73**
1518 work on **S. Giovanni dei Fiorentini 69**
interior, **S. Maria di Monserrato 68**
1520 Director of the fabric of **St Peter's 63**
1523–24 Mint now Banco di Santo Spirito
1534–49 Sala Regia & Capella Paolina, Vatican **52**
1537– Porta Santo Spirito
1538–44 **Santo Spirito in Sassia,** facade & interior **74**

1483 Raffaello Sanzio: ' RAPHAEL' 1520
born Urbino
† Rome
1509–36 **S. Eligio degli Orefici 66**
1513–16 **Santa Maria del Popolo 56,** Chigi Chapel
1514–20 co-director of the fabric of St Peter's
with Fra Giocondo, Giuliano da Sangallo

1507 Iacopo da VIGNOLA 1573
born Vignola
† Rome
1550–55 **Villa Giula 80** with Ammanati
1550–55 **Sant'Andrea in via Flaminia 81**
c1562 *Treatise on the Orders*
1564 Succeded Michelangelo as Capomaestro at St Peter's

1511 Giorgio VASARI — 1574

born Arezzo

1553–55 **Villa Giulia 80** with Ammannati, Vignola

1511 Bartolomeo AMMANNATI — 1592

born Florence

1550– worked in Rome in service of Julius III

† Florence

1553–55 **Villa Giulia 80** with Vasari, Vignola

1555 moved to Florence

1533/39 Giacomo della PORTA — 1602

born Genoa

† Rome

1573–1602 archt in charge of fabric of **St Peter's 63**

completion of **Il Gesù 87**

1580 **Madonna dei Monti 90**

1580–83 Sant'Anastasio dei Greci

San Giuseppe dei Falegnami 95

1580 –84 façade, **San Luigi dei Francesi 67**

Palazzo Maffei (later Marescott)i

Palazzo Crescenzi (later Serlupi)

Palazzo Capizucchi

Palazzo Paluzzi (later Spinola)

Fountains in Piazza Colonna, Piazza Aracoeli, Piazza delle Tartarughe & at Madonna dei Monti & others

1543 Domenico FONTANA — 1607

born nr Lake Lugano

† Naples

1585 **Sistine Chapel, S. Maria Maggiore 31**

1585–90 Plan for Rome with G Fontana

1585– **Quirinal Palace 88**

1586–89 **Acqua Felice**

1587–90 **new Vatican Library**

Erection of **obelisks in Piazza di San Pietro, Piazza Santa Maria Maggiore, etc**

1592 returned to Naples

1490 1500 1510 1520 1530 1540 1550 1560 1570 1580 1590 1600 1610

At the beginning of the thirteenth century, Innocent III carried out works to the Lateran Palace and established Santo Spirito in Sassia **74** as a hospital and pilgrim hostel, and in 1208 he started what was to become the Vatican Palace north of St Peter's. Towards the end of the century, the popes presided over a brief period of high artistic activity. In 1300 two million visitors attended Boniface VIII's Holy Year, but two years later he was deposed by the French, and for much of the century Rome, its buildings decaying and its population shrinking to fewer than 20,000 souls, had to manage without the papacy which ruled from Avignon. St Catherine of Siena is credited with persuading Gregory XI to return to Rome, but it was only in 1420 that his successor Martin V began to restore it, summoning artists from northern Italy and starting a programme that his successors continued through the century.

The Renaissance and Mannerism 1475–1574

While cities in northern Italy were rediscovering and reinventing classical antiquity (Brunelleschi had begun the Ospedale in Florence in 1421 and the new Duomo in that city was consecrated in 1436), the first indication of the new architecture in Rome was the Palazzo della Cancellaria **58** of 1486–98. Its unknown architect, possibly Bramante, was strongly influenced by Alberti's Florentine work. The subsequent Renaissance flowered with an energetic programme of patronage of artists and architects from the northern cities. Bramante, Raphael, Antonio da Sangallo the younger and Michelangelo, who had variously worked in Milan, Umbria and Florence, were summoned by the pope to Rome where they established studios to serve him, their cardinal patrons and the local aristocracy and land owners.

On his arrival, Bramante, aged 56, studied and recorded the ruins of Roman antiquity. In 1500 he was commissioned to build the Tempietto **62**, in 1504 the cloister at Santa Maria della Pace **122**, and with Raphael and Michelangelo to enlarge the Vatican Palace. The ten years of the pontificate of Pope Julius II (1503–13) conveniently encompass the very brief Roman High Renaissance. He employed Raphael to paint a series of rooms in the Vatican Palace, and Michelangelo to paint the ceiling of the Sistine Chapel. In 1506 Julius held a competition to rebuild the Constantinian basilica of St Peter's **63**. Bramante won the competition, proposing a radical Greek cross plan, its centre surmounted by a colossal hemispherical dome with a diameter only slightly smaller than that of the Pantheon. The design celebrated the completion of that appropriation of pagan Roman antiquity which had first begun in

Florence but which was now identified with the very centre of Western Christianity. But Julius died in 1513, and when Bramante died a year later only the piers for the crossing to support the dome had been built. Work on the enormous project continued intermittently and with many changes of design for the next hundred years, carried out by among others Michelangelo, Raphael, Peruzzi, Sangallo and Vignola. Leo X (1513–21) and his successors continued the projects started by Julius, but all building work was abandoned when Rome was occupied and sacked in 1527 by German mercenaries of the Emperor Charles V.

The Church responded vigorously to the Reformation in the northern countries: new religious Orders, Oratorians and Capuchins, were established requiring new buildings. In 1540, the Jesuit Order was sanctioned and two years later the Inquisition was reintroduced. The Council of Trent was set up in 1545 and deliberated for the next two decades. It established a severe, austere regime accompanied by a new religious fervour. In architecture, earlier experiments with centralising plans were abandoned: the new churches had long wide naves for processions and preaching, and the chapels which lined them could be devoted to individual saints. The areas for the clergy were clearly separated from those for the laity. The church of the Gesù **87**, started in 1568, is the clearest expression of the architectural response to Tridentine requirements. Its architecture, like the late work of Michelangelo, embodies the characteristics of what was later to be called 'Mannerism': the deliberate exploration of tensions, ambiguities and uncertainties compared with the forthright proposals of the Renaissance. As well as new churches for the new Orders, in mid-century a number of churches were built for the various national communities which had established themselves in Rome including the Florentines (San Giovanni dei Fiorentini **69**), Lombards, the French (San Luigi dei Francesi **67**), Serbs and Dalmatians.

Counter Reformation and the Baroque 1575–1674

The Council of Trent succeeded in checking the progress of Protestantism in the north, and the victory over the Turks in the battle of Lepanto of 1571 contained the expansion of Islam to the east. During the fifty years since the Sack of Rome in 1527, the city had hugely increased its stock of churches, and Pope Sixtus V (1585–90) was able to devote himself to a thorough programme of improvements to the infrastructure of the city. With his architect Domenico Fontana, he established new long straight streets which cut both across open land and through medieval building blocks. These

The Baroque in Rome 1595–1675

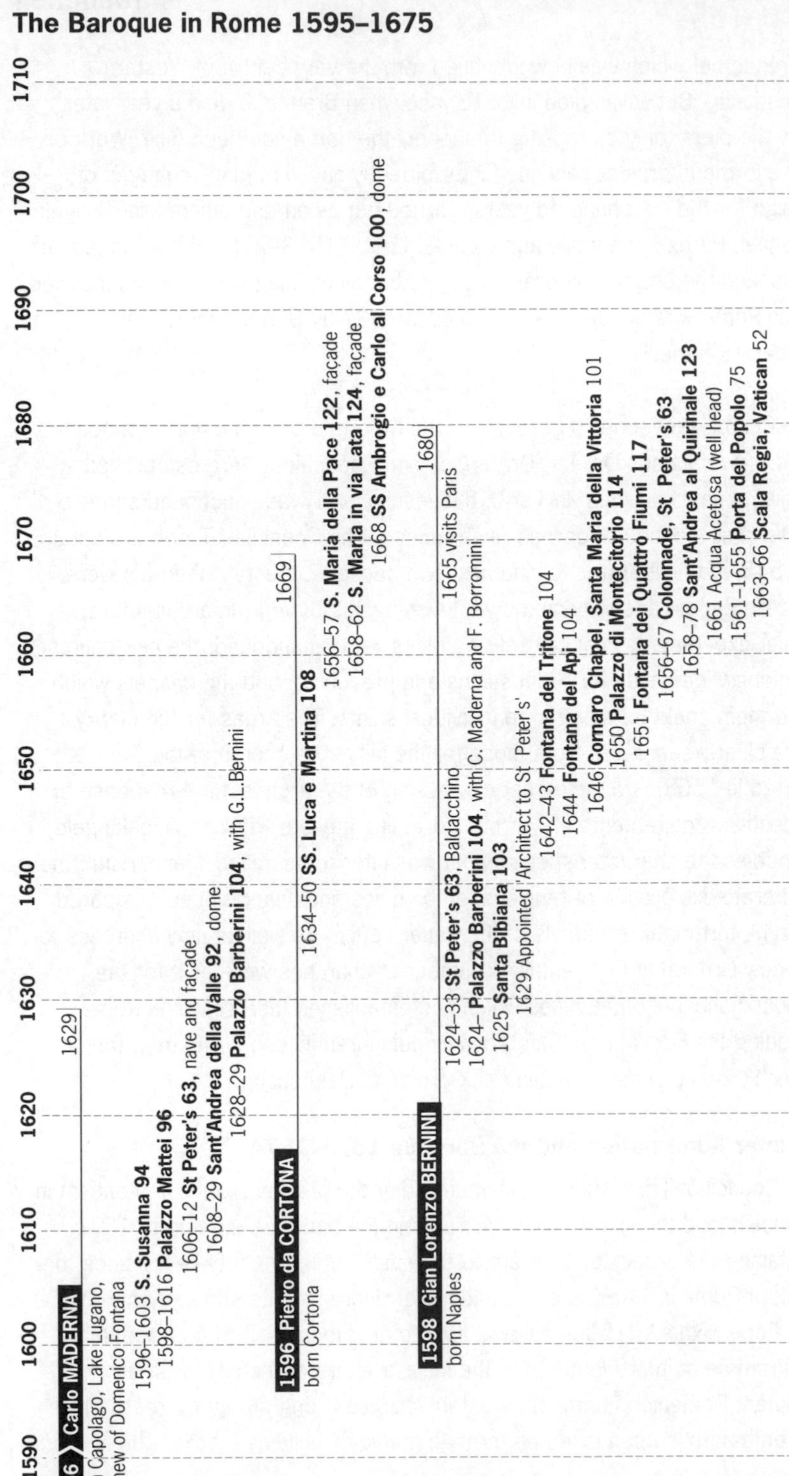

1590
1600
1610
1620
1630
1640
1650
1660
1670
1680
1690
1700
1710
1556 Carlo MADERNA
born Capolago, Lake Lugano, nephew of Domenico Fontana
1596–1603 S. Susanna 94
1598–1616 Palazzo Mattei 96
1606–12 St Peter's 63, nave and façade
1608–29 Sant'Andrea della Valle 92, dome
1628–29 Palazzo Barberini 104, with G.L.Bernini
1629
1596 Pietro da CORTONA
born Cortona
1634–50 SS. Luca e Martina 108
1656–57 S. Maria della Pace 122, façade
1658–62 S. Maria in via Lata 124, façade
1668 SS Ambrogio e Carlo al Corso 100, dome
1669
1598 Gian Lorenzo BERNINI
born Naples
1624–33 St Peter's 63, Baldacchino
1624– Palazzo Barberini 104, with C. Maderna and F. Borromini
1625 Santa Bibiana 103
1629 Appointed 'Architect to St Peter's'
1642–43 Fontana del Tritone 104
1644 Fontana del Api 104
1646 Cornaro Chapel, Santa Maria della Vittoria 101
1650 Palazzo di Montecitorio 114
1651 Fontana dei Quattro Fiumi 117
1656–67 Colonnade, St Peter's 63
1658–78 Sant'Andrea al Quirinale 123
1661 Acqua Acetosa (well head)
1561–1655 Porta del Popolo 75
1663–66 Scala Regia, Vatican 52
1665 visits Paris
1680

born Como

1633, 1667 **S. Carlo alle Quattro Fontane 107**
1637–40 **Oratorio di San Filippo Neri 109**
1642–60 **Sant'Ivo 110**
1646–49 **Palazzo Falconieri 111**
1646–1736 **S. Giovanni in Laterano 112,** nave
1652–66 **Sant'Agnese in Agone 117**
1653–65 **Sant'Andrea delle Frate 119,** cupola & campanile
1662 **Collegio di Propaganda Fide 126**, façade and chapel

1611 Carlo RAINALDI – 1691
born Rome, son of
Girolamo Rainaldi (1570–1655)
1652–66 **Sant'Agnese in Agone 118**
1661–65 **S. Andrea della Valle 92**, façade
1662–79 **S. Maria in Monte Santo, S. Maria dei Miracoli, Piazza del Popolo 75**
1663–67 **S. Maria in Campitelli 125**
1673 **S. Maria Maggiore 31**, rear façade

1616 Giovanni Antonio De ROSSI – 1695
born Rome
1650–60 Palazzo Altieri
1662 **Palazzo d'Aste Rinuccini Bonaparte** 55
1681 **SS. Pantaleo e G. Calasanzio 130**
1685 **S. Maria in Campo Marzio 128**
1695–99 **S. Maria Maddalena 129**

1638 Carlo FONTANA – 1714
born nr Como
1650s Clerk of works to Cortona, Rainaldi and Bernini
1665 S. Biagio in Campitelli
1671 **S. Andrea della Valle** 92, Capella Ginetti
1682–83 **S. Marcello al Corso 70**, façade
1683–87 **S. Maria del Popolo 56**, Capella Cibò
1692–98 **St Peter's 63**, Baptismal Chapel
1705 S. Sebastiano, Capella Albani

1590 1600 1610 1620 1630 1640 1650 1660 1670 1680 1690 1700 1710

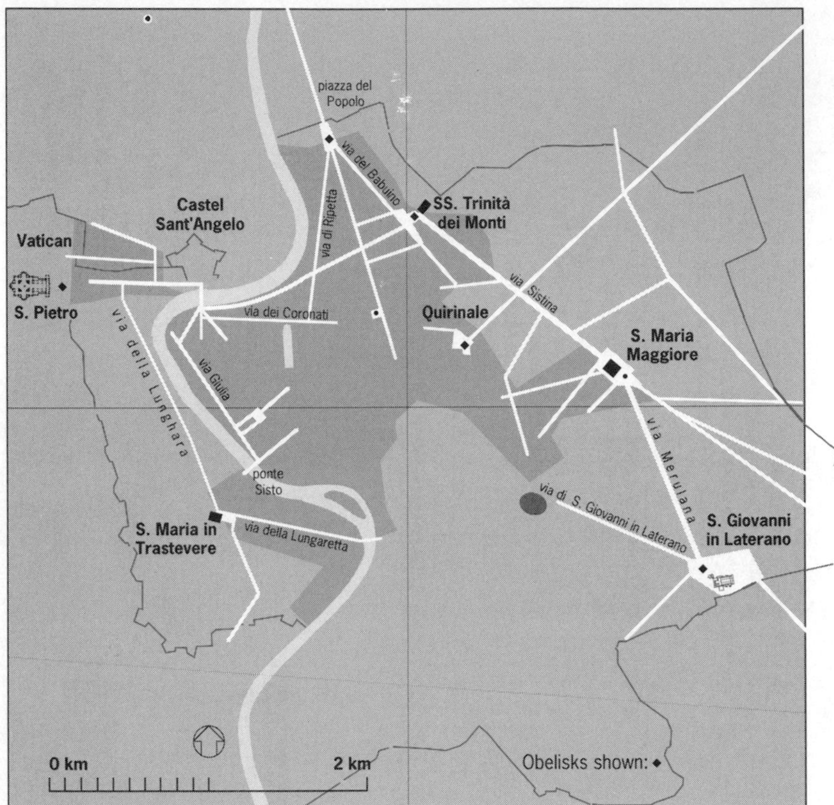

Sixtus V's new streets

streets, cutting also across the ancient radial routes, connected the various scattered monuments and piazzas in a great arc running from St Peter's in the north-west to San Giovanni in Laterano in the south-east. Sixtus started the fashion for setting up antique obelisks or fountains at the intersections of the new streets, and more usefully improved the water supply by extending the Aqua Felice into the centre of Rome. During his reign, the dome of St Peter's was finished to Michelangelo's design by Giacomo della Porta and Fontana, and the papal palaces at the Vatican and Lateran were extended.

Sixtus' reign had reversed the austerities promoted by the Council of Trent, and his immediate successors found themselves made increasingly wealthy by offerings both from northern Europe and from the countries colonising the Americas. At the very end of the sixteenth century, three men were born who, with their respective patrons Urban VIII (1623–44) and Alexander VII (1655–67), were to determine the Roman architecture of much of the seventeenth: the painter and architect Pietro da Cortona (1596–1669), Gian Lorenzo

Bernini (1598–1680) and Francesco Borromini (1599–1680). (See the Chart, pages 18–19.) The ground for their rejection of Mannerism had been prepared by such architects as Carlo Maderna (1556–1629) whose serious façade for Santa Susanna **94** of 1596–1603, and whose nave and façade of St Peter's, completed in 1612, had suggested that it was possible to develop the classical language beyond Michelangelo's idiosyncrasies.

The first significant commission of Urban's reign was to the young sculptor Bernini to decorate the crossing of St Peter's: the result was the exuberant bronze baldacchino over the site of St Peter's tomb, the first of a series of works which span the next forty years and constitute a substantial proportion of the Roman Baroque canon. Much of the balance was carried out by Bernini's rival Borromini whose patrons included both Alexander and religious Orders such as the Oratorians. Their architecture, now called Baroque, is characterised by its knowing rhetoric and its appeal to both the emotions and the intellect. The preferred forms were the curve, especially when inflected, the complex and, in plans, the oval; in sculpture coloured marbles were used both naturalistically and for effect, and the boundary between sculpture and architecture was frequently indistinct. Borromini finally detached the column from the regular grid with which it had always been associated, and severed the connection between the orders and their original tectonic metaphor. Other architects soon found ways of spacing and clustering columns for plastic effect. Bernini developed the use of polychromy using coloured marbles to code the different elements of his architecture as, for example, at Sant'Andrea al Quirinale **123**. The scale of buildings became larger, and orders were often required to span more than the two storeys which Michelangelo had first introduced at the Capitol. The design of the Roman palace front had apparently been finally established by that of the Palazzo Farnese **73**, but Bernini gave it the new form which was to provide the model to the world for the next two centuries in his design for the Palazzo Chigi-Odaleschi **102.** Borromini died in 1667, and Bernini in 1680, but they had each completed their last works in the 1660s.

Classicism and neoclassicism 1675–1869

Their successors in taste and practice pursued not a reaction against the strong flavour of the High Baroque, but either a milder, less individualistic restatement influenced by the French taste emanating from the court of Louis XIV, or a reworking of the themes of the earlier generation. The first is exemplified in the influential and widely copied works of Carlo Fontana (1634–1714), such as the façade of San Marcello **70** of 1683, the Cappella Spada in the Chiesa Nuova **89**, and the Cappella Cibò in Santa Maria del Popolo **56**; the second in Antonio Gherardi's Cappella Avila in Santa Maria in Trastevere **47**, and Cappella di Santa Cecilia in San Carlo ai Catinari **99**.

By 1730 when Pope Clement XII was elected, the reaction against the Baroque had finally taken hold. For his small building programme promoted largely by competitions, the pope called the Florentine architects, Alessandro Galilei (1691–1736) and Ferdinando Fuga (1699–1781) to Rome, and patronised the Roman Nicola Salvi (1697–1751). Galilei won the competition for the design of the façade of St John Lateran **112** and built that of his 'national' church San Giovanni dei Fiorentini **69**, while Salvi is now best known as winner of the competition for design of the Trevi Fountain **133** begun in 1732. Fuga's classical taste is seen in the Palazzo della Consulta **134** of 1739, the façade of Santa Maria Maggiore **31** and his later very dry Sant'Apollinare. By mid-century scarcely any official building was being carried out in Rome, but important theoretical work and publication was being done by Gian Battista Piranesi whose only built works in Rome, the entrance court and church of Santa Maria del Priorato **138** of 1764–65, stand on the Aventine. In 1798 Napoleon's army entered Rome and the French Senate declared it a Republic. Pope Pius VI was taken prisoner, in 1809 the Papal States were annexed to France, and two years later Napoleon pronounced his son 'King of Rome'.

The popes had first brought neoclassicism to Rome's interiors by commissioning extensions to the Vatican Museum in 1776. A decade later, the first series of garden ornaments for the Villa Borghese **139** exhibited the style outdoors. The most prominent architect practising in Rome at the beginning of the nineteenth century was Giuseppe Valadier (1762–1839). After an early period in which he produced theoretical studies influenced by Piranesi and the elemental geometrical forms of Ledoux, Boullée and Gilly, he was employed for most of the official work of the time. Pursuing his own staccato interpretation of neoclassicism, he reconstructed the Ponte Milvio **4**, laid out the piazza del Popolo **75** and Pincio gardens above with their Casina **142**, introduced thoughtful archaeological methods to the first reconstruction of the Arch of Titus **7**, and built the city's second modern theatre, the Teatro Valle **143**.

After Napoleon's defeat in 1814, the Pope, now Pius VII, returned to a Rome which settled down to its previous role as country town and religious and cultural centre, under continued papal rule, but largely unaffected by the development of industry in the north of Europe or Catalonia. (The first factory in Rome, opened in the 1860s, was devoted to tobacco processing **145**.) At mid-century, the population stood at about 180,000, and the built-up area, much of it still of medieval stock, occupied only about one third of the land enclosed by the Aurelian Wall. In 1849, the French army again occupied Rome, but on this occasion opposition came not from the popes but from the soldier, and later statesman, Giuseppe Garibaldi who had gathered an informal army of 'Redshirts' devoted to the establishment of a unified Italian state. In 1857 he founded the Italian National Association for unification under Piedmont, and in 1860 the first Italian Parliament met in Turin. Garibaldi's army sailed to Sicily and launched the successful campaign to occupy the peninsular from the south. Meanwhile, Vittorio Emanuele, King of Sardinia, had invaded the Papal States whose army was defeated at Castelfidardo. Garibaldi proclaimed Vittorio Emanuele King of Italy, and the new kingdom was ratified by the Italian Parliament in 1861.

Capital of Italy 1870–1921

In 1870, the army of the new Italian state, led by Garibaldi, entered a Rome defended by its walls for the last time. While other cities such as Florence and Turin had been considered for the role, Rome's symbolic attraction proved overwhelming, and it was declared the capital of a united Italy. Accommodation was required for the new institutions of the state, and the Parliament first met in the Palazzo Montecitorio **113**, the Senate in the Palazzo Madama **114**. Government ministries first used expropriated monasteries, but their armies of clerks needed offices and housing. The city required new arrangements for its traffic. A planning authority was set up, commissioning Alessandro Viviani's plan of 1873 which, though never ratified, did serve as a guide to development. This proposed a new ceremonial road, the straight via Nazionale, between the site of the new railway station and the Palazzo Venezia in the heart of the old city, and its continuation as the serpentine Corso Vittorio Emanuele which cut through the medieval district towards the Tiber. The road tunnel, the Traforo Umberto I, was started in 1873 to connect two of the many new streets: the via del Tritone with the via Nazionale. In 1876, to prevent the frequent flooding caused by the Tiber which had affected the city since Roman times, work was started to equip the river's entire length within the city with tree-lined embankments. Over the next twenty-five years, both banks were lined with roads and new bridges built.

New residential areas, mostly laid out in simple rectangular grids, were to be established to the east and north of the old Rome, and on the western side of the Tiber north of Castel Sant'Angelo. These housed the new bureaucracy, the people displaced from demolished medieval districts and migrants from Rome's rural hinterland and from the south of Italy.

The architecture of *Roma Capitale* was developed either from current Parisian practice, or from precedents of not necessarily Roman palazzi of the Italian cinquecento (sixteenth century). The most prolific and influential architect of the time was Gaetano Koch (1838–1910) of whose huge output only a selection is included in this guide. His first works of the 1870s were modest blocks of flats and small office buildings, so modest that they are now almost eclipsed by their more rhetorical neighbours. His later commissions, however, included the gigantic piazza Vittorio Emanuele south-east of Santa Maria Maggiore, and the piazza della Repubblica **154** which attempted to provide a significant termination to the northern end of the via Nazionale. Both were derived from Torinese examples, and brought Rome its first arcades. The first buildings constructed with cast iron frames were introduced in Rome in the 1880s, and many examples survive, including De Angelis' Galleria Sciarra **152** of 1883 and blocks of offices near it.

At the beginning of the twentieth century, Rome had most of the equipment of a European capital city and a population of about half a million. In 1909 a new Plan was introduced by a new radical mayor which was to influence the pattern of residential development for the next forty years. It proposed three types of residential zone: *giardini* of luxurious detached houses which could not occupy more than one twentieth of their plots; *villini* of two or three storeys; and *fabbricati* of flats up to twenty-four metres high. The densest areas were to be separated by parks or zones of *villini*. Shortly after the introduction of this plan, in 1911 a fourth type was added: the four-storey *palazzina*, nineteen metres high and with a modest garden. In the same year, Rome celebrated its recently acquired international status by holding the Esposizione Universale which added new public buildings to her stock. The centrepiece of these was Bazzani's huge Galleria d'Arte Moderna **167** which was connected to an area of experimental housing across the Tiber by the new Ponte del Risorgimento **168**.

Roman intellectuals and architects had been aware of two interlinked strands of thought which had been emerging in England and Germany since the end of the nineteenth century: the conservation and garden city movements. In 1875 a group had founded the Roman *Associazione artistica fra i cultori di architettura* (the Artistic Association for the Patronage of Architecture). The Association started publishing scholarly studies of medieval Rome, but graduated to actual restoration work, and in 1892 received its first commission to restore the ancient church of Santa Maria in Cosmedin **49**. The Association's cause found an influential voice with the publication in 1916 of Marcello Piacentini's *Sulla conservazione della bellezza di Roma e sullo sviluppo della città moderna* ('The preservation of the beauty of Rome, and the development of the modern city'). He argued against the grandiose (the Vittorio Emanuele monument had finally been completed in 1911), and for the 'contextual' and picturesque. Both his book and the continuing authority of the Association had a strong influence in the development, starting in 1920, of Rome's first workers' garden suburbs of Garbatella **173** and Aniene, sponsored by the ICP (*Istituto per le case popolari*). Here two- and three-storey maisonettes in a mixture of rustic, medieval and 'characteristic' styles were arranged along picturesquely winding roads which radiated from a neighbourhood centre of shops and a school.

The Fascist era 1922–43

In 1922 Benito Mussolini with his Blackshirts 'marched' on Rome and King Vittorio Emanuele III invited him to form a government. In the following four years the democratic constitution was annulled and the Partito Fascista Nazionale established as the single political party. Rome was ruled not by an elected mayor but by a directly appointed governor. One of the new regime's first acts was to set about a second equipment of Rome, this time to make it a suitable setting as capital of the new Italian Empire which would be a direct descendant of that of the Caesars. The plan of 1930, commissioned from Marcello Piacentini, proposed a variation of the three dwelling types, introducing an even more dense version of the *fabbricato*, the *intensivo* which could be up to thirty-five metres high. A relatively coherent example of the use of the *intensivo* can be seen in the area planned around the piazza Bologna, which includes Mario De Renzi's block **182** of 1930. Other districts fared less well and the broadly laissez-faire implementation of the Plan produced large areas of chaotically arranged and over-dense housing.

The Plan contained two further proposals: the first for new wide avenues such as the two leading from either side of the Vittorio Emanuele monument, the via dei Fori Imperiali **178** and via del Teatro di Marcello which was intended eventually to reach the coast at Ostia. These were partly intended to improve traffic circulation but they also provided settings for political and military displays. The second proposal was to clear the Imperial monuments of their medieval accretions, to consolidate and restore them, and to provide new settings for them. Monuments thus exposed included the Mausoleum of Augustus and Ara Pacis **10**, the Largo Argentina, the Imperial Fora, and the Theatre of Marcellus **9**. Much of this work was completed by the mid 1930s, but other schemes followed: the via della Conciliazione **190** was started in 1937 but only completed in 1950.

The Fascist regime is now largely but wrongly associated solely with the sometimes pompous and usually reactionary 'official' architectural style, the 'stile Littorio' exemplified in Piacentini's later work. Patronage, however, lay in the hands of various ministries and agencies who were free to choose their architects, and who did so from a surprisingly wide range of tendencies. In 1927 the Milanese 'Gruppo 7' of seven young architects had been launched, its manifestos calling for a 'rational' modern architecture. A year later, two Roman architects, Adalberto Libera (1903–63) and Gaetano Minucci (1893–1980) introduced both the word and the movement to Rome where they organised the first 'Esposizione del'architettura razionale'. The Roman rationalists received their first official commission when Libera and Mario De Renzi (1897–1967) won one of the competitions for the four new 'postal centres' for the city, that of the Via della Marmorata **187**. The 'rationalists' were represented too among the many architects involved in the construction of one of the other new planned 'centres', the Città Universitaria **184**, started in 1932, and planned by Piacentini, where the architecture ranged between the monumental and the playfully modern.

The greatest planning enterprise of the regime was, however, intended to be the Esposizione Universale di Roma ('EUR') **191**, to be held in 1942 to celebrate the twentieth anniversary of the March on Rome. Modelled at first on world fairs of the sort held in Chicago in 1933, the programme became conflated with Mussolini's desire to unite Rome with the sea and his slogan '*Roma al mare*'. A site of 400 hectares near Ostia was chosen, and Piacentini commissioned to design the layout. Although this was of the extreme simplicity associated with the regime, architects of modern persuasion were selected to design some of the more important buildings. With the outbreak of the Second World War, plans for both the exhibition and work on the site were abandoned.

During the war, while heavy fighting occurred in the towns and countryside around Rome, especially following the Allied landings at Anzio and Nettuno in 1944, the only serious physical damage the city sustained was to the church of San Lorenzo fuori le Mura **36** whose nave was destroyed by bombing in 1943. Fascist rule had collapsed in 1943 and a provisional government was set up at the king's invitation. Fighting their way north, in June 1944 the Allied army entered Rome as its liberators. In April 1945 Mussolini was captured and killed.

The first Republic 1945 to the present

The referendum held in 1946 favoured a republican constitution: King Umberto II left Italy, Alcide de Gasperi was appointed provisional head of state and Rome confirmed as capital of the new Republic. Housing programmes interrupted by the war were restarted both to improve conditions and to cater for a new influx of population from the south of Italy. Various acronymic state agencies were responsible for providing this housing, but they carried out their activities in the almost complete absence of planning. The result was the explosive growth at the edges of the city which brought its population to two million and which reached its climax in the middle of the 1960s.

This expansion, together with the start of an aggressive policy of road-building, has produced the present unhappy surroundings to the nineteenth-century city. In the 1950s, some local attempts had been made to suggest patterns of housing different from the mindless *intensivi*, including INA-Casa's 'neo-realist' quarter at Tiburtino **200**, and the Case a Torre in the viale Etiopia **201** designed by a team led by Ridolfi. In spite of a ferment of architectural polemics in Rome, progressive building was to be found in the north of Italy where the simplicities of international modernism were being challenged in Milan by the eccentricities of Neo-Liberty, and such buildings as Gio Ponti's Pirelli offices and BBPR's Torre Velasca; and in Venice by Ignazio Gardella's work. Luigi Moretti's Girasole flats **197** of 1947–50 had supplied Rome's only example of a similar dissidence, and ten years later Albini and Helg's *Rinascente* department store **206** brought Milanese sophistication to the piazza Fiume. Many Roman architects who before the war had pioneered international modernism, or who had had a part in inventing the *stile Littorio*, later seemed anxious to work in any style except those associated with the earlier period. The consequences were often surprising and frequently trivial. One strand of innovation, however, seemed to offer a positive path whose forms could not be associated in any way with the earlier regime. This was the use of engineering structure to determine architectural form, and Rome acquired some distinguished works by such internationally known Italian engineers as Pier Luigi Nervi (the Palazzo **191** and Palazetto dello Sport **204**), and Riccardo Morandi (Leonardo da Vinci airport terminal and hangars **207**).

The signing in 1957 of the Treaty of Rome, which established what was to become the European Union, left no architectural evidence in the city. In 1962, a new regulatory plan proposed a new by-pass to the east of the city linking Montescaro and EUR. This was to have been lined with new business districts, but while little came of the plan, EUR itself was gradually and successfully developed as one such centre and now provides a civilised and modest counterpart to La Défense in Paris, or London's Docklands, without the tall buildings which were thought necessary in both those places. When the Olympic Games of 1960 were held in Rome, the old Foro Italico **176** of 1927–35 which had been intended for an earlier Games was dusted down and modernised. Pier Luigi Nervi's magnificent arenas **204** were built, together with the athletes' housing village **205** and associated new roads and bridges.

The Christian Democrats who had run Rome since 1945 were replaced in 1976 by a Communist administration under C. G. Argan. With the advice of such distinguished architect-critics as Carlo Aymonino, various planning initiatives were suggested, including a serious one to dismantle the via dei Fori Imperiali, and a possibly frivolous one completely to reconstruct at least one of the Imperial Fora. Neither has happened, but the antique Metropolitana system originally started to connect Termini station and EUR was modernised and extended, and the new line 'A' built.

With the growth of its population now almost at a standstill and the expansion in Italy's industry and services largely taking place in the corridor between Turin, Milan and Venice, and in competition with other former national capitals of a slowly federating Europe, Rome seeks to define a role for itself. For the visitor, tourist or pilgrim, it remains a pungent and exasperating city, much of it overwhelmed by its traffic. Many of its streets, though, still support the rich outdoor life characteristic of the countries surrounding the Mediterranean, and continue to exhibit the two millennia of extraordinary architectural wealth recorded here.

Ara pacis Augustae: detail of frieze

Republic and Empire 753 BC–AD 315

1Bk **Servian Wall** 378 BC

Rome's second wall, about eleven kilometres long, was built in the Republican period and enclosed the 'seven hills' but not the flat land later called the Campo Marzio on which many buildings of the early Empire were subsequently erected. It was built of large blocks of tufa, and one of the best preserved portions (illustrated right) can be seen in the forecourt of the Stazione Termini **198**.

2De **Circus Maximus** 329 BC
Via dei Cerchi/via del Circo Massimo

M B Circo Massimo

Perhaps established in the seventh century, the first and subsequently largest circus (race-track) in Rome was set up on flat land to the south of the walls of 'Roma Quadrata', the fortified Palatine hill. Destroyed, rebuilt, enlarged and reconstructed in Imperial times, little is left of the marble with which it was originally equipped, but now, cleared of later accretions, its shape is clearly visible in the contoured grass: a square end to the north-east, and a turning circle at the south-western end where a few of the estimated between 150,000 and 400,000 seats are still visible. The slightly raised long hump running down the centre marks the position of the *spina* round which chariots and athletes separately raced. (For a complete reconstruction of a similar stadium, with chariots, emperor and spectators, see the film *Ben Hur* of 1959.)

Circus Maximus, left, and Palatine: Modello plastico EUR

Rome's later circuses included that of Domitian, now visible in the shape of the piazza Navona **117**, and that at the palace of Maxentius on the Appian Way, which is still being excavated.

☞ The conspicuous and ostentatiously guarded office building at the south-eastern end of the circus has since 1951 been the headquarters of the FAO, the United Nations Food and Agricultural Organisation. The original building, designed by Ridolfi and Frankl with Sabbatini and others, was started in 1938 as the Ministero dell'Africa Orientale, but work was stopped during World War II. It was finally extended and completed in 1952 with Vittorio Cafiero as architect.

3Ch **Temple of Hercules Victor** ex **'Temple of Vesta'** about 180 BC

Piazza Bocca della Verità, opposite Ponte Palatino

Like the nearby Temple of Portunus **5**, this is from the Republican period, and the earliest surviving marble building in Rome. While the walls of the cella and the peristyle of twenty Corinthian columns remain, the entablature together with the possible dome suggested in Palladio's restoration have vanished. (Palladio the surveyor notes that the internal diameter of the cella is the same as that of the height of the columns.) The present provisional tiled roof with its straw-hat profile deprives it of its dignity. The temple, together with its near contemporary 'Temple of Vesta' at Tivoli, was important among the precedents for the plans of the centralised churches of the Renaissance.

☞ Temple of Portunus **5**, Santa Maria in Cosmedin **49**, the Casa dei Crescenzi **45.**

4Eb **Ponte Milvio** or **Milvius** 109 BC, 1805

Via Flaminia/piazza Cardinale Consalvi

The first Roman bridge over the Tiber, well north of the Servian and Aurelian Walls, remained until the nineteenth century one of Rome's two strategic connections with the Italian peninsular to the north. (The other bridge was that which carried the via Nomentana over the Aniene.) It was the focus of many military events in the city of Rome's history, including the battle in 312 when the forces led by the Christian Constantine defeated those led by Maxentius who was thrown into the river. The present bridge retains the form of the original but it has frequently been destroyed and rebuilt. In 1805 Valadier redesigned the gate tower to the north which is clothed in the neat neoclassical military dress of rustication, quoins and an attic. Garibaldi's troops blew up the bridge in 1849 to prevent the advance of a French army: it was rebuilt by Pius IX in the following year. It was last restored in 1985 when it was closed to wheeled traffic.

5Ch **Temple of Portunus** ex **Temple of Fortuna Virilis** 100–80 BC

Piazza Bocca della Verità, opposite Ponte Palatino

Showing Greek influences in its order, but Roman in its plinth, this small temple while unremarkable in its form is one of the few to survive intact from the many which must have existed in the period of the Republic.

☞ Temple of Hercules Victor **3**, Santa Maria in Cosmedin **49**, Casa dei Crescenzi **45**.

6De **Palatine**

Entrance to enclosure from via di San Gregorio near the Arch of Constantine

Restoration: EUR modello plastico

The Palatine hill was one of the two summits on which the settlements which were later to become the city of Rome were established. It was first occupied in the ninth century BC, and its ruins are evidence of continuous building activity over more than two thousand years, from traces of the early huts, via aristocratic mansions of the Republic to the various palaces of the Imperial period (our word 'palace' is derived from the name), a Greek monastery of the twelfth century and a villa of the sixteenth century.

Modern archaeological work began in 1860s, and the excavated but mainly inaccessible ruins of the **Palace of the Flavian Emperors** or **Domus Augustana** are now exposed over much of the south-west corner of the hill. This palace, one of the few Roman buildings whose architect's name, Rabirius, has been recorded, was initiated by Domitian and first used in AD 92, and subsequently extended and completed by Hadrian. Its plan is now best appreciated in drawings of its reconstruction, but its largest feature, the so-called walled 'stadium', is clearly visible, although its surrounding two-storey colonnades have vanished. The terraces and vaults which extend out from the hill and which supported both this and other parts of the palace are best seen from the Circus Maximus **2** from which side the palace was entered.

The **'House of Livia'** to the north-west of the palace may not be accessible. Probably part of Augustus' palace, it was excavated in 1869 and contains fine wall paintings. To the north, the **Cryptoporticus**, a vaulted tunnel 130 metres (430 feet) long runs beneath the hill and connects the various structures above. Its fine original stucco ceilings have been replaced with casts.

Apart from the Orti Farnesiani and their terraces, described separately at **85**, other remains are very incomplete, excavations continue, and many of the ruins are only occasionally accessible. The hill is best enjoyed as an escape from the bustle of the city below: a pleasantly landscaped park with plenty of shade and good views to the north-east over the Roman Forum.

☞ The entrance ticket to the Palatine also allows access to the Forum **7**.

7Da **Roman Forum**

Entrances to enclosure from via di San Gregorio near the Arch of Constantine, or from via dei Fori Imperiali

Curia Senatus

The Forum lies on the flat land between the Palatine and Quirinal hills where settlement first took place. At first a burial ground for those communities, the site later became the focus for their religious, political and commercial activities, and buildings to house these were constructed on the flat land and on the Capitoline hill to the north-west over a period of about a millennium. The via Sacra, the processional way, ran from the Capitoline hill to the south-east and connected the various structures. The original nucleus was greatly extended in the Imperial era when Emperors constructed the series of self-contained Imperial Fora. Julius Caesar built the first which was followed by those of Augustus, Vespasian, Nerva, and Trajan **14**. The continuity of these with the original Forum was lost when the wide via del Impero, now the via dei Fori Imperiali **178**, was constructed diagonally across the site in 1932.

Arch of Titus

What is visible in the area today is the result of war, accidents and changing fashions in archaeology, and only those buildings which can be visited from within the modern enclosure and which are still recognisable as architecture are described below in chronological order.

The **Curia Senatus** or Senate House was originally built between 80 BC and 44. It housed the Senate, the 'S' in 'SPQR', the government of Rome in the Republican period, and its nominal government during the Empire. Rebuilt after a fire

Temple of Antoninus and Faustina

Arch of Septimus Severus

in 283, it was converted into the church of Sant' Adriano in the seventh century, but its present form owes as much to the twentieth century as any other. Originally flanked by other large buildings its now exposed façade is dominated by three large windows. Its plain brick has been stripped of the original stucco, traces of which are still visible below the entablature. The interior is a large plain hall, its marble floor stepped for the senators' chairs.

The **Arch of Titus** of AD 81 lies on a summit at a bend in the via Sacra where it turns to avoid the Temple of Venus and Rome. It was started by Titus to celebrate his conquest of Jerusalem in AD 66, and employs the simplest format of the triumphal arch: the arch itself is flanked by blind bays, and the whole is topped by a deep attic whose central panel contains the dedicatory inscription. It was clad in white Pentelic marble, and the Composite capitals were among the earliest examples of their use in Roman monumental architecture. The Arch was one of the first buildings to be subject to modern notions of representation: its restoration was begun by Raffaello Stern in 1817 and continued by Valadier who in 1821 completed the work, adding new capitals and repairing the masonry in travertine to distinguish the repairs from the original. The restored Arch became highly regarded and its composition was, for example, the model for the country side of the Porta Pia **83**.

Now the church of **San Lorenzo in Miranda**, the **Temple of Antoninus and Faustina** was begun in 141. Commissioned by Antoninus to honour his late wife, it is an unremarkable example of a late Imperial temple, well-preserved through having been converted into a church whose Baroque façade of 1602 now forms the back wall of the portico.

The **Arch of Septimus Severus** of 203, to the south of the Curia and forming a gate to one of the two approaches to the Capitoline hill, was built to mark the tenth anniversary of the emperor's reign. It is the finest remaining complete example of the most developed form of the triumphal arch. The central arch is flanked by two lower ones; the blind panels between its projecting order provide opportunities for sculpture, and the continuous deep attic a setting for the fine inscription of bronze letters. In 1988, one half of the Arch was cleaned to allow citizens to decide whether they preferred the clean or dirty half; in 1994, they had still not decided.

☞ The Basilica of Maxentius or of Constantine of 306–12 **23**, can be reached from the enclosure of the Forum, and the entrance ticket to the Forum also allows access to the Palatine hill **6**.

8Cd **Ponte Fabricio** or **'dei Quattro Capi'** 62 BC

Lungotevere Cenci to Isola Tiberina

After the early Romans emerged from the fortified Palatine, the strategically important banks of the Tiber on either side of the Isola Tiberina were among the first land to be occupied, and a crossing must have existed here from very early in the city's development. The Ponte Fabricio is now the earliest remaining bridge, and is still in use. Its span divided into two simple arches, it is a characteristically Roman work of engineering, and the spare architectural decoration is limited to the columns flanking the arch which rises from the central pier.

☞ One remaining arch of its predecessor, the **Pons Aemilius** of 179–142 BC, the first stone bridge across the Tiber which was finally washed away in 1598, can be seen to the south of the island and next to the modern Ponte Palatino. The church of **San Bartolomeo** on the Isola Tiberina was built in the twelfth century and is similar to other churches of the period such as San Crisogono **48** and Santa Maria in Trastevere **47**, but it was substantially altered in the seventeenth century. It has a basilican plan like those of San Crisogono and Santa Maria in Trastevere, with a nave arcade and raised transepts.

9Cd **Theatre of Marcellus** 44 BC –13 or 11 BC

Via di Teatro di Marcello

Julius Caesar commissioned the building of this theatre but it was completed by Augustus, who named it after a nephew. It held about 11,000 spectators, who were arranged in three semi-circular tiers of seats facing a shallow flat stage, this still unexcavated. The seats were surrounded by and reached from the external arcaded ambulatories built of travertine, the lower two of which are decorated with the Doric and Ionic orders. The third, top, storey which may have been constructed of timber is now completely missing. Converted into a fortified mansion in the middle ages, and later into a palace for the Savelli family, much of the exterior of the building has survived. The arcades were last cleaned and the remnants of the interior gentrified in 1993.

☞ The former church of **Santa Rita** of 1665, one of Carlo Fontana's earliest works, was moved in 1940 to make way for the via di Teatro di Marcello which it now faces at the corner of via Montanara. To the north-west of the theatre is an arch and part of the colonnade of the **Portico d'Ottavia**: this was built by Augustus and rebuilt in the third century. To the south along the via del Teatro di Marcello is the church of San Nicola in Carcere **50**.

Santa Rita

10Al **Ara Pacis Augustae (altar)** 13–9 BC, reconstructed and enclosed 1937–38

Lungotevere in Augusta/via di Ripetta

Ⓜ A Spagna

This splendid ceremonial altar is one of the few significant remains of Augustus' revolutionary transformation of monumental Rome. Originally standing in the open and at a much lower level than its modern surroundings, it was reconstructed and housed in 1938 as part of the programme to represent Imperial glories. The diffident glass-walled enclosure was designed by Vittorio Ballio Morpurgo. The altar is a cross between a building and a piece of furniture: a wall surrounds a nearly square enclosure in which stands the altar itself, raised on a stepped plinth, the whole made of Carrara marble from the quarries opened by Augustus. The sculpture with which the wall is covered, carried out for the first time in Rome by Greek masons introduced by Augustus, is of the highest quality, and the upper half with its frieze of figures portraying the dedication ceremony of 4 July 13 BC is touching in its humanity (illustration, page 8). For a fine fictional recreation of the ceremony see Allan Massie's *Augustus*. The lower half is decorated with a pattern combining acanthus leaf scrollwork and swans.

☞ **Mausoleum of Augustus/Tumulus Caesarum now Augustan Museum** 28–23 BC.

This was a very large example of a type erected earlier for aristocratic burials. Built by Augustus for his own tomb and those of his family, its circular concrete drum with a diameter of 88 metres (290 feet) was originally faced in travertine, and contained an elaborate series of passages and compartments with niches for funerary urns. It was surmounted by a tumulus of earth crowned with a colossal statue of Augustus set in a grove of black poplars. Subsequently used as a fort for the Colonna family, a bull ring, a theatre and a concert hall, its present state and setting date from 1938 when the Augustan Museum was installed, the surrounding medieval buildings were cleared away and the new flaccid piazza arranged. The churches of San Rocco **116** and **San Girolamo degli Schiavoni** which face the Tiber were isolated when the Mausoleum was cleared.

11Cp **Pyramid of Gaius Cestius** 12 BC

near Porta San Paolo

Ⓜ B Piramide

Those monuments built near the Aurelian Wall and which have been preserved are idiosyncratic (compare the Baker's Tomb next to the Porta Maggiore **12**). This pyramidal tomb for the Praetor Gaius Cestius was built of brick and clad in fine white limestone. While the form of the tomb was never copied, it became one of the identifying features in the Rome of the early guide books, and occurs frequently in paintings imagining antiquity. The obelisks set up by Sixtus V are crowned with pyramids, and the entrance to the Foro Italico **176** has a gilded one on the modern re-working of the obelisk form at its entrance.

☞ The Post Office **187** of 1933–34 is through the gate to the north in via Marmorata.

12Ee **Porta Maggiore** AD 52

Piazza di Porta Maggiore

M A Vittorio, San Giovanni

While Caligula unaccountably destroyed the end of the Aqua Virgo, he also began the construction of two new aqueducts, the Aqua Claudia and the Aqua Anio Novus, but the work was left unfinished at his death. Claudius ordered their completion, extending them into Rome, and spanning two of the main roads to the south, the Via Prenestina and via Labicana. The two arches of the aqueduct were later incorporated into the Aurelian Walls as one of their gates, the Porta Prenestina. Built entirely of travertine, the Porta Maggiore demonstrates the growing sophistication in the architectural treatment of engineering structures. The base of massive rusticated blocks, much copied by the architects of the Renaissance, is contrasted with the smooth masonry of the attic which houses the water channels and exhibits the beautifully lettered dedicatory inscription.

The small travertine structure outside the gate is the **Tomb of M. Virgilius Eurysaces**, of about 30 BC, which commemorates a baker and his wife. The plain circular openings, which were to provide the architects of the *Stile Littorio* with one of their much used motifs, represent oven doors, and the sculptures in the frieze above show the various stages of baking.

Tomb of M. Virgilius Eurysaces

☞ **Aqua Claudia (Claudian Aqueduct)** AD 38–52, the workmanlike continuation in brick to the south and west of the stone Porta Maggiore. The **Basilica of Porta Maggiore** is an important survival of the underground place of worship for a Neo-Pythagorean sect of the mid first century AD, but it is accessible only with permission. On the east side of via Eleniana, the **Cabina dell'ACCA**, an electricity sub-station of 1934, is a huge cube, less a design, more an assemblage of motifs, including in the surrounds to the windows a direct quotation of the flat circular openings from the Baker's Tomb.

13Db **Flavian Amphitheatre/'Colosseum'** AD 72–80

Via dei Fori Imperiali

M B Colosseo

Vespasian, the head of the second Imperial Roman dynasty, emerged the victor from the civil war which followed the death of Nero in AD 68. He started several large buildings of which the Colosseum has proved the most conspicuous and enduring. Its position was determined as much by political considerations as by those of accessibility: it occupies the site of the artificial lake which was designed to be overlooked by one wing of Nero's Domus Aurea (Golden House) on the slopes of the Oppian hill to the north-east, and its building was the first step in eradicating the repellent reminder of the excesses of the previous dynasty. (The present name for the amphitheatre was not used in antiquity: it may derive from the colossal gilded statue of himself which Nero set up near the Temple of Venus and Rome to the south-west.)

Built to serve the needs of Rome's growing population, and as a popular gesture, the building is remarkable not for its architectural innovations (its exterior is no more sophisticated than that of the Theatre of Marcellus **9** of ninety years earlier), but for the elegant geometry of its plan, the ingenuity of its circulation system and the organisational assuredness required to build it. A foundation of thick concrete was laid over the bed of Nero's lake, and this was covered with travertine blocks. Over this was raised the building whose oval plan measured 188 by 142 metres (620 by 470 feet). The seating for spectators was supported on radiating

walls of travertine and tufa which supported concrete vaults and the marble-covered seating for about 50,000. The two main lower tiers of seats and the raised top tier were reached via stairs and ramps from double barrel-vaulted ambulatories which surrounded the perimeter. The four projecting ceremonial entrance porches which were placed on the main axes have disappeared.

The architecture of the exterior, carried out entirely in travertine, subsequently provided a mesmerising model for generations of architects. One of the three Orders is used to decorate each of the three arcaded storeys: Roman Doric for the base, Ionic for the middle, and Corinthian for the top. Corinthian pilasters decorate the blind attic. This bears the projecting sockets used to support the wooden poles from which were strung ropes to support a sailcloth awning (the velarium) which shaded the seating. The rope from each pole was secured at ground level to one of a series of bollards placed round and away from the perimeter of the building, and the whole apparatus was operated by a platoon of sailors.

Apart from its size, and stripped of its marble fittings and without a floor to the arena, the interior now offers few clues to its original appearance. Fortunately, Hollywood has supplied several restorations of both its aspect and its cruel entertainments: *Quo Vadis* of 1951, although set in Nero's time, is probably the best.

☞ **Domus Aurea (Golden House of Nero)** AD 64-68. The remains of the Golden House, the huge country villa which Nero established in the heart of Rome, are the most important remaining indications of the discovery by Roman architects of techniques of spatial intricacy which played such an important part in the subsequent development of Roman architecture, and whose rediscovery underground in the sixteenth century profoundly affected the decorative art of the Renaissance. Unfortunately the ruins are now housed in cellars accessible only with permission.

The remains of the **Temple of Venus and Rome** stand in the park on the small eminence to the west of the Colosseum. This huge building was erected by Hadrian in about 135 using Greek Pentelic marble rather than Roman Carrara, and Greek artisans to work it. It contained two identical cellas back to back. The original straight dividing wall between them was replaced by Maxentius with apses covered with semi-domes when he repaired the Temple after a fire in 307. The Arch of Constantine **24** stands to the south of the Colosseum at the beginning of via di San Gregorio, and beyond it is one of the entrances to the Palatine and Forum.

14Da **Trajan's Forum, Column** and **Markets**

110–13

Via dei Fori Imperiali/Largo Magnanapoli

Apollodorus of Damascus

The tradition of Imperial forum building started by Julius Caesar, and continued by Augustus, Vespasian and Nerva, concluded with that of Trajan whose contribution was more extensive than the total area of all its predecessors. Its form is also more complex and reflects Trajan's eclectic architectural taste: the forum established by Caesar had a temple raised on a high base situated at one end of a walled enclosure, the long sides of which were lined with colonnades which provided shelter.

Trajan's Forum reconstructed: from modello plastico, EUR

The innovatory design of Trajan's architect Apollodorus provided *two* enclosed courts. These were separated by a very large hall, the Basilica Ulpia ('Ulpius' was Trajan's family name), beyond which the second court contained a temple. In front of this stood the memorial Column, now standing free, but originally flanked by two libraries. Large parts of the Quirinal were cut away to provide space for the new construction: the height of the Column records the original ground level before excavation. To the north-east of the first court Trajan developed a new commercial area which rises up, and is further cut into, the Quirinal hill.

Shops on the curved street

The area was fully excavated and partly restored in the 1930s, but the subsequent construction of the via dei Fori Imperiali and its associated landscaping has made it difficult to see or to imagine the original scheme, and the area itself is inaccessible. The first court, originally approached through an arch, is now almost completely obscured, but some of the double rows of granite columns of the Basilica Ulpia and its double-square ground plan are visible. To the south-east of these, the Column rises, now lacking both its setting of the libraries and the temple which lay beyond, between the two present churches of Santa Maria di Loreto and the Nome di Maria. The Column, built of Carrara marble, records in a novel way Trajan's successful military campaigns in Dacia: a continuous narrative frieze of bas reliefs of very high quality runs in a spiral from bottom to top. The Column's square base, intended as Trajan's tomb, displays the inscription whose subtle and beautiful letter forms have become the model for all inscribed 'Roman' lettering.

The markets, accessible from Largo Magnanapoli, comprise a confusion of several streets and halls set on and into a steeply sloping site on four levels. The view we now have from the via dei Fori Imperiali of the rather grand row of shops laid out on a segmental plan was not available in antiquity. These shops, at the lowest level of the commercial section of the Forum, originally formed one side of a curved street; the other was formed by the blind outer wall of one of the two exedrae which flanked the Forum's first court. The remaining shops, built entirely of brick-faced concrete, include a nearly complete street of three storeys, visible from the Largo Magnanapoli. This is lined with shops of the *taberna* type which are found all over the countries which border the Mediterranean: the high barrel-vaulted room, entered through a single wide square opening above which a window provided ventilation, or light to an optional timber mezzanine floor. Many of the shop entrances are still protected by a continuous cantilevered canopy of concrete vaulting. Above this street are the remains of a market hall of two storeys, its vaulted roof still in position.

15 **Villa Adriana (Hadrian's Villa)** 113–38

off via Tiburtina, Tivoli

Hadrian reigned for twenty-one years (117–38) and his remarkable building programme included the religious Pantheon **16** and Temple of Venus and Rome, as well as the secular reconstruction of the port of Ostia. But unlike his predecessors he chose not to live on the Palatine and started this combination of official court residence and country villa only a year after his accession and continued building until his death.

With the collapse of the Empire, the undefended Villa was abandoned, sacked, and used as a quarry. During the Renaissance, however, interest was revived, and at the end of the fifteenth century Cardinal Alessandro Farnese and Pope Alexander VI started excavations, but with more interest in finding art treasures than in archaeology. In the sixteenth century, Cardinal Ippolito d'Este commissioned his architect Pirro Ligorio to survey the ruins, and carried away many finds of antique sculpture. Piranesi surveyed and drew the site in the eighteenth century. In 1870 the Villa was transferred to the care of the state, and systematic excavation and conservation was started, and continues today. The model in the hut opposite the present car park is helpful in suggesting the extent and splendour of the original, and the small converted villa to the west houses a modest exhibition about the history of the site.

The choice of site is mystifying: an undistinguished patch of undulating low-lying land inconveniently remote from both Rome and Tivoli. The arrangement of the huge complex of buildings is equally baffling: there appears to be no organising principle informing the sprawling layout, and most of the parts lack the ruthless geometrical clarity of Hadrian's other monuments. Geometrically self-contained complexes are strewn across the site and abut each other with no apparent reason. It would be tempting to try to see a precursor of eighteenth-century notions of Picturesque planning, except that it is impossible to trace a route through the buildings which would have afforded the eighteenth-century experience of surprise and carefully contrived views. Indeed it is hard to imagine that the original occupants did not often get lost, although many of the buildings were connected by a system of large underground service corridors. There are few written clues about the symbolic or allegorical programme which may have informed the building, and many of the names which have been given to the various structures are fanciful, conjectural or incorrect. The ruins are described in the order suggested by the signposts.

From the car park, the visitor enters the **Poikile.** This is the largest enclosure on the site, a walled rectangle 232 by 97 metres (760 by 318 feet) with curved ends. Modelled on the Stoa Poikile at Athens, the space was originally surrounded by a roofed colonnade, the positions of its column bases now marked by trees. At its centre was a large pool around which races might have been run. The north-east corner of the Poikile gives access to the **'Naval Theatre'** (illustrated above), an enclosure containing a circular island reached by a movable bridge. On the island stand the restored remains of a delicate and complex open structure of circular colonnades, a setting perhaps for entertainment. The northern exit from the 'theatre' connects with the outside of the walls of the 'Greek Library'. This stands next to what has been identified as the Imperial Palace which was irregularly arranged round three courts, the largest of which is the '**Court of the Libraries**'. South of the palace and via an extensive Nymphaeum lie the large and small **Thermae** or baths. Much of their original vaulting has fallen, but some fine stucco decoration remains on that which still stands. Beyond the baths and set in an excavated shallow valley lies the **Canopus**, a long canal, its surrounding colonnade partly restored, at the end of which is the **Serapaeum**, a shrine and grotto whose design was derived from that of the original shrine to Serapis in Alexandria.

To enjoy a visit, choose a fine day, take a picnic and for an insight into Hadrian's life and his eclectic imagination read Marguerite Yourcenar's *Memoirs of Hadrian.*

☞ Villa d'Este, Tivoli **79.**

16Ap **Pantheon** 118–25

Piazza Rotonda

Agrippa's inscription, 'ME AGRIPPA FECIT...' below the pediment refers to an earlier building on the site which was destroyed by fire and of which nothing remains. Its replacement was commissioned by Augustus' son-in-law Hadrian, whose remarkable building programme is described in the Introduction. It has subsequently captivated generations of western architects, prompting reworkings from Palladio at Maser to Thomas Jefferson at both Monticello and the University of Virginia. In 608 it became one of the first Roman temples to be converted into a church, Santa Maria Rotonda, and it has never been a ruin: the continuous admiration it has excited probably owes as much to its state of preservation as to its intrinsic qualities, its 'perfection', and the appeal of its universal programme.

The temple was originally set at the long end of a narrow square lined with colonnades: for a reconstruction of the setting, see the model in the Museo della Civilità Romana at EUR **191**. It comprises two elements: the first a conventional but deep porch supported by unfluted granite columns, its plinth originally approached via a flight of steps. This crudely abuts and provides the entrance to the second: the highly unconventional circular temple with its hemispherical dome. The dome springs from a drum whose height is exactly that of the radius of the dome, that is, the diameter of the interior is the same as its height of 43.2 metres (142 feet) from floor level to the oculus. It remains one of triumphs of Roman civil architecture, both in its unprecedented size and in the care and daring of its concrete and brickwork construction, and in its sophisticated modelling of

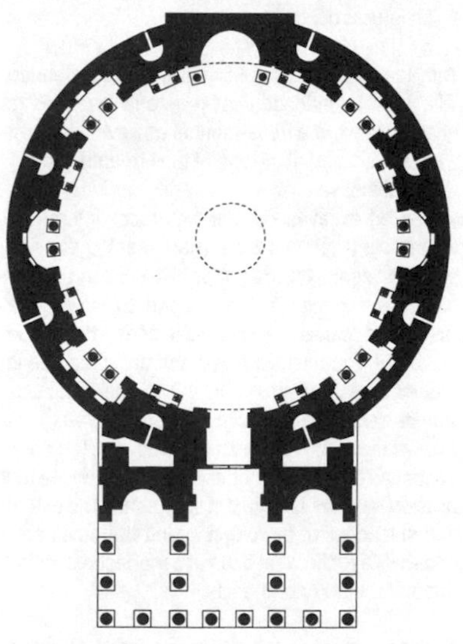

space. For the purposes of decoration, the drum is divided into two storeys, the lower pierced by six shallow exedrae carved into the seven-metre thick walls and separated from the main space by screens; the only recognition of the axis suggested by the entrance is the apse facing it. The upper storey is decorated with sixteen blind windows altered in the sixteenth century but some of whose form and surrounding facings were later plausibly re-Romanised. The platonic geometry is not insistent: this rhythmic division into sixteen is not repeated in the coffering pattern of the dome, which instead has twenty-eight divisions.

The building's present form and setting are the consequence of nearly two millennia of adaptation and restoration. During the middle ages two small towers one either side of the portico were added; they were copied by Palladio in his Maser church, re-styled by Bernini, and then removed in a restoration of 1883. Earlier, in the 1620s, the decorative bronze coffers of the ceiling of the porch had been removed and melted down to provide the material for Bernini's baldacchino at St Peter's.

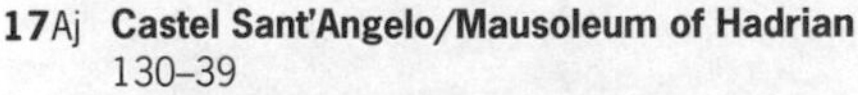

17Aj **Castel Sant'Angelo/Mausoleum of Hadrian**
130–39

Lungotevere Castello/Ponte Sant'Angelo

M A Lepanto

After nearly a century of Imperial burials the Mausoleum of Augustus had become full, and Hadrian undertook this replacement, one of the few imperial monuments to be sited on the west bank of the Tiber. The new tomb was modelled on its predecessor, but its form was more complex, infused with the platonic geometry of the other buildings commissioned by Hadrian. The cylindrical Mausoleum with a diameter of 64 metres (210 feet) and 21 metres high (69 feet) housed a spiral ramp, and was raised on a podium 84 metres (275 feet) square and 10 metres (33 feet) high. Over the drum was raised a mound of earth planted with cypresses and crowned with a statue of the emperor. For a picture of the original architectural intentions, see the models in the museum which now occupies the building. As the papacy established itself near the shrine of St Peter, in the middle ages the tomb was converted into a fortress which terminated the eastern end of the Leonine Wall: its marbles were removed, the interior of the drum hollowed out, and the present bulky battlement and superstructures added. In the sixteenth century the base was greatly enlarged with further fortifications and polygonal salients which were subsequently remodelled by Bernini.

☞ Hadrian also commissioned a bridge, the Pons Aelius now the **Ponte Sant'Angelo**, finished in 134, to connect the new mausoleum to the city. It was replaced in 1892–94 when the Tiber embankments were built.

18Ap **Temple of Hadrian** begun 145

Piazza di Pietra

An unusually successful if unintentional example of pastiche: eleven of the remaining Corinthian columns which flanked the cella of the temple dedicated by Antoninus Pius to his father Hadrian have been incorporated into the rear wall of the Borsa (Stock Exchange) and now preside over a small square dedicated to parked cars.

19Ap **Column of Marcus Aurelius** 180–96

Piazza Colonna off Corso

Two of the columns set up by emperors to commemorate their activities survive: this one and the Column of Trajan **14** of seventy years earlier. The format here is the same: above a square base (restored by Domenico Fontana in 1589 when the original statues of the emperor and his wife were replaced by that of Saint Paul), marble drums are carved with a continuous spiral of sculptures which celebrate Marcus Aurelius' military victories over the Germans and Sarmatians. The column was originally surrounded by other monuments of which the fragments of Hadrian's Temple **18** are all that remain. It is now encircled by buildings which date from all the centuries between the seventeenth and the present one.

☞ On the east side of the square, the Galleria Colonna **169**; on the north-east corner is *La Rinascente* **162**. To the north, one flank of the Palazzo Chigi. On the south side of the piazza is the small church of **San Bartolomeo dei Bergamaschi**.

20Dj **Thermae/Baths of Caracalla** 212–17

Via delle Terme di Caracalla

Ⓜ B Circo Massimo

Trajan had established the tradition of providing great Imperial public bath buildings, but the present scant ruins of his baths on the Oppian hill now suggest nothing of the scale and grandeur of the type. The remains of Caracalla's baths of a century later are more extensive if no more complete, and considerable imagination is required to attempt to reconstruct the building. An external recreation is supplied in the model at the Museo della Civilità Romana at EUR **191**, but for the qualities of the interior only modern examples such as McKim Mead and White's Grand Central Station in New York offer any guidance, and there the decoration is muted and the light wrong.

The baths were composed of two elements: a very large walled rectangular enclosure 300 metres (984 feet) by 245 metres (804 feet), with exedrae on its short sides, which housed the water cisterns and which was laid out as a park and stadium. Within this was arranged a compact rectangular block 200 metres (656 feet) by 100 metres (328 feet), its main elevation facing south-west and planned around two cross axes. At the intersection of the axes, in the centre of the block were the baths proper, clustered around the main central hall, the *frigidarium*, tall, and of three cross-vaulted bays. On either side of this hall, at the ends of the long axis, were the *palaestræ*, open-air exercise yards. Along the full length of the south-west side a separately planned sequence of rooms with large windows faced the afternoon sun, at their centre the large projecting circular and domed *calidarium*, the steam room.

Suggested restoration, EUR modello plastico

Most of the concrete vaults have fallen, and only visible now are the weathered remains of the massive brick structure of the building which indicate no more than its size. Its enclosure, enormous vistas, the sumptuous and probably excessive decoration are all missing, though archaeology has supplied hints of the last. The floors were of black and white mosaics, the walls were entirely covered in polychrome marbles and fully equipped with statuary, and the vaults were clad in stucco or mosaic, the whole lit by shafts of sunlight from the high windows under the vaults. For an indication of the qualities of the interior of the *frigidarium*, we have the later Baths of Diocletian, now the church of Santa Maria degli Angeli **84**, but even here the original decorations have not survived.

☞ The little church of **Santi Nero ed Achilleo** is near the entrance to the Baths, stranded in a park and next to the main road. Founded in 524 it was rebuilt in 1597, but its triumphal arch retains an original mosaic. On via di Santa Balbina, to the west of the baths, are the church and convent of **Santa Balbina**, the pleasantly dishevelled convent now a conference centre, and the church having been stripped almost bare in a restoration of the 1940s.

21Eb **Catacombs of Priscilla** from about 250
Via Salaria 430

This is the only example of the catacomb included here. While not exactly a building type and rarely having any more architectural sophistication than a rabbit warren, it has become established in the imaginative reconstruction of the Rome of the early Christians in popular fiction (*Quo Vadis?*), and cinema (*Ben Hur*). The type evolved from an underground cemetery outside the walls of the city: there is no evidence that it was used as a place of meeting or refuge. The shelf-tombs were excavated out of the earth or rock, and stacked above each other on either side of a meandering corridor. Bodies were generally interred sideways, and then sealed with an inscribed terracotta or marble slab. Most of the Christian catacombs are now cleared of human remains: in an enthusiastic programme of relic gathering undertaken in the ninth century, the bones were redistributed to Rome's churches to be venerated as those of the martyrs. The Catacombs of Priscilla are among the least visited and therefore the least crowded of those accessible. The tombs themselves are characteristically arranged, but they are approached via an underground *cryptoporticus*, a vaulted room with vaults on either side, one of these containing the 'Greek chapel' in the form of an excavated 'T' with an apse, all decorated with original simple paintings.

☞ On the west side of the via Salaria, the grounds of the ex **Villa Savoia** are now an enormous park larger than the Villa Borghese, and planted with indigenous species of tree including small forests of umbrella pines.

22 **Aurelian Wall** 272–79

Ever since Rome defeated Carthage in 146 BC, and given her naval supremacy in the Mediterranean, by the third century the only military threat to the Empire came from the north: from those German tribes who had never been subdued. In about 269 an army of these crossed the Alps and invaded the valley of the River Po, prompting the building of a complete new city wall to supersede that of Servius **1**. The boundary of the Empire had been brought from its extremities to its capital. The area enclosed was very large, including much open land outside the built-up area, and the new walls often cut through aristocratic country estates. To the south, the Baths of Caracalla, which had been built outside the Servian Wall, were included within the new, and to the north-east the walls of the camp of the Praetorian Guard were incorporated into the new construction. Many tombs and mausolea which up till then law had required to be situated outside the city became included. On the west bank of the Tiber, the enclosure of much of what is now Trastevere, including a gate for the via Aurelia, followed after the main campaign.

The walls, with a total length of about 19 kilometres (12 miles), were built in a single prodigious campaign lasting nearly ten years. They were constructed of concrete rubble faced in brick, about 3.5 metres (11 feet 6 inches) at the base and 7.6 metres (25 feet) high with a walk on top protected by a slotted parapet. Three hundred and eighty square towers were placed at intervals of two arrow-shots or one hundred Roman feet (29.6 metres, 97 Imperial feet), and a gate of standard design placed to guard each of the

Porta Appia, now Porta San Sebastiano

Porta Asinaria, now Porta San Giovanni

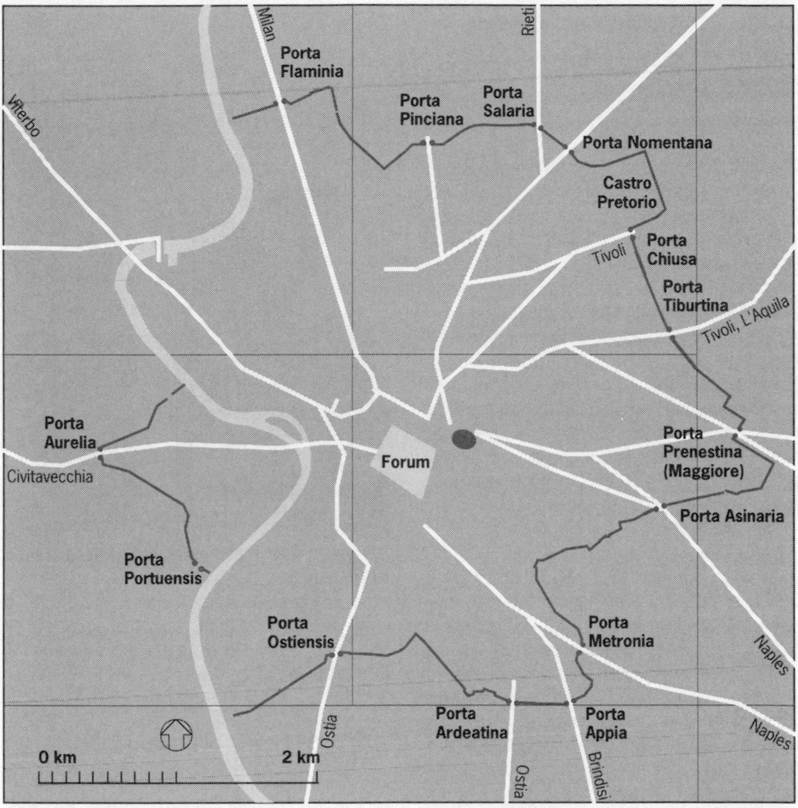

Aurelian Wall, and gates with their original names

eighteen main roads. The gates originally had either one or a pair of arches set between semicircular towers. Many of them have, for reasons of defence, traffic circulation or ceremonial, since been considerably rebuilt. The **Porta Appia** (now San Sebastiano) and **Porta Asinaria** (next to the Porta San Giovanni) to the south retain most of their Roman features; and the **Porta Tiburtina** (now Toscolana) to the east is the best preserved.

Under Maxentius, in 309–12 the walls were raised, and were raised again by Arcadius and Honorius in 402–3 to their present height of about 15 metres (50 feet). They were never breached until 1870 when the nascent Italian army destroyed a section near the Porta Pia and entered Rome.

Porta Tiburtina, country side

23Da **Basilica of Maxentius** or **of Constantine/ Basilica Nova** 306–12

Via dei Fori Imperiali

M B Colosseo

One of the last Imperial public buildings in Rome, this basilica was also one of the largest, and with the Pantheon **16**, one of the Empire's greatest achievements in civil architecture. Its form is derived from the central spaces or *frigidaria* of the Imperial Baths and consists of a huge rectangular hall 80 metres (265 feet) long, 25 metres (82 feet) wide and 35 metres (115 feet) high, of three bays each roofed with a cross vault of concrete. Subsidiary tunnel-vaulted shallow bays on either side buttress the main vault. The building techniques had been developed two centuries earlier, for example in the Colosseum, and in successive Imperial Baths: it is the scale and daring extension of those techniques which are remarkable here.

The original entrance was through a porch at the eastern end, and a vaulted segmental apse terminated the western. All the original marble and stucco decoration has been stripped, but the coffers of the vaults and the remaining corbels of the vaults, each of which would have been supported by a column, suggest how the bare forms were articulated. (One of the remaining columns is now re-erected in the piazza in front of Santa Maria Maggiore.) Begun by Maxentius, but left incomplete at his death in the battle at Saxa Rubra in 312, the building was completed by his successor Constantine who moved the entrance to the southern, long side, and constructed a new apse in the central bay facing it. He placed a colossal statue of himself in the apse left by Maxentius: parts of this are now in the museum at the Campidoglio.

24Df **Arch of Constantine** 315

Via di San Gregorio/piazza del Colosseo

M B Colosseo

Constantine concluded the Imperial tradition of building arches to celebrate victories in battle, erecting this one to commemorate his victory with divine help over Maxentius in 312. Its design is conservative, and closely follows the model of that of Septimus Severus of 203 to the west at the opposite end of the Forum. The attic here, however, is not continuous, but is divided into three parts corresponding to the arrangement of the arches below. Some of the sculptured panels including those at the bases of the columns were newly commissioned but carried out in an old-fashioned style; others were taken from the earlier arches of Trajan and Hadrian, and those in the attic from a monument of Marcus Aurelius.

Although partly submerged by the rising ground level of later Rome, the Arch remained visible to the surveyors and scholars of the Renaissance. Its motifs of three arches, and the decorative use of the column with its entablature projecting from an associated wall, immediately entered the small repertoire of classical architecture.

25Dd **Pavilion in the Licinian gardens/'Temple of Minerva Medica'**: early fourth century

Via Giovanni Giolitti

M A Vittorio

A sad relic in a sad setting sandwiched between road and railway, this garden pavilion or *nymphaeum* is now significant only for its illustration of late Roman building techniques. It has a ten-sided plan 25 metres (82 feet) in diameter and ringed by nine projecting apses. Above, a drum lit with large round headed windows supported a dome of concrete without the usual separate transitional pendentives. The dome, which until it collapsed in 1828 was a model for many architects of the Renaissance, is divided into segments by non-structural brickwork ribs.

Archaeology has been unable to determine what purpose the builders intended these to serve: they may form movement joints for the otherwise monolithic construction, or they may have made building the dome easier.

26De **Arch of Janus Quadrifons/Arco di Giano**
about 315
Via del Velabro

An extraordinarily incompetent undertaking which powerfully suggests the rapid collapse of Classical architectural values during and after Constantine's reign, the four-sided arch was designed to provide shelter at a crossroads for the cattle dealers from the Forum Boarium, the market nearby. It is constructed of brick and covered with marble sheets punctuated with ninety-six niches for statues.

☞ The church of San Giorgio in Velabro **38**, inaccessible in 1995.

Christian and medieval Rome 316–1474

27Ec **Mausoleum of Constantia/church of Santa Costanza** before 354

Via Nomentana/via di Santa Costanza

This mausoleum was built by Constantine's daughter on her estate to house her own tomb and that of her sister Helena. Its form is pre-Christian, with the standard circular plan of a pagan tomb of an aristocratic Roman. The drum of the central domed space is supported on arches carried on pairs of columns. The arcade is surrounded by an ambulatory whose barrel vault is entirely covered in magnificently preserved and restored mosaics in panels. Abstract geometrical patterns alternate with scenes of secular life, wine producing, for example, which contain no apparently explicit Christian symbolism and are a good guide in imagining some of the decoration now stripped from earlier pagan Roman buildings. The recess off the ambulatory and facing the entrance now contains a copy of Constantia's tomb. The exterior is very plain, and the narthex which may originally have formed the approach to the entrance has nearly disappeared.

☞ The Basilica of Sant'Agnese fuori le Mura **28** lies immediately to the north and can be reached either by the path through the gardens opposite the entrance to the mausoleum, or from the via Nomentana. The large ruins of Constantia's **Basilica** of 337–50 which served a Christian cemetery near her mausoleum can be seen from the gardens and better from via Bressanone to the west. The former Istituto Romano dei Ciechi di Guerra **180** of 1930 lies to the south-west.

28Ec **Basilica of Sant'Agnese fuori le Mura** (337–50), 625–38

Via Nomentana/via di Sant'Agnese

This church was built over a large cemetery and catacombs to replace the basilica which had been erected by Constantine's daughter Constantia to commemorate the martyred Saint Agnes. It has been restored several times in its long life. Its plan is of the standard basilican type, with narthex, nave, aisles and apse. Its section was, however, varied by the insertion above the aisles of galleries (*matronea*) for women worshippers who could observe services through the delicate arches above the nave arcades. Above these again are clerestories, resulting in an unusually tall section in proportion to the width of the nave. The walls of the apse are decorated with what may be the original marble cladding, and the semi-dome is covered with a seventh-century mosaic showing against a gold background Saint Agnes flanked by popes, one of whom carries a model of the Basilica. Beneath the church are the Catacombs of Sant'Agnese, but the tour is less architecturally interesting than that of the Catacombs of Priscilla **21**.

29Di **Santa Prisca** 350

Via di Santa Prisca, Aventine

The date is deceptive: the small basilica was heavily restored by Carlo Lambardi in 1600 when the nave arcades were strengthened with piers, and the aisles were given barrel vaults. Lambardi also contributed the new façade.

30Eg **San Paolo fuori le Mura** 384, rebuilt 1823–54 and 1893–1910

Via Ostiense

M B San Paolo

Originally built during the period of confusion before the final split of the Roman Empire into Eastern and Western parts, and intended to claim Saint Paul for Rome as an Apostle with the same standing as Saint Peter, the church is Rome's largest after St Peter's, its nave 25 metres (82 feet) wide. In 1823 it was severely damaged by fire, and after much controversy the decision was taken to demolish the surviving parts of the nave, transepts and campanile and to build something new. Luigi Poretti's design, built on the original plan of a nave flanked by pairs of aisles, is a raw, regular neoclassical reconstruction the glossiness of whose materials has more connection with the reconstructions of Hollywood than with the more authentic character of surviving basilicas such as that of Santa Sabina **32**. Of the original foundation only the triumphal arch of the apse decorated with its much-restored mosaics now remains. Undamaged in the fire, the bronze entrance doors of Byzantine design were set up in 1070, and the small cloister with pairs of twisted columns covered in mosaic dates from the beginning of the thirteenth century.

Replacing the original quadriporticus and built between 1893 and 1910, Guglielmo Calderini's colonnaded courtyard and screen through which the church is approached are more original, and combine elements both from antiquity and from the Renaissance. The screen is particularly inventive and is derived from an enlarged version of the cloister of San Giovanni in Laterano **112**. Its three rows of columns are spanned by a tunnel vault on the inner face and by single barrel vaults running at right angle to this on the outer.

31Bo **Basilica of Santa Maria Maggiore** 420–40, 1673, 1743

Piazza Esquilino

M A B Termini

A century after the first church building campaign initiated by Constantine, Sixtus III began a second which was continued by his successor Leo I, 'the Great'. It included the basilicas of Santa Maria Maggiore and of San Lorenzo fuori le Mura **36**, and the re-modelling of Constantine's Lateran baptistery **112**. The popes' aim was to consolidate the importance of the papacy in a city now deserted by its Emperor, their means a revival of the forms of classical antiquity of the period before Constantine. Sited on one of the summits of the Esquiline hill, the first church of Santa Maria, started in about 420, had a standard basilican arrangement: an arcaded nave flanked by aisles and terminating in a semi-circular apse. Two features distinguish it from earlier work: its size– the nave is 17 metres (56 feet) wide and 86 metres (282 feet) long; and the Ionic order of the columns and entablature of the colonnades, last used in Rome in Trajan's Forum and here confidently and correctly revived. The triumphal arch and the panels between the paired pilasters of the walls above the colonnade carry a magnificent cycle of contemporary mosaics of biblical scenes.

The church remained unaltered until the middle of the thirteenth century when the fine Cosmatesque pavement was laid. At the end of the century the east end was rebuilt: transepts were added; the apse remodelled with a polygonal plan and furnished with mosaics by Torriti; and a new west façade, subsequently obscured, was built.

In the sixteenth century, the axes of the transepts were extended. On the north side, Domenico Fontana's **Sistine or Holy Sacrament chapel** of 1585 was added to house the tomb of Sixtus V. In the form of a domed Greek cross, its decoration is a sumptuous display of patterned and coloured marbles, contrasting with the statues of Sixtus and

Pius V in white. Set in the floor outside the chapel, is the tomb of the Bernini family. To the south, the **Borghese chapel** was designed by Flaminio Ponzio in 1611. Next to this, towards the west end, is the **Sforza chapel** with its complex vault, completed by Giacomo della Porta who followed a late design by Michelangelo.

A 'façade' to the apse, with flanking wings which fill out the corners of the plan, was designed by Carlo Rainaldi and added in 1673 when the magnificent flights of external stairs were provided.

The present western façade was commissioned in 1743 from Ferdinando Fuga, whose design was required to span the width of the church itself and to include the flanking canons' houses. He used the standard Roman device of a façade of two storeys, the lower wider than the upper, but extended it to cover the five doors of the church rather than the more usual three. The brief required a papal benediction loggia and a vestibule for pilgrims, and the design is developed in depth as a series of voids framed by bays capped with alternating triangular and segmental pediments. At the same time, in the interior, Fuga also added the present baldacchino and slightly modernised the nave.

☞ **Flats,** 1926, via Napoleone III/via Gioberti by Vincenzo Fasolo: an attempt to vernacularise a 'palazzina' flat block with overhanging Florentine eaves and loggias, and irregular projecting Roman balconies like those in the street at Trajan's Market **14**.

32Cl **Basilica of Santa Sabina** about 425–32
Piazza Pietro d'Illiria/via Santa Sabina, Aventine hill

M B Circo Massimo, Piramide

Few of the earlier Christian basilicas in Rome have survived in their original form: many were damaged by fire or war, others modernised or rebuilt. Santa Sabina, now tactfully restored, remains the best example of the type in the city, rivalling in magnificence the contemporary churches of Ravenna. The first basilica to be built in what was, and still largely is, a quiet upper-class suburb, it belongs to the phase of church building which took place about a century after Constantine christianised the Roman state. This included the first basilica of San Paolo fuori le Mura **30**, since burnt and rebuilt, and that of Santa Maria Maggiore **31**.

Compared with the often improvisatory quality of the first official churches the style here is precise, assured and calm: classicism was already being revived for the first time. The plan is of a pure basilican form: the tall nave, lit by very large clerestory windows and separated from the aisles by arcades of re-used matching grey marble Corinthian columns, terminates in a semi-circular apse with a vault of half a hemisphere. The enclosure for clergy and choir, the presbytery, is

contained within a marble wall. The design of the modern grilles to the windows was deduced from surviving fragments of the originals. Of the first decorative scheme, the marble opus sectile surrounds to the arches remain. The walls above, the arch over the apse, and the vault of the apse were completely clad in mosaic of which the magnificent dedicatory inscription of gold letters on a blue ground on the west wall remains. The wooden doors below this panel, of the fifth century and probably contemporary with the foundation of the church, are remarkable both for their preservation and the carvings of biblical scenes on the exterior.

☞ Next to Santa Sabina and north-east: a small park with fine views west over Trastevere and north to Monte Mario; the church of **Sant' Alessio**; G. B. Piranesi's Piazza Cavalieri di Malta **138**.

33Db **San Pietro in Vincoli/Basilica Eudoxiana** 442 onwards
Piazza di San Pietro in Vincoli

M B Cavour

The first basilica on this site was founded by the Empress Eudoxia to house the chains (*vincoli*) with which St Peter had been bound. These are housed in the open crypt under the high altar. Of the original church, the very wide nave with its arcade of Doric columns, and the east wall with its three apses remain; the shallow segmental barrel-vaulted ceiling is of the seventeenth century. The present delicate Renaissance portico was provided in 1475. The reason that the church attracts large numbers of tourist coaches is to be found in the chapel in the south transept, where the projected **Tomb of Julius II** is to be found. Julius, who died in 1513 and was the great patron

of the artists and architects of the High Renaissance, including Bramante, Raphael and Michelangelo, is in fact buried in St Peter's. Having quarrelled with the pope, Michelangelo never finished work on the tomb, and while the general layout, the statues of Moses in the centre and the flanking Leah and Rachel are his, the remaining sculptures are by his pupils.

34Df **Santo Stefano Rotondo sul Celio** about 475
Via di Santo Stefano Rotondo/piazza Navicella

Ⓜ B Circo Massimo

The basilicas of Santa Maria Maggiore **31** and Santa Sabina **32** were built at the beginning of the Christian classical revival of the fifth century. Their rectangular halls were adapted from the Roman basilica. Completed about fifty years later, Santo Stefano was the last church of that revival, but its complex and enigmatic circular plan shows that by then other influences were also at work, possibly those of late Roman Imperial work or of the Near East. After years of neglect, in 1993 the church was handsomely restored under the *Roma Capitale* programme, and can now be appreciated as Santa Sabina's circular peer. Its present white paint is, however tasteful, inauthentic: the walls were originally covered with brilliantly coloured paintings and mosaics, and the sixteenth-century paintings covering the outer wall are no substitute: a catalogue of martyrdoms, their horrible events usefully captioned 'A' and 'B'. They are by Nicolò Circignani.

In the centre is a tall circular central space 22 metres (72 feet) wide and high, its perimeter colonnade of granite columns whose flat architrave supports the drum. This space is inexplicably bisected by a diaphragm wall supported on arches carried by Corinthian columns. An outer, now blind, arcade of marble columns forms the outer wall and defines a circular ambulatory. Beyond this arcade was a further outer circular wall towards which four transepts extended. This was demolished in 1450, and only two of the transepts now remain, one used as the entrance porch, the other as a chapel. The church was noted by the scholars and architects of the early Renaissance, and was certainly a useful precedent in furthering the fashion for later centrally planned churches.

☞ **Santa Maria in Domnica/della Navicella** 817–24. Nothing remains of the original church which was originally laid out with three apses, but substantially remodelled in the sixteenth century. The nickname comes from the stone Roman boat placed in front of the church by Pope Leo X. The entrance to the **Villa Celimontana** formerly **Mattei**, now the seat of the Società Geografica Italiana, its gardens now a lush, quiet public park, is to the north of the church. To the north again, the **Arch of Dolabella and Silanus** marks one end of the via San Paolo di Croce. The arch of AD 10 was incorporated as a single bay of the aqueduct built by Nero to serve the Palatine. To the north is the **Ospedale militare del Celio** of about 1885 by Salvatore Bianchi. The ward blocks are arranged in two rows stepping down the hill and connected by cast-iron galleries similar to those at the contemporary Policlinico **161**.

35Da **Santi Cosma e Damiano** 527
Via dei Fori Imperiali

The church was formed out of the conversion in the sixth century of two antique buildings: a Roman prefect's audience hall, and a part of the 'Temple of Romulus' built during Maxentius' reign. Approached through a courtyard into which parts of the temple intrude, it was reconstructed in the seventeenth century when the present ceiling was installed, and now consists of a short but broad nave connected to an apse of nearly the same width. The mosaics on the triumphal arch and in the semi-dome of the apse are of the sixth century and contemporary with the original foundation: of the six saints portrayed, the figure on the left is Saint Felix IV, the founder of the church, shown presenting a model of it to Christ in the centre.

36Ee **Basilica of San Lorenzo fuori le Mura**
579, 1216
Piazzale San Lorenzo

Ⓜ B Policlinico

The church was among the few buildings in Rome which were bombed in World War II. Its subsequent rebuilding removed evidence both of its earlier reconstruction by Vespignani and others in the nineteenth century, and of the painted flat ceiling of the nave. The earliest church on the site was built in the sixth century to accommodate pilgrims to the tomb of San Lorenzo in one of the catacombs for Christian burials which had been located like all Rome's cemeteries 'outside the walls'. It was unconventionally oriented with its entrance to the east. Its nave of two storeys had broad colonnaded and arcaded galleries and was terminated at its west end by an semi-circular apse. At the end of the twelfth century, this apse was demolished and a new basilica dedicated to San Lorenzo was constructed, its nave extending westwards. The nave of the new church with its colonnade of recycled antique granite columns follows the pattern of the earlier Santa Maria in Trastevere **47** and San Crisogono **48** of the previous century, but without their transepts. The nave of the earlier church, its upper level inserted between the existing colonnades, was used as the new 'apse' or chancel: it was this transformation which gave the present church its unique longitudinal section. The pavement and the fine marble walls of the choir, decorated with mosaic, and its ambo and lectern are contemporary with the nave in which they stand, but the prominent baldacchino of the high altar was originally built in 1128 for the older church, and moved to the newer on its completion. A porch was built at the western end of the nave, and the plain cloister and the campanile to the south completed the programme.

☞ Opposite the front of the church, to the west, the campus of the Città Universitaria **184** abuts the piazzale San Lorenzo. The entrance to the extensive **Cimetero Campo Verano** lies immediately to the south. Its romantic neoclassical monumental lodge and gates were designed by Virginio Vespignani as part of a large programme of reordering and extension for which he was responsible between 1859 and 1874.

37Da **Santa Maria in Aracoeli** about 650
Capitoline hill

The original church was built on one of the two eminences of the Capitoline hill on the site of a Roman fortress, possibly occupied by the soothsaying Sibyl. Its present form was established in the twelfth century when it was substantially rebuilt as a regular basilica with a wide nave, its colonnade formed of unmatched antique columns; and aisles, a transept and a single apse. The aisles are lined with continuous square chapels whose cross walls do not align with the nave columns, with consequent difficulties in setting out the vaulting of the aisles. In 1571, the former open roof trusses were concealed by the sumptuous gilded ceiling installed to celebrate the victory over the Turks at the naval battle of Lepanto. The breathtaking flight of stairs which provides access from the modern via di Teatro di Marcello were erected in 1348 in thanks for reprieve from a plague.

☞ The piazza del Campidoglio, the Capitol **76**, can be reached from the door in the right transept of the church.

38De **San Giorgio in Velabro** about 700
Via Velabro

A bomb was exploded in the street outside the church in 1993, and restoration work to the damaged church and surrounding monuments was being carried out in 1995. The small building has a basilican plan notable for its geometrical irregularity. The campanile was added in the twelfth century, when the porch was restored. The church itself was restored in 1876 by Andrea Busiri Vici, and in 1926, and again in 1995.

☞ Next to the church the **Arcus Argentoriorum**, a small shrine of 204, was erected by money changers to honour the Emperor Septimus Severus. The Arch of Janus Quadrifons **26** lies across the west end of the street.

39Ch **Santa Cecilia in Trastevere** 817–24
Piazza dei Mercanti, Trastevere

The church is approached via a screen of 1741-42 designed by Ferdinando Fuga which leads into a large atrium from which a portico provides entrance. Of the interior of the original ninth-century basilica only the restored apse now remains, with its fine contemporary mosaic in the semi-dome showing Christ between saints, who include Cecilia (now patron saint of music). In 1724 the nave was converted by Luigi Berrettoni and Domenico Paradisi into a space more like an eighteenth-century ballroom by enclosing pairs of the original columns in new piers, installing a barrel-vaulted ceiling whose section follows a four-centred curve, by letting in plenty of light through enlarged windows, and then by decorating the whole in flat plaster painted in white and gold. The stairs to the left (south) of the main door lead to a crypt containing the excavations of two Roman houses, one of them perhaps that of Saint Cecilia, and a tannery. The intensely decorated crypt which houses the bodies of Saint Cecilia and other saints, was designed in 1901 by Gustavo Giovenale.

☞ In the small via dei Genovesi to the north-west of the church is the church and convent of **San Giovanni Battista dei Genovesi**, founded in the late 1400s. The church was reconstructed by Francesco Cellini in about 1850, but the original two-storey arcaded cloister is intact and accessible from via Anicia. To the south-west and past the enormous bulk of the former children's workhouse founded in 1683 and now the Istituto di San Michele is the church of **San Francesco a Ripa**, notable for the statue of Beata Lodovica Albertoni of 1671–74, one of Bernini's last works, in the Albertoni chapel, the last chapel on the north. Its façade of 1681–89 is by Mattia De Rossi.

San Francesco a Ripa

40Bo **San Prassede** 822

Via Santa Maria ai Monti/via Santa Prassede

Ⓜ B Cavour

Embedded safely in a small enclave unaffected by later main roads cut in the nineteenth century, the church has not been stripped of its surroundings. It is best approached from via Santa Maria ai Monti through the porch from which a covered flight of stairs leads to an atrium. The church was among those built at the instruction of Pascal I (817–24) after the coronation of Charlemagne, and the arrangement of atrium and church looks back to the practice of early Christianity, particularly to the old Constantinian basilica of St Peter's. The nave, now interrupted by diaphragm arches supported on piers and inserted in the middle ages, was originally defined by a simple colonnade flanked by aisles. The sanctuary and apse are raised in order to provide for a chapel under the high altar where martyrs' bones collected from the catacombs were reinterred to be visited by the devout. The baldacchino over the high altar was designed in the 1730s by Francesco Ferrari who incorporated antique elements from the original church.

The splendour of the church is its mosaic decoration. These are contemporary with its foundation, and the revival of the craft in the ninth century was part of Pascal's cultural programme for the renaissance of the Church in the reign of the new emperor. The mosaics cover both faces of both the arches defining the sanctuary, and the apse vault depicts Christ between six saints, with the flock of the faithful below. Mosaic is used most vividly and extensively in the **chapel of San Zeno**, off the north aisle, where its decorative scheme reinforces the architectural form: a diminutive plan in the shape of a Greek cross. Built by Pascal I as a mausoleum for his mother, the chapel is approached through a porch made of a collage of salvaged antique remnants. Its vault shows the central figure of Christ supported by four angels whose bodies lie on the diagonals of the room. The polychrome marble memorial tablet to G. B. Santoni on the pier outside the chapel is an early work of Bernini.

41Cc **San Salvatore in Onda** 1090

Via dei Pettinari

Among the number of churches built around the end of the eleventh century which included, for example, that of Santa Maria in Cosmedin **49**, this was drastically restored and retains little of its original structure or decoration except the antique columns of the nave arcade. But the restoration was carried out not, as was more usual in Rome, in the seventeenth or eighteenth centuries, but in 1877–78 by Luca Carimini using a late neoclassical style more considerate of the original. The plain façade was renovated in 1845 by Vincenzo Pallotti.

☞ The narrow and decaying **Ponte Sisto** at the southern end of the street was built at the order of Pope Sixtus IV in 1473–75. Its engineer was probably the Florentine Baccio Pontelli who constructed new arches on earlier Roman piers. The cantilevered iron walkways were added in 1877 though they are now unsafe.

42Df **San Clemente** 1110–30

Via di San Giovanni in Laterano/via Celimontana

Ⓜ B Colosseo

Like the churches of Santa Maria in Cosmedin **49** and San Giovanni a Porta Latina **43**, that of San Clemente was among the many built or rebuilt around 1100. Here, uniquely, the earlier basilica of the fourth century was not completely demolished, but used as the foundation of the new. This first, lower, church was itself built over Roman buildings which included a Mithraeum, and the present complex, excavated from 1861 onwards, now records three different periods each at a separate level.

The later entrance to the upper church was removed in a recent restoration: it used to provide access to the simple square atrium whose roofs are supported by an Ionic colonnade. Off this are the entrances to the canons' houses and the church. The upper church retains much of its delicate medieval layout and character although its walls are now covered with paintings of the eighteenth century. It is of regular basilican form with a nave flanked by aisles of different widths. Like those at Santa Maria in Cosmedin, the columns of the nave colonnade are interrupted at their mid point by a pier which marks the extent of the choir. The apse and its triumphal arch are decorated with mosaics among the finest of the period in Rome. The fittings, and the richly decorated enclosure of the choir made of large marble slabs, were reinstalled from the lower church, and the elaborate fine marble pavement was one of the first of its kind.

The lower church is of no intrinsic architectural interest, but houses rescued frescoes. The level below this, however, includes the well-preserved Mithraeum of about AD 300, a barrel-vaulted chamber housing an altar for ritual meetings of the cult; the extensive remains of a large Roman house of the first century AD; and later Christian catacombs.

☞ The church of Santi Quattro Coronati **46** lies to the south, and is entered from via dei Santi Quattro.

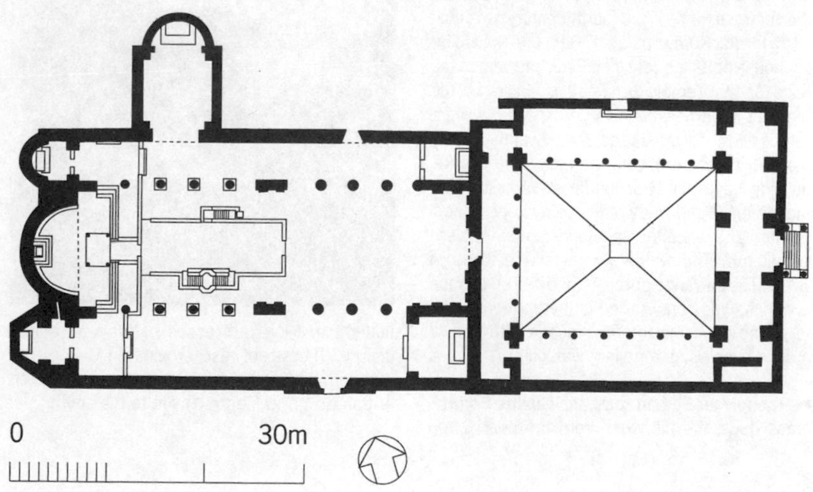

43Do **San Giovanni a Porta Latina**
late eleventh century
Via di Porta Latina

Of the large number of parish and monastic churches started towards the end of the eleventh century, only a few now retain their original form. This small basilica was, however, characteristic of that programme, and has perhaps survived unmolested by later cardinals because of its unshowy, tranquil location near the Aurelian wall in what remains one of the most rural areas of Rome. Originally founded in 550, and last restored in 1940, the later church has a nave separated from the aisles by columns re-cycled from earlier monuments. The apse is illuminated by windows of selenite. Fragments of original frescoes remain at high level in the nave and in the apse. The modest narthex contains on the left the base of the campanile, and on the right an earlier terminal from the chapel of San Giovanni in Oleo.

☞ **San Giovanni in Oleo**, towards the Porta Latina. A sixteenth-century octagonal chapel, attributed without strong evidence to Bramante, whose present colour scheme suggests a neoclasscial garden ornament of the eighteenth century. Borromini added the frieze of roses and acanthus leaves. The **Parco degli Scipioni** is a public park in which are the **Tomb of the Scipios**, of the third century BC, and the **Columbarium of Pomponius Hylas**, of the first century AD. The Porta Latina and Porta San Sebastiano **22** are to the south.

44Df **Santi Giovanni e Paolo** (fourth century), 1084–1118
Piazza di Santi Giovanni e Paolo, off Clivio di Scauro

Ⓜ B Colosseo

The church, one of the first to be established near the centre of Rome in the fourth century, was built into a former Roman palace, later supposed to be the house of Saints John and Paul, and next to the ruins of the Temple of Claudius. Parts of the temple's travertine masonry can be seen incorporated into the lower stages of the twelfth-century campanile on the north side of the piazza. Rebuilding began in 1084 under Robert Guiscard the Lombard and was continued by Pope Pascal III until 1159 when the apse and campanile were completed. The whole was again restored in 1718. The entrance porch, supported on antique columns, was constructed in the thirteenth century, and conceals the first façade with its five arches over which a gallery was built.

☞ The former Roman road, the **Clivius Scauri**, leads down the hill west from the piazza and under the flying buttresses of the wall of the church. The street also provides a view of the arcaded Lombard apse of the church. The church of San Gregorio Magno **106** is to the south.

45Ch **Casa dei Crescenzi** now **Centro di Studi per la Storia di Architettura** about 1100

Via del Teatro di Marcello, near piazza della Bocca della Verità

Stripped of its densely packed setting when the via del Teatro di Marcello was built, this is now Rome's unique example of the lightly fortified medieval mansion. The heavily fortified is represented by the Palazzo Anguillara in Trastevere. The upper parts which would have made it a tower have disappeared, but its paraphrases in brick of classical usages combined with some genuine antique fragments suggest an attempt by its aristocratic builder to revive a former Roman grandeur.

☞ San Giorgio in Velabro **38**, the temples of Portunus **5** and of Hercules Victor **3**, and Santa Maria in Cosmedin **49**.

46Dg **Santi Quattro Coronati** 1116

Via dei Santi Quattro

Ⓜ B Colosseo

The history of this collection of buildings is more significant than its present architectural remains: the church itself has been 'restored' almost to extinction, and its approaches via a suddenly apparently suburban district of Rome are dishevelled and awaiting money for a new restoration campaign. The original basilica of the ninth century burnt down in 1084 and a new much smaller church built over part of its site. Its only departure from the standard basilica type is the arcaded gallery which occupies the storey above the nave arcade. The church is approached through two courtyards, the second guarded by a tower. The cloister, reached through a door, usually locked, on the left side of the church, was probably the first to be built in Rome, and may be the earliest which survives. The buildings of the convent which now lie to either side of the church were added in the twelfth and thirteenth centuries. Their situation on the side of the hill adds to the fortified appearance of the complex.

☞ The church of San Clemente **42** lies at the foot of the hill to the north in via di San Giovanni in Laterano.

47Cg **Santa Maria in Trastevere** 1120–43
Piazza di Santa Maria in Trastevere

The earlier church founded in the fourth century was, like the churches of San Clemente **42** and Santi Quattro Coronati **46**, rebuilt in the twelfth. It has a long broad nave separated from the aisles by an colonnade of re-cycled ancient columns, and the walls above were originally perforated with much smaller windows. The sanctuary and apse are raised above the level of the nave and separated from it by an arch supported on two large Corinthian columns. The half-dome of the apse and the panels to the sides of the triumphal arch are decorated with fine contemporary mosaics; those of the walls below were placed in the thirteenth century. Much of the rest of the decoration of the church was carried out in the nineteenth century.

The Cappella Avila off the middle of the south aisle is one of four in Rome designed by the painter Antonio Gherardi in about 1680 (see also the Cappella di Santa Cecilia in San Carlo ai Catinari **99**). Having learnt the Baroque techniques of decoration and of manipulating space and light from Bernini and Borromini, Gherardi added his own experience as painter to produce this small but busy confection in which the lantern is split into two detached cylinders, the inner one supported by angels.

The porch to the piazza and the fountain which stands in it, were designed by Carlo Fontana in 1702, but the façade's present nineteenth-century appearance is the responsibility of Virginio Vespignani who restored it in 1869.

48Cg **San Crisogono** 1123–30, 1620–27
Piazza San Sonnino, near Ponte Garibaldi

This was one of several churches started or reconstructed in the surge of building which took place at the beginning of the twelfth century (for example San Giovanni a Porta Latina **43**). They were all built to the same pattern: a revival of the type established in the first Christian basilicas, with a nave colonnade or arcade supporting clerestory walls and flanked by aisles; and an apse framed by an arch. San Crisogono retains the form, its colonnade carried on re-used antique columns, but restorations have robbed the church of either patina or the air of the primitive still present in some of its contemporaries. Giovanni Battista Soria carried out a general tidying-up of the interior between 1620 and 1627, when he also designed the new façade and porch. Bernini designed the Holy Sacrament chapel to the right of the apse.

☞ The **Palazzo Anguillara** lies opposite and towards the lungotevere. This is Rome's only remaining instance of a twelfth-century fortified manor house, one of the predecessors of the 'palazzo', but it has been over-restored, and would not originally have stood in isolation. It is now the home of the Dante Society. To the west in the street behind the church is the very long two-storey façade of a hospital, the **Ospedale di San Gallicano** of 1724–29, designed by Filippo Raguzzini. An early example of a purpose-built type, it is still in use and its interior inaccessible.

Palazzo Anguillara

49Ch **Santa Maria in Cosmedin** 1123

Via Santa Maria in Cosmedin/piazza Bocca dell Verità/via del Circo Massimo

The present church is the conversion of its eighth-century predecessor which was built inside the shell of a building of a century earlier, a *diaconia* or Christian welfare centre. This in turn re-used one wall of a Roman building for inspectors of the cattle market, parts of which remain at the east end of the nave. The touchingly simple hall of today is the outcome of two campaigns: the first a drastic rebuilding of the early twelfth century, a period when many Roman churches were built and rebuilt; the second the enthusiastic renovation of the 1890s which included the reconstruction of the porch. This was undertaken by the *Associazione artistica fra i cultori di architettura* as its first live project. In 1993 another restoration, including that of the campanile, was under way.

The plan departs from that of the standard Roman basilica in retaining the three apses of the earlier church, one apse at the ends of the nave and aisles; and its nave colonnade is more ambiguous than most in being articulated by two wide piers which approximately delineate the areas for chancel, choir and congregation. Earlier arched diaphragm walls which spanned the nave and further emphasised the division have since been removed. The marble fittings of the choir, so admired by Le Corbusier in his *Vers Une Architecture* of 1923, are by members of the Cosmati family, but the baldacchino which they also designed was replaced by the present Gothic one at the end of the thirteenth century.

The **Bocca della Verità** ('Mouth of Truth'), a former drain cover of one of ancient Rome's main sewers, is erected on the left side of the porch.

☞ San Giorgio in Velabro **38**, the temples of Portunus **5** and of Hercules Victor **3**, and the Casa dei Crescenzi **45**.

50Cd **San Nicola in Carcere** 1128
Via del Teatro di Marcello/piazza di Monte Savello

This typical basilica of the twelfth century was built on the site of three Republican temples, the remains of one of which, that of Juno Sospita, can be seen built into the exterior of the south wall. It has a flat-ceiling nave separated from the aisles by a colonnade supporting a flat architrave. The choir and apse are raised to allow the shrine to be sunk below the high altar. The church was remodelled and a façade provided by Giacomo Della Porta in 1599, and it was separated from its medieval surroundings during the building of the via del Teatro di Marcello in 1932.

51Da **Santa Francesca Romana al Foro** ex **Santa Maria Nova** 1161, 1615
Entrance from stairs off via dei Fori Imperiali

M B Colosseo

The church was founded in the ninth century, its apse partly built into the ruins of Hadrian's Temple of Venus and Rome to the east. It was enlarged in the twelfth century when the present campanile was built, and systematised in 1615 by Carlo Lambardi. The interior still retains the layout of the original, with a simple nave and an apse and sanctuary both raised above it, the latter to accommodate the crypt housing the skeleton of the medieval Saint Francesca Romana, patron saint of Roman motorists. (Given Rome's problems with the motor car, she should be de-canonised immediately.) Lambardi also provided the present façade. Though he was born in Arezzo, his work may have been influenced by Palladio's designs for church façades, and this one appears to be a paraphrase of that of the church of San Giorgio Maggiore in Venice, but with scrolls replacing the gables of the model.

52Ai **Vatican Palace** begun 1208
Entrance to Museums from viale Vaticano

M A Ottaviano

The buildings to the west and north of St Peter's now lie in what is the walled State of Vatican City. They are described in chronological order of their construction. Not all of them are necessarily accessible to the public.

Pope Innocent III (1198–1216) set up a fortified house next to St Peter's in 1208, but the official urban papal residence continued to be at the Lateran Palace until 1378 when the popes returned from Avignon. Nicholas V (1447–55) made the first substantial addition to the original house when he built the **Cortile del Pappagallo (a)** (Court of the Parrot, named after the frescoes of the birds which decorated it). In 1473, Sixtus IV added the chapel named after him, the **Sistine Chapel (b)**, a large hall 40 metres long, 13 wide and 21 high (131 by 43 by 69 feet) to house conclaves and designed by Giovanni de'Dolci. Architecturally unremarkable, the chapel is now celebrated as the setting for Michelangelo's frescoes on the ceiling of 1508–12 and *The Last Judgement* of 1535–41 on the west wall above the altar.

Innocent VIII (1484–92) built the first **Belvedere (c)** designed by Giacomo da Pietrasanta on top of the hill to the north of the church. Pope Julius II (1503–13) made the single most important addition to the palace when, as well as confirming Bramante's success in the competition to design a new St Peter's, he also asked him to provide a setting for the papal collection of antique sculptures. Bramante proposed the gigantic new **Cortile del Belvedere** which extended north from St Peter's to connect the palace to Innocent VIII's

Belvedere. Work started in 1505. The courtyard, 100 metres wide and 300 long (328 feet by 984 feet) was divided into three terraces of different sizes stepping up the hill, and lined by colonnades and loggias three storeys high to the south, and of one storey at the top of the hill to the north. The first section, nearest St Peter's, was laid out as an open-air theatre, the central terrace had steps and areas for seating, while the top had a garden and a double flight of semi-circular steps in front of a small exedra which screened the original Belvedere villa. The best view of this extraordinary work would have been obtained from Julius' private suite on the top floor of the rooms to the north of the Cortile del Pappagallo. When Bramante began work on St Peter's, the courtyard was continued by his pupil Baldassarre Peruzzi, and by Antonio da Sangallo. After Julius' death, alterations were made to the north wall by Pirro Ligorio who replaced the exedra by a niche covered with a semi-dome. Pirro Ligorio also later designed the little **Casino**, **(d)** of 1559–62 which lies in the garden to the west of the Belvedere courtyard. This little Mannerist masterpiece was built by Pius IV as a setting for discussions.

Twenty years after completing the church of Sant'Andrea in via Flaminia **81** with its oval dome, in 1572 Vignola introduced a thorough-going oval plan into the chapel of the papal grooms, **Sant' Anna dei Palafrenieri (e)**, in via Sant'Anna to the east of the Belvedere courtyard. Its exterior is visible through the gate in via di Porta Angelica.

Sixtus V (1585–90), while creating new vistas in the city, destroyed that of Bramante by building a library, the **Biblioteca Sistina (f)** of 1587–89

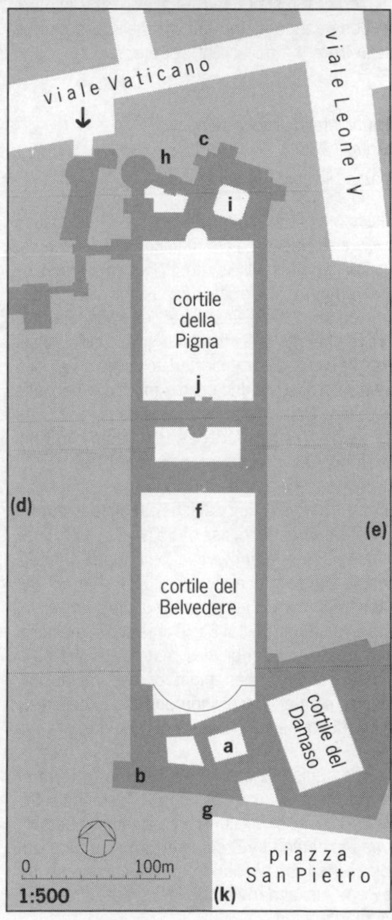

across the middle of the courtyard's central section. Both this and the new block extending from the Cortile San Damaso and which now overlooks the Piazza di San Pietro were designed by Domenico Fontana. The **Scala Regia (g)** of 1663–66, the stairs which provided a new ceremonial entrance to the palace from the new piazza in front of St. Peter's, run between the basilica and the Sistine Chapel. They were one of the most masterly Baroque syntheses of architecture, story telling and sculpture, and continued Alexander VII's patronage of Bernini. The architect exploited the fact that the walls between which the new stairs were required converged to produce for the visitor a scenographic effect of enhanced depth. Lighting adds to the drama: the vestibule is brightly lit, the pope's exuberantly modelled coat of arms above the arch receiving most light. The half landing is dramatically lit from the side, while the window at the top of the stairs causes glare. The sculpture of Constantine at the foot of the stairs can be seen from the portico of St Peter's.

After the peak of the Baroque, very little new work was done at the palace for the next hundred years. The Museum of Pagan Antiquities was founded by Clement XIII (1758–69), and work was undertaken by his successors to provide a setting for a **Museo Pio-Clementino (h).** Designed by Michelangelo Simonetti, this took place first in the Belvedere itself where the original courtyard was converted to the **Cortile Ottagono (i)**, then in 1776 in severely classical new buildings to the north, near the modern visitors' entrance, where the new rooms included the **Sala Rotonda** and **Sala a Croce Greca**. Yet more accommodation for the papal collections was needed, and between 1800 and 1823 Pius VII added the **Braccio Nuovo (j)** (New Wing) across the Cortile della Pigna. The only building of distinction added since the beginning of the nineteenth century has been Pier Luigi Nervi's semi-underground **Audience Hall** named after Paul VI and completed in 1971, which is sited south of St Peter's. Its flank with the large window in the shape of an eye rears over the boundary wall.

53Ap **Santa Maria sopra Minerva**
begun 1280
Piazza Minerva/via dei Cestari

The name of this church derives from its situation over a former temple dedicated to Minerva, Roman goddess of wisdom. Commissioned by the Dominican Order, the disposition of its Gothic vaulted nave and aisles closely follows that of the Order's church of Santa Maria Novella in Florence, with its wide nave designed for preaching, and vestigial transepts. Its authors may have been the Florentine Dominicans Ristoro da Campi and Sisto da Firenze. The plain façade was added in 1453 and its stucco most recently replaced in 1993.

On the left of the choir is Michelangelo's sculpture *Christ bearing the Cross* of 1514–21, its bronze drapery added later by a censor. Filippo Raguzzini decorated two chapels: in 1724 that of the baptismal font at the beginning of the south aisle, and a year later that of San Domenico in the north transept. The interior was restored in the nineteenth century when most of the implausibly regular painted decoration and the excessively cheerful stained glass were carried out.

☞ The sculpture called the **Pulcino** (a term of endearment for a pet) of 1665–67, stands in the piazza in front of the church. Designed by Bernini, it was executed by Ercole Ferrata. The elephant has carried the obelisk from Africa to present it to Pope Alexander VII (Bernini's great patron) for his glorification.

Il Pulcino

54An **San Onofrio** 1439

Via di Gianicolo

Facing a raised terrace, an open 'L'-shaped cloister shelters the entrances to the church in front and to the convent on the left. The unremarkable church was restored in the nineteenth century, and its celebrity rests in the chapel off the south aisle which houses the tomb of the poet Torquato Tasso (1544–95), and which was designed by G. De Fabris in 1857. The rectangular two-storey cloister of the convent is pretty but without architectural pretensions.

55Ap **Palazzo** and **Palazzetto Venezia** now **Museo di Palazzo Venezia** 1455–91

Piazza Venezia

The palazzo, its ceremonial rooms last used for functions of state by the fascist regime, is now occupied by a number of institutes, including a section of the scattered Museum of Rome which is the only part open to the public. The courtyard of the Palazzetto can be seen from some of the museum's galleries, but the church of San Marco, now embedded in the palace, is often closed. The monumental staircase by which entrance to the Museum is now gained is a retrogressive work completed in 1930 and designed by the Venetian architect Luigi Marangoni.

Commissioned by Cardinal Pietro Barbo in 1455, enlarged in 1464 when he became Pope Paul II, the palace was completed in 1491. It was the first large palace built in Rome in which the influence of the Renaissance in the north of Italy was evident, most clearly in the unfinished arcaded courtyard which may have been designed by Antonio da Sangallo the elder. The architect of the palazzo is unknown, but the five possible candidates include Alberti. Its organisation was that of a type intermediate between the earlier fortified manor house such as the Palazzo Anguillara in Trastevere, and the later Palazzo della Cancelleria **58** where no trace of the castellated enclosing wall remained, and the façade became a medium for architectural representation.

The **Palazzetto**, which was considered to obstruct the view of the Monument to Vittorio Emanuele, was moved and rebuilt in its present position between 1911 and 1913. Alberti again has been credited with the design of its complete courtyard of 1467, but so too has its Florentine mason, Meo del Caprino also known as Amedeo di Francesco.

☞ To the north of the Palazzo, on the corner of via del Plebescito and via del Corso, is the **Palazzo D'Aste** or **Napoleone** of 1658–65 designed by Giovanni Antonio De Rossi. Its position, commanding the piazza Venezia, for once allows the composition of its tall façade to be fully appreciated. Its delicate urbane refinement represents a late stage in the evolution of the palazzo type over the two hundred years between the completion of the first stages of the Palazzo Venezia and the sophistication of the Baroque.

56Ah **Santa Maria del Popolo** 1472–77

Piazza del Popolo

Ⓜ A Flaminio

Although an Augustinian foundation, the earlier church of 1227 originally had a plan modelled on those introduced by the Cistercians to Italy in the twelfth century. The nave, however, was remodelled by Bernini, and its main architectural interest now lies in the chapels and the façade. In the apse beyond the high altar, the small niche with its delicate shell vault is perhaps one of Bramante's first works in Rome.

In the north aisle, the octagonal chapel for the banker Chigi (who also commissioned the Villa Farnesina **65**) was started by Raphael and worked on by him between 1513 and 1516, but suspended at his death in 1520. The mosaics in the dome are to Raphael's design, but were carried out after his death. The chapel was finally altered and completed by Bernini for Chigi's descendant Alexander VII, and Raphael's original scheme, intended as a Renaissance synthesis of the arts of architecture, has been completely overlaid by the work of later painters and sculptors.

The Cappella Cibò (1682–87), the second in the south aisle, was designed by Carlo Fontana and shows this architect reacting to what he regarded as the excesses of the Baroque and lining the chapel in marble in a comparatively restrained manner.

The competent façade of two storeys, perhaps by the Romans Giacomo da Pietrasanta or Meo del Caprina da Settignano, shows the influence of Alberti's Santa Maria Novella in Florence, although the Albertian scrolls which connect the upper storey to the lower were added in the seventeenth century.

☞ Porta del Popolo, Piazza del Popolo **75**, the churches of Santa Maria dei Miracoli and Santa Maria in Montesanto.

The Renaissance and Mannerism
1475–1599

57Ao **Sant'Agostino** 1479–83, 1756–61

Via di Sant'Agostino, east off piazza delle Sette Lune

Giacomo da Pietrasanta and Sebastiano Fiorentino

Very little is known about Fiorentino, one of the two architects associated with the design of this Augustinian church, but Giacomo da Pietrasanta's family were masons from the quarries near Lucca, and he is known to have worked on the additions to the Palazzo Venezia **55**. One or other must have been familiar with Alberti's Florentine work, and with the church of Santa Maria Novella in particular. The plan is that of a northern Cistercian type developed in the twelfth century, but the façade, of two storeys linked at their sides with scrolls was an Albertian invention. However, the execution here is botched by the inclusion of the intermediate element, a cross between an entablature and a pediment, which spans the full width of the façade. Such were the stumbling beginnings of the arrival of Renaissance ideas in Rome. The church was thoroughly modernised by Vanvitelli in 1756–61, but the façade was restored to something like its fifteenth-century appearance in 1993–94.

☞ Beyond the arch to the west of the church, in via Giuseppe Zanardelli is the **Palazzo Altemps** formerly **Riario.** Originally built in 1480, the arrangement of accommodation round a courtyard is that of the palazzo, but its style retains hints of the earlier medieval fortified manor from which the later true palazzo developed. This may, though, be merely the result of the historicising tendencies of its various restorers who included Peruzzi and both the older and younger Longhis. In 1994 it was being converted to house part of the Museo Nazionale Romano.

58Ao **Palazzo della Cancelleria** ex **Riario** 1486–98

Piazza della Cancelleria/corso Vittorio Emanuele II

Built originally as the residence of Cardinal Riario and later used as the papal chancellery (*cancelleria*), this palazzo is significant as the first building in Rome to be informed by the revival of antique forms and the literature of antiquity which started in northern Italy earlier in the fifteenth century and

which we now call the Renaissance. There is no documentary evidence for the identity of its architect, but Alberti and Bramante have been proposed as possible authors, together with Andrea Bregno whose Palazzo Torlonia **60** has a similar façade.

The building's irregular plan includes a courtyard, and it incorporated the reconstructed fourth-century church of San Lorenzo in Damaso. The design of the courtyard's upper two storeys appears to be derived from that of the Palazzo Ducale at Urbino of 1470–75, but here the arcade is repeated. In particular, the 'L'-shaped piers at the corners at Urbino and here are identical: a fifteenth-century innovation without classical precedent. The ground floor arcade incorporates columns from the first church of San Lorenzo.

The façade, 90 metres (295 feet) long and 26.5 metres (87 feet) high, presented a formidable architectural task for which antiquity offered few models. Its lightly rusticated wall surface is strongly divided vertically by cornices and string courses, and its ends are very slightly projected. The broad horizontal bands of the upper storeys are subdivided into bays by triplets of delicate pilasters, the central pair of which enclose an arched or square window opening. The arrangement is derived from a synthesis of two buildings designed by Alberti: the Palazzo Rucellai in Florence of 1446–51, which has regularly spaced pilasters, and the A–B–A rhythm of the façade and bays of the nave of the church of Sant'Andrea at Mantua.

59Bi **Santissima Trinità dei Monti** 1493, façade 1570–84

Viale della Trinità del Monti

Ⓜ A Spagna

The interior of the church, begun in 1493, is architecturally unimportant. The west façade, its twin towers perhaps derived from those proposed by Bramante for St Peter's, was designed by Giacomo Della Porta in 1570–84. On the ridge of a hill, the site provided a splendid scenographic opportunity which was taken up by Domenico Fontana who used the church and a relocated obelisk as the focus of two of the new straight roads, the via Sistina and the via Condotti, which he laid out for Sixtus V. In 1587, Fontana himself designed the ramp and double stairs which now provide access to the church. In the 1720s, the last stage in establishing the church in countless postcard views as an icon of Rome was arranged by De Sanctis when the Spanish Steps **131** were built.

☞ The **Palazzo Zuccari** lies to the south of the church at the pointed junction of the via Sistina and the via Gregoriana. Its little porch and covered balcony are the work of Filippo Juvara, of 1711.

60Aj **Palazzo Torlonia** ex **Castellesi Corneto**
1499–1504
Via della Conciliazione 30
Andrea Bregno (?)

The authorship of this palace is unclear. Built for Cardinal Adriano Corneto, it has been attributed to the same architects as those who worked on the Palazzo della Cancelleria **58**, the Palazzo Turci **61** and the Palazzo Venezia **55** towards the end of the fifteenth century, and these include Bregno, with perhaps Bramante or Antonio da Sangallo the elder in a supervisory role. The detailed design of the façade is very similar indeed to that of the Cancelleria, the whole being treated with pilasters, doubled and enclosing arched openings on the first floor, and extending into the double attic. The design here is more satisfactory than that of the much longer Cancelleria: the façade's elevation of only seven bays approximates to a double square, and the result is neat and comprehensible.

☞ The Palazzo dei Convertendi **127** lies to the east; the church of Santa Maria in Transpontina **86** to the west, and the **Palazzo della Rovere** or **dei Penitenzieri** (now the Hotel Columbus) of 1484–90 and designed by Baccio Pontelli or Meo del Caprino, is opposite on the south side of the road.

61Ao **Palazzo Turci** about 1500
Via del Governo Vecchio

Like the large Cancelleria **58**, this tiny building of three by four bays has been attributed to Bramante on stylistic grounds, understandably but without authority. Undoubtedly influenced by Alberti's Florentine palaces, the façades consist of panels of fine brickwork framed vertically by very flat pilasters and horizontally by delicate cornices, and every opening in each of its four storeys is arched.

☞ Opposite on the north side of via del Governo Vecchio is the **Palazzo Nardini** or **del Governo Vecchio** of 1473.

62Cf **Tempietto, San Pietro in Montorio**

1500– about 1505

Piazza San Pietro in Montorio, via G. Garibaldi, Gianicolo

Donato Bramante

Bramante arrived in Rome in 1499. His first commission, in that year, was for the cloister at Santa Maria della Pace **122**; his second was for this diminutive chapel to commemorate the site of Saint Peter's crucifixion. Its arrangement in what was intended to be a cloistered square fulfils all Alberti's requirements for the ideal church: it stands on a platform and can be seen from all sides. Its circular plan, which may be derived from Bramante's studies of Roman tombs and circular temples such as that of Vesta **7**, or later Christian shrines to house the remains of martyrs, brought the ideas of the northern Renaissance to Rome, particularly those of the centrally planned church, which were subsequently to play such an important role in the selection of an architect and a design for the rebuilding of St Peter's. Its severity is enhanced both by the first use of the Tuscan Doric order with its unfluted granite columns, and by the almost complete absence of decoration except for that of the frieze where the symbols of the Mass and the attributes of Saint Peter are displayed. Bramante had originally proposed a hemispherical dome, and the somewhat more pointed one built does not follow his design. The walls of the interior have four large shell-vaulted niches which alternate with narrow windows. The dome was originally painted with ribs which framed a blue ground sprinkled with gold stars.

The tiny building captivated and strongly influenced subsequent generations of architects: later in the sixteenth century Palladio considered its recreation of antiquity so authentic that he included it in the fourth of his *Four Books*, as the only modern example in his collection of *ancient* Roman buildings, saying: 'Since Bramante was the first who brought to light good and beautiful architecture which from the time of the ancients to his day had been forgotten, it seemed to me correct that his work should have a place among the ancients.' And always ready with instruction on how to build, he further tells us that 'the columns are of granite, their bases and capitals of marble, and the rest of travertine'.

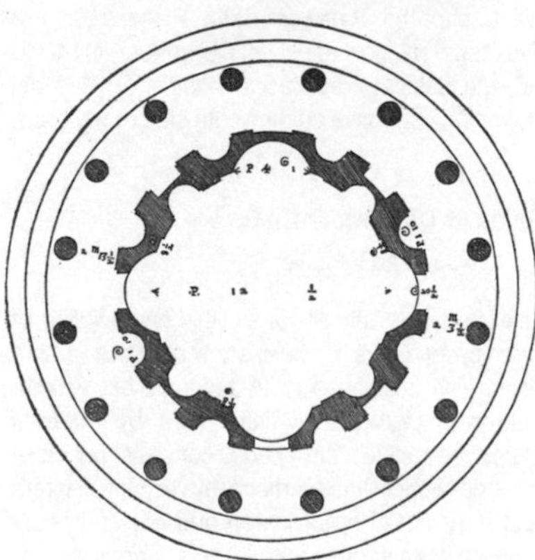

Plan from Palladio, *Quattro Libri*, Book IV

☞ To the south-west, the **Monumento ai Caduti di 1849–70**, a memorial to those who died defending Rome in the war to liberate and unify Italy, by Giovanni Iacobucci of 1941, and heroically inscribed 'Roma o Morte'. To the west, the Aqua Paola **98**, and further up the hill the Porta San Pancrazio **144**. To the north at the sharp bend of via Garibaldi is the church and convent of **Santa Maria dei Sette Dolore** of 1643–67 with its chapel (which is, however, not accessible, and no appeal to the viciously rude nuns will make it so), and unfinished façade both by Borromini. To the north of the convent and set back from the road is the entrance to the **Bosco Parrasio**, a terraced garden (usually closed), laid out in 1725 and designed by Antonio Canevari to provide a setting for the proceedings of the literary society the Accademia dell'Arcadia.

63Ai **Basilica of San Pietro in Vaticano ('St Peter's')** 1506–1626

Piazza San Pietro

M A Ottaviano

Graffiti from the second century record that the site of the present basilica was then already visited by Christians who believed that Saint Peter had been entombed there. Constantine started to build the first basilica to mark the site in 319, its crypt housing the tomb. The new church immediately became Rome's most important attraction for pilgrims, and has remained so ever since. Nine centuries later, Pope Nicholas III (1277–80), in his bid to establish Rome as 'the very diadem of all the world' and consolidate the papacy's rule over the Campagna, began the restoration of the basilica and started the construction of the Vatican Palace.

Three years after his accession in 1503, Julius II held a competition for designs for a new basilica. Bramante won with his proposal for a centralised church with a plan in the form of a perfect Greek cross set in a square of about 182 metres (600 feet). The crossing of its arms was to be covered with a hemispherical dome about 45 metres (150 feet) in diameter. The central space was surrounded by a broad ambulatory with smaller domes at its corners, and the square of the plan was filled out with towers at each corner. Architects in northern Italy had been proposing centralised churches for much of the fifteenth century, and a few had been built, for example, Giuliano da Sangallo's Santa Maria delle Carceri at Prato near Florence. Shortly after first arriving in Rome, Bramante himself had designed the tiny circular chapel of San Pietro in Montorio **62** only a few years before gaining the approval of the pope who brought one of the most potent architectural ideas of the Renaissance to the heart of Western Christianity.

When Julius died in 1513 much of the western end of the Constantinian basilica had been demolished, but of the new work only the four large piers to support the drum of the dome had been built. Bramante died in the following year leaving no more than inconsistent sketches of how the work might be continued. Raphael was appointed Director of works, but died four years later to be succeeded jointly by one of Bramante's studio, Baldassarre Peruzzi, and Antonio da Sangallo the younger. But work was interrupted by the sack of Rome in 1527, Peruzzi died in 1536, and Sangallo prepared a modified design proposing a departure from Bramante's strict bi-axial symmetry: a large vestibule on the eastern arm of the Greek cross.

Sangallo died in 1546, and was succeeded by the seventy-two year old Michelangelo who spent the remaining eight years of his life producing a new definitive design for a drastically simplified square plan in which the dome became the single overwhelming feature supported on massive piers. The simple square perimeter of Bramante's plan was smudged by a high sinuous wall which wrapped its way round the apses and the corners of the plan, and a single entrance was to be provided, covered by an enormous portico with a projecting central bay. Michelangelo died in 1564 leaving detailed models for the construction of the dome, in which he had abandoned Bramante's hemisphere and substituted the more Florentine pointed version

raised on a high drum which we see today. Two of the four cupolas proposed by Michelangelo for the corners of the ambulatory were added in 1546 by Vignola, his successor with Pirro Ligorio. The dome, constructed of two skins of brickwork with stone ribs supporting the lantern, was finally finished by della Porta and Fontana between 1590 and 1595.

A century after the foundation stone had been laid, the ideas of the Renaissance had largely been forgotten or crushed by the proceedings of the Council of Trent. New liturgical requirements, and the need to house a larger congregation than the existing church could accommodate, finally brought about the end of the centralised dream: Maderna was commissioned to complete the work. He ingeniously added three bays to the eastern side of the ambulatory, thereby creating a nave flanked by aisles the thickness of the crossing piers. This and the colossal eastern portico and façade were all finished by 1612. The two outer bays of the façade were built as the lower stages of two proposed towers, but these were never continued and in 1788 Valadier finished off the stumps with the two clocks.

The startlingly large interior, its length exactly the same as that of one side of Bramante's first square plan (182 metres, 600 feet), is dominated by the strong light which falls from the ample windows in the drum of the dome. These and the windows in the apse provide the only direct lighting to nave and

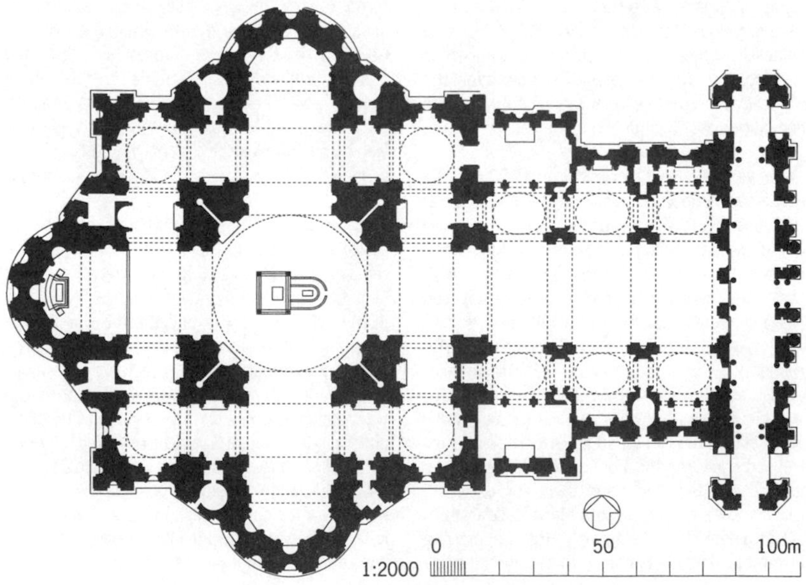

crossing. The main decoration and articulation is provided by the single giant Corinthian order of pale grey stone (or plaster painted to look like stone) which rises past the subsidiary arches of the nave to support the cornice at the level of the arches which carry the drum of the dome. The baldacchino and the painted and gilded decoration with which the interior was gradually covered, while initially shocking to Protestant taste, is in fact quite restrained and coherent compared with the later wilder and even more theatrical excesses of the seventeenth century.

Baldacchino

Bernini was twenty-six when in 1624 his patron Urban VII gave him his first commission: to decorate the crossing of the church. His scheme was in two parts, the first the massive **Baldacchino** which marks the site of Saint Peter's tomb and covers the altar. This extraordinary work, carried out in bronze taken from the portico of the Pantheon, is now the most conspicuous feature of the interior. The twisted columns supporting the canopy are copied from those which stood around the altar in the Constantinian basilica and which were supposed to have come from the Temple in Jerusalem. The welding of architecture and its sculptural decoration make the work one of the first and most complete examples of what was to become the Baroque. Bernini's scheme for the crossing itself was finally completed in 1633–40 when he provided the niches which house statues of early saints, and above these the galleries, their niches decorated in innovative coloured marbles. Bernini's last and most theatrical work in the church is the **Cathedra Petri** of 1657–65 at the western end, where all the plastic arts, painting, sculpture, coloured glass and an architectural setting, are harnessed to celebrate the legitimacy of the papacy as successors to Saint Peter.

Since 1612 Maderna's façade had faced a muddy yard encroached on by medieval houses to the east and south, and by the Vatican Palace to the north. Alexander VII commissioned Bernini's great half-oval **Colonnade** in Roman Doric in 1655, and its completion in 1667 finally provided an appropriate setting for outdoor ceremonies and processions, and a viewpoint for what had become the grandest architectural composition of the Baroque.

64Bm **Santa Maria di Loreto** 1507–34

Via dei Fori Imperiale/piazza di Venezia

Antonio da Sangallo the younger

Bramante is credited with the first proposal of about 1507 for the design of this church, but the nave and apse were executed by Antonio da Sangallo the younger and finished in 1534, and the design may be his alone. In any case, they were overwhelmed by the gigantic dome on its octagonal drum designed by Jacopo Del Duca but completed in 1576 after he had returned to his native Sicily. Del Duca had been one of Michelangelo's assistants in the work of converting the Baths of Diocletian into the church of Santa Maria degli Angeli **84**, and the dome here follows the pointed profile of that of Michelangelo's for St Peter's. The detail is, however, his own, including the peremptory buttresses, and the splendidly elaborate lantern.

☞ The church to the east on the corner of via S. Eufemia is that of **Santissima Nome Di Maria** of 1736–38 designed by Antonio Derizet.

65Cb **Villa Farnesina** now **Accademia Nazionale dei Lincei** 1508–11

Via della Lungara 230, Trastevere

Baldassarre Peruzzi

The villa was built by Agostino Chigi, a banker from Siena and one of richest men in Europe, as a *villa suburbana*. This type had interested many architects of the Renaissance who made designs based on the detailed description of such a building by the classical Roman author Pliny the younger in his *Letters*. Chigi required his villa for entertaining clients and friends in a countrified setting, across the Tiber but conveniently close to the centre of Rome and his own palazzo. The Siennese architect Peruzzi provided a simple two-storey block, its plan a double square, with wings extending towards the garden and enclosing a loggia on the ground floor. Raphael was commissioned to supply the decorative programme for the loggia and his studio provided the paintings. In 1520 the Sala delle Prospettive was created on the first floor. Here Peruzzi's paintings at either end of the room supply ideal views of what would have been visible from the first floor of a country villa, prevented here because of the low lying ground on which it stands.

Chigi died in 1520 and the villa was bought by Cardinal Alessandro Farnese after whom it became named. Michelangelo's plan to make the villa a 'casino' or garden pavilion of the cardinal's palazzo on the east side of Tiber by building a connecting bridge was not realised. The offices and library of the learned institute, the Accademia Nazionale dei Lincei, have occupied the building since 1927.

☞ The **Palazzo Corsini**, housing part of the Galleria Nazionale d'Arte Antica, is immediately opposite the Villa on the other side of via della Lunghara. Rebuilt to Ferdinando Fuga's design in 1732–36, its plan is 'E' shaped and, approached through a columned vestibule, a grand dog-leg staircase lit from windows on both sides fills the central leg of the 'E'. It provides one of the few accessible examples of a Late Baroque interior. The former **Museo Torlonia**, now converted into flats, lies to its south with the **Porta Settimiana** at its corner. This was last reconstructed in a general programme of the restoration of the walls sponsored by Popes Innocent VIII and Alexander VI, and supervised by Antonio da Sangallo the elder.

66Ao **Sant'Eligio degli Orefici** 1509 (?), 1516–36

Lungotevere Tebaldi

Donato Bramante (?), Raffaello Sanzio/'Raphael', Baldassarre Peruzzi

Bramante's first design for St Peter's with its hemispherical dome supported on the arms of a Greek cross captivated the architects of the 1500s, but few were able to realise it. This tiny church distils the spirit of its model, and since Bramante's work at St Peter's was never completed, it remains the most complete realisation of his idea so that both he and Raphael have been credited with the design but without documentary evidence. It may have been designed in 1509 by Bramante, who died in 1514, or by Raphael in 1516. The project was executed by Baldassarre Peruzzi who continued with the work after Raphael's death in 1520, and who completed the dome in 1536. Between 1602 and 1615 Flaminio Ponzio tidied up the exterior, finished the façade and painted the whole interior in the white which can now be regarded as essential to the perfection of the architectural idea.

67Ao **San Luigi dei Francesi** 1518–89

Via della Scrofa

Façade designed by Giacomo della Porta

The body of the church for French nationals was started in 1518, but the present appearance of its interior is the result of a much later neoclassical decorative scheme carried out in 1756–64 by Antonio Dérizet. The façade, designed by Giacomo della Porta but realised in 1588–89 by Domenico Fontana, is a Baroque innovation and an alternative to the two-storey format derived from that of Santa Maria Novella in Florence.

68Ao **Santa Maria di Monserrato** 1518–95

Via di Monserrato/via della Barchetta

Antonio da Sangallo the younger

Sangallo designed this, the national church of the Spanish, in 1518, but work proceeded slowly. After Sangallo's death in 1546 the otherwise unknown Bernadino Valperga continued the supervision of the original design. The high altar was consecrated in 1594 and the lower storey of the façade was completed a year later by Francesco da Volterra. The very deep apse was designed by Gian Battista Contini and added in 1673–75. The Camporeses, uncle and nephew, restored the church in the 1820s, but the flat upper storey of the façade was only completed in 1925–26 by Salvatore Rebecchini, whose design makes an abrupt connection with the earlier work.

69An **San Giovanni dei Fiorentini** started 1519
Piazza d'Oro/via Giulia
Iacopo Sansovino

The construction of the large national church of the Florentines has a history almost as long and complicated as that of St Peter's, and what we now see is the result of two centuries of intermittent building activity. Sansovino won the competition promoted by Leo X in 1519 with a design for a new church with a Latin-cross plan. Antonio da Sangallo the younger became supervisor in 1520 and started the foundations. Work was interrupted by the Sack of Rome in 1527, by shortage of funds, and by interference from Michelangelo. By 1546 the nave and aisles, now to Sangallo's design, were completed. Maderna designed the dome which was completed by 1620. In the 1630s Borromini made a design for the high altar which in 1634 started under Pietro da Cortona's supervision. Carlo Fontana completed the body of the church between 1667 and 1669. Finally, in 1733, the Florentine Alessandro Galilei, who in the previous year had won the competition for the design of the façade of San Giovanni in Laterano, obtained the commission for that of San Giovanni, the second of his two works in Rome. The proportions of the church and the absence of requirements for balcony or vestibule, allowed him to develop, within the traditional Roman format, a strong horizontal emphasis reinforced by paired columns.

☞ Just to the south of the church in via Giulia, a street lined with palaces, is the **Palazzo Sacchetti** at number 66. This was built in 1542–46 by Antonio Sangallo the younger as his own house. It was enlarged after his death by Nanni di Baccio Bigio between 1553 and 1555.

70Ap **San Marcello al Corso** 1530, 1682–83
Via del Corso/via dell'Umilità
Iacopo Sansovino

Of ancient foundation, the church was completely reconstructed by Sansovino in about 1530 to a simple plan with a single flat-ceilinged nave lined with chapels and a semi-circular apse. The façade, added much later in 1682–83 to the designs of Carlo Fontana and one of the few works which he was able to execute, is a regularisation of the earlier Baroque experiments of, for example, Borromini and Cortona. The surface of the singly curved wall is modulated only by the depth of the columns which emerge from it, or which are placed against it. The design represents a shift from the novelties, torments or triumphs of the High Baroque towards a drier and more comprehensible architecture and classical taste, and as such it was much admired and easily copied.

71Ao **Piccola Farnesina** now **Museo Barracco**
1523
Piazza San Pantaleo, Corso Vittorio Emanuele II
Antonio da Sangallo the younger

This large house or little palace originally faced the street at right angles to the Corso. Its 'U'-shaped plan results in the unusual deep notch in the façade. The elevation to the Corso, designed by Enrico Guj, is a pastiche of the original composition put in place in 1898–1904 when the flank was exposed to the newly-cut Corso Vittorio Emanuele II.

72Ao **Palazzo Massimi alle Colonne** 1532–36
Corso Vittorio Emanuele II/Corso del Rinascimento
Baldassarre Peruzzi

The façade of the Palazzo, Peruzzi's last work, is the best example in Rome of Mannerist architecture, the elegant and contradictory style for connoisseurs which succeeded that of the solid certainties of the patrons and architects of the High Renaissance. Some of the peculiarities here may be responses to the convex street line which follows the shape of the underlying Odeon of Domitian, others are innovations. The conventional division into base, middle and top has been subverted. The deep shadowed entrance is delineated by a portico of paired columns in severe Roman Doric, whose architrave extends right across the front to produce a sharp horizontal division below which the residual rustication is no more emphasised than that of the upper storeys. This event is contrasted with the flatness and unenergetic modelling above. While the hoods of the windows of the *piano nobile* are pronounced, their sides are flatter and less emphasised than would have been acceptable to architects of the High Renaissance (compare for example the Palazzo Farnese **73**). Those of the second-floor and attic windows are reduced to delicate atectonic picture frames.

The plan of the palace is highly irregular: there are two courtyards: the Roman Doric of the portico is extended into the first and larger; beyond is a further tiny courtyard decorated with frescoes now in picturesque decay.

73Cc **Palazzo Farnese** now **French Embassy**
1534–48

Piazza Farnese

Antonio da Sangallo the younger, Michelangelo Buonarroti and others

Cardinal Alessandro Farnese commissioned this greatest of Roman palaces in 1517, but when he was elected Pope Paul III, work on an enlarged design was started by Sangallo in 1534. His design became highly influential: the arrangement is so general that it was subsequently copied for banks, offices and London clubs. Its plan is a rectangle 58 by 74 metres (190 by 242 feet), symmetrical about its long axis. A central courtyard, 25 metres (81 feet) square, is reached through a grand tunnel-vaulted vestibule opposite which is a loggia facing the garden. (The garden side of the palazzo can be seen from a gate in the via Giulia.) From one corner of the courtyard a single wide staircase rises to provide access to the principal rooms on the first floor, the *piano nobile*. These rooms can be reached from the formerly open loggia surrounding the courtyard, and they are all connected *en suite*.

The design of the front, towards the piazza Farnese, started as a comparatively straightforward exercise in the usages established in the High Renaissance. It is divided horizontally into its three storeys by small cornices or string courses which form bases for the plinths of the window surrounds. Rustication, in travertine stone quarried from the Colosseum, is used only for the quoins which hold the corners. The alternating triangular and segmental hoods to the windows of the *piano nobile* are correctly supported on columns, emphasising the importance of the rooms at that level. Sangallo died in 1546, and the balanced design he had sought was upset by the idiosyncratic contributions of Michelangelo, who added the gigantic cornice to the exterior and designed the top storey of the courtyard, finished in 1548.

Sangallo's design for the first two storeys of the courtyard employed the scheme of the exterior of the Theatre of Marcellus **9**. The ground floor has a Roman Doric order and the first an Ionic; arches, originally open, are set between the columns and span onto a smaller version of the appropriate order. For the top storey, Michelangelo, who was still engaged in work on St Peter's, ignored the ancient precedents of the design below. He separated the bays with triple overlapping Corinthian pilasters. Between these are set windows whose segmental hoods are not supported by the corbels at the sides.

The palace first became the French Embassy in 1635, and although its use has not been continuous, it remains so today. There are no 'open-days', and the courtyard and the rooms of the *piano nobile* can only be visited with written permission.

74Aj **Santo Spirito in Sassia** 1538–44

Borgo Santo Spirito/via dei Penitenzieri

Antonio da Sangallo the younger

An earlier church of 1471–73 designed by the Tuscan Baccio Pontelli, of which only the handsome campanile now remains, was completely replaced to Sangallo's design. The cramped site only allowed for a wide nave lined with semi-circular chapels. There are no transepts, and the apse is an extension of the nave, separated from it by two arches. The façade, to a design by Sangallo but executed by Ottaviano Mascherino, is another attempt to adapt the design of the two-storey front of Santa Maria Novella in Florence to a Roman church. The profile of the nave is capped with a pediment, and the lower storey which screens the sides of the chapels is connected to the upper by scrolls.

☞ The southern end of via Penitenzieri is spanned by the **Porta Santo Spirito**, an unfinished gate of 1543–44, also by Antonio da Sangallo. To the south of the church and extending to the Tiber is the large **Arcispedale di Santo Spirito**. The former hostel and hospital, now containing several museums devoted to the history of medicine, was founded in 726 and rebuilt in 1204 and again in 1474–82. The present east wing, designed by Gaspare and Luigi Lenzi, repaired the demolition necessary when the Tiber's embankments were constructed, and was completed in 1933.

75Ah **Piazza del Popolo** 1538 onwards

Latino Giovenale Manetti and others

Ⓜ A Flaminio

Until the first Stazione Termini was built, the piazza on the city side of the gate was always one of the main points of arrival for visitors to Rome from the north, and it still is for the cars which continue to swirl round it. While the via del Corso continued the straight line of the Roman via Flaminia into the heart of the city and to the Capitoline hill, the piazza itself was one of the first public spaces to receive attention from the urbanists of the Renaissance and it was first consolidated in 1538 by Manetti. It was chosen as one of the points from which two of the new streets planned for Sixtus V by Domenico Fontana would radiate. The via di Ripetta to the west of the Corso skirted the Tiber, and to the east the via del Babuino extended to the Piazza di Spagna. In 1589, an obelisk which had stood in the Circus Maximus, having been brought by Augustus

from Heliopolis in Egypt, was erected at the intersection of the new streets.

In 1662, Carlo Rainaldi designed the twin churches which occupy the points of the street intersections, **Santa Maria dei Miracoli** to the north and **Santa Maria in Monsanto** to the south. Both were continued by Carlo Fontana, and between 1675 and 1679 Bernini and Fontana designed the theatrical and unusual freestanding porticoes in the form of pedimented temple fronts, more neoclassical than Palladian in spirit. To celebrate the arrival in Rome of Queen Christina of Sweden in 1655, Bernini also redesigned the inner face of the gate, the **Porta del Popolo**. Its lower parts are restrained, and the exuberance is confined to the garlanded setting for the crest.

The last contribution to the piazza was made by Valadier who, at first working for Napoleon, designed several projects between 1810 and 1820 for its enhancement, including one to open and extend the piazza to the bank of the

Tiber. Eventually Pope Pius VII chose a more modest scheme, its enclosure provided by two walled hemi-cycles with new customs houses and barracks at the corners. The obelisk was set in a new fountain with sculpted lions.

☞ The church of Santa Maria del Popolo **56** is on the north-east side of the piazza; beyond the gate and to its north is one of the entrances to the Villa Borghese **97**, **139**.

76Da **Campidoglio (Capitol), Palazzo Senatorio**

1539–92

Piazza del Campidoglio

Michelangelo Buonarroti, Giacomo della Porta

The Capitoline hill had formed the north-western boundary of the Forum, and its northern summit had been crowned by ancient Rome's most important temple, that of Jupiter Capitolinus. In the middle of the twelfth century, when it briefly appeared possible that Rome could become a free city, a palace for a re-established Senate of Rome was started on a hollow between its two ancient summits. By the beginning of the fourteenth the Palazzo di Senatori was finished: it remains the seat of the secular administration of Rome. In 1528, the antique bronze equestrian statue, thought to be that of Constantine but actually of Marcus Aurelius, was to set up in front of the Palazzo, and in 1538 Michelangelo's advice was sought about its setting. It is a tribute to the power and simplicity of his proposal that the present ensemble, built over the next century under the supervision of several architects, has retained its integrity.

In one of the first examples of town planning, the design of a coherent group of buildings together with the space they address, Michelangelo proposed a new square in front of the Palazzo and facing away from the Forum, with the statue at its centre. A new façade to the existing Palazzo was to be framed by two new buildings and the whole approached by a wide stepped ramp from the open north-west side. Work on a new façade for the Palazzo began immediately, to be finished in 1592, and the southern of the two flanking buildings was started in 1546. However, it was unfinished when Michelangelo died in 1564, and the final construction was achieved by Giacomo della Porta. Its twin to the north was built to Michelangelo's design a century later. The only vertical feature in the ensemble, the campanile, was built in 1579. In the design of the two new buildings Michelangelo introduced one of his most widely copied innovations: the giant order of Corinthian pilasters which span the height of the two storeys to support a single heavy architrave. The ground floor has a recessed colonnade its openings framed by a subsidiary Ionic order and a flat architrave.

The Capitoline Museums, the first public museums of Greek and Roman art, were founded by Clement XII and Benedict XIV. They are now housed in Michelangelo's buildings and their extensions to the north contain collections of Roman sculpture including the statue of Marcus Aurelius removed for its protection from its position in the centre of the square. The Palazzo Conservatori to the south gives access to the Museo Nuovo, the Museo del Palazzo, the Pinacoteca Capitolina and the Sale dei Conservatori. These house the several papal collections of antiquities, sculpture and paintings, including the colossal white marble head, hand and foot of a statue of Constantine from his Basilica **23**.

☞ From the north-east corner of the piazza, stairs lead to the side entrance of Santa Maria in Aracoeli **37**.

77Cc **Palazzo Spada** or **Capodiferro** 1548

Vicolo de Venti

Giulio Mazzoni (?)

The palazzo was built for Cardinal Capodiferro, but its authorship is uncertain. Mazzoni, a plasterer, carried out the highly modelled stucco decorations which are the main feature of the façade and the elevations to the courtyard, and he may or may not also have been the architect. Unlike many other palaces, for example those on the via Giulia, this has always been free-standing on three sides, and the gap on the south side of the plot was ingeniously filled by Borromini, who carried out alterations to the Palazzo between 1635 and 1653, with the *galleria prospettica*, an eye deceiving and charming architectural decoration of a barrel-vaulted arcade rendered by perspective to appear much deeper than it is. The idea may have been suggested by scenic decorations of Palladio and Scamozzi for the Teatro Olimpico at Vicenza. It was built earlier than Bernini's Scala Regia at the Vatican whose form it closely resembles.

78Ah Villa Medici now French Academy 1540–85

Viale della Trinità del Monti

Nanni di Baccio Bigio, Annibale Lippi, Bartolomeo Ammannati

Ⓜ A Spagna

The first villa on this privileged site on the side of a hill and bounded by the Aurelian Wall to the north-east was built by Cardinal Ricci of Montepulciano and designed by Nanni di Baccio Bigio (Giovanni di Bartolomeo Lippi) succeeded by his son Annibale Lippi between 1564 and 1568. In 1576, this villa was bought by Cardinal Ferdinando de' Medici, who commissioned the Florentine Ammannati to enlarge it to house his collection of antique sculpture (now mostly transferred to the Uffizi in Florence). To complement the first tower, a second was added to the south and connected to it by a balcony; the façade to the garden was reconstructed and decorated with antique sculptural fragments; a sculpture gallery was housed in a new wing; and a formal courtyard projected as an approach to the villa.

The work was finally completed in 1625, but the courtyard was not constructed. The garden was planned at the same time, and was laid out in a rectangular grid of paths with works of sculpture at their ends. While the garden had no general iconographic programme, an artificial mound, the 'Mons Parnassus', was created in its eastern corner as a home for the Muses whom de' Medici patronised.

In 1801 Napoleon bought the villa, and since 1803 it has housed the French Academy, where students of architecture from the École des Beaux Arts in Paris who had won the Prix de Rome were sent for three years to study Rome's monuments.

☞ The church of Santissima Trinità dei Monti **59** and the Spanish Steps **131** lie to the south; the Pincio and the Casina Valadier **142** are to the north.

79 Villa d'Este, gardens 1550–72

Piazza Trento, Tivoli

Pirro Ligorio and others

In 1550 Cardinal Ippolito d'Este was appointed Governor of Tivoli, then part of the Papal States. His official residence was the former thirteenth-century monastery set on the edge of the hill on which the town stands. The grounds extended down the hill to the north and west where the city wall formed their boundary. The Cardinal, competing with one of his rivals, Cardinal Farnese who had begun building his palace and gardens at Caprarola in 1559, started to decorate two suites of rooms in the monastery and to remodel its grounds in 1565. His advisor was the Neapolitan painter and architect Pirro Ligorio whom he had already employed to survey the ruins of Hadrian's Villa and as consultant on the purchase of antiquities. Ligorio had also previously surveyed the Temple of Fortune at Prenestina, which is set on a hilltop and reached by a system of transverse ramps.

Viale delle cento fontane

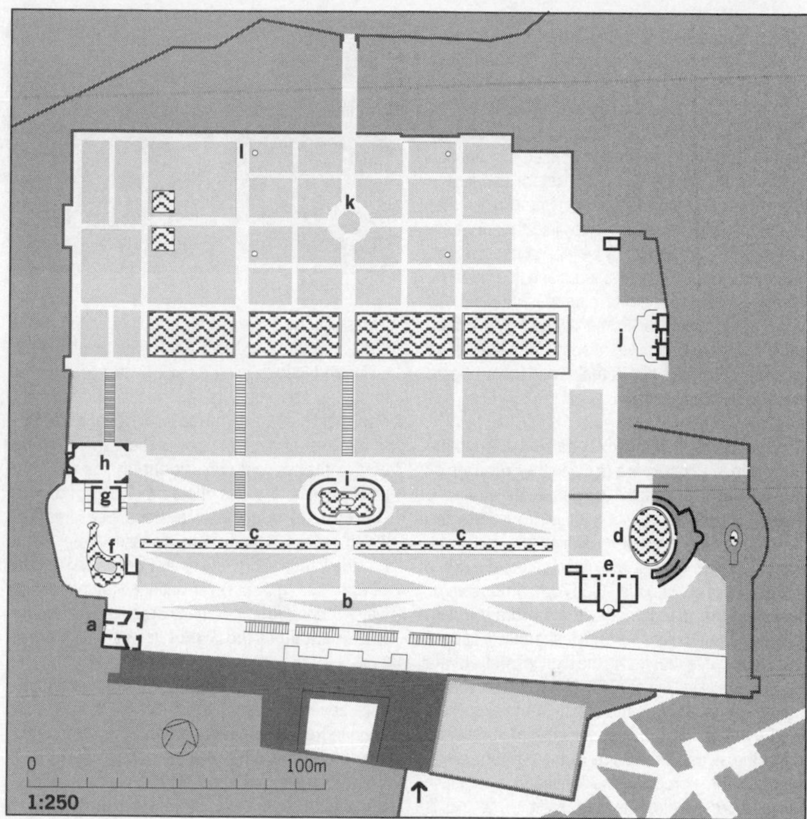

An aqueduct from the River Aniene was constructed, and the lower part of the grounds formed into a broad terrace, its edges filled up against the city wall. Two slopes were formed down to this terrace, a broad one from the monastery itself, the other and narrower from the north-east following the fall of the hillside. Across this warped surface, a rectangular network of paths was laid, connected by stairs or transverse ramps. The layout was disposed around a central axis running from a new two-storey loggia set against the façade of the monastery towards the original entrance to the site, which was from the road skirting the city wall below. All the paths running from east to west are terminated at the boundary of the site by a feature or view point.

Ippolito died in 1572, by which time the ground works were substantially completed, although few of the fountains were finished. His d'Este family successors continued the work over the following century and a half until the villa was sold in 1743. It passed to the Austrian Habsburgs in 1803, and in 1945 it became the property of the Italian state.

The features of the gardens are described from south to north, starting on the terrace which runs across the Villa's garden front. (Some of the names of the fountains have been different at different times: they are given here in English.) The eastern end of this terrace is terminated by the **Grotto of Diana (a)** whose stucco caryatids carry baskets of golden apples. These probably refer to Ippolito's coat of arms, two of whose quarters contain three of the golden apples of the Gardens of the Hesperides. This mythical region may provide an allegorical framework for the ornaments of the garden. At the western end of the terrace are the little **Fountain of Thetis** and the **Grotto of Esculapius**. A path leads north from these to the small **Fountain of Pegasus**.

On the first path just below the terrace, on the axis of the garden, is **Fountain of the Big Glass** or **of the Shell (b)** (Fontana del Bicchierone) of 1661–62, designed by Bernini. Transverse ramps lead down to the **viale delle Cento Fontane (c)**, a path flanked by a continuous basin fed by jets of water emerging from the wall. Originally decorated with terracotta panels illustrating the *Metamorphoses* of Ovid, both wall and jets are now charmingly overgrown with ferns and moss. To the west, this path ends at Ligorio's **Fountain of Tivoli (d)**, or **Oval Fountain**, with to its right the **Grotto of Venus (e)** which originally housed an antique statue of the goddess. At its eastern end lie the **Rometta (f)** and Fountain of Proserpine. The Rometta, 'Little Rome', is a toy-like model of ancient Rome, surrounded by water representing the Tiber from which a boat-shaped island, the Tiberina, emerges, with an obelisk for its mast. Behind this is a seated statue of Rome flanked by models, originally more extensive, of some of the buildings of antique Rome, and of Romulus and Remus being suckled by the she-wolf.

Steps to the right of the Rometta lead down to the **Fountain of Proserpine (g)**, and the **Fountain of the Owl and the Birds (h)** the sound of whose water supply was originally made to imitate the calls of birds and of the crowning owl, now vanished. On the central axis just below the Shell Fountain and cut into the slope is the **Fountain of the Dragons (i)**, named after the dragon who guarded the Gardens of the Hesperides. Also on this slope but to the west is the flight of steps of the 'Bollori' ('boiling'), lined with masks from whose mouths water splashes turbulently into basins which feed the next mask. Straight flights of stairs lead down the slope to the edge of the flat terrace on which the three broad basins or fishponds establish the main cross axis of the composition. This axis is terminated to the east by the spectacular **Fountain of the Organ (j)** set high above against the hillside.

The fish ponds

It was built by Bernini in 1661 and crowned by the eagle from the Cardinal's crest. The fountain originally produced music by using water to force air through organ pipes. Its waters cascade down the slope past high jets to the basin of Neptune of 1927 at the level of the fish ponds. The gardens to the north of the fish ponds are laid out in squares. On the path on the axis lies the former **Rotonda dei Cipressi (k)**, a circle of cypress trees most of which have succumbed to disease, while at the boundary to the north the small **Fountain of Diana of Ephesus (l)** displays an antique statue of Diana, water flowing from her many breasts. Nearby, the little **Fountain of the Swans** lies against the wall.

☞ The town of Tivoli is of ancient foundation, but was severely damaged in World War II. Two antique Republican monuments, the rectangular **Temple of the Sibyl** and the circular **Temple of Vesta**, lie next to the river Aniene in a park reached from via della Sibilla. **Hadrian's Villa 15** lies below the town from which it can be reached by the bus to Rome.

80Eb **Villa di Papa Giulio/'Villa Giulia'** 1550–55

Viale delle Belle Arti

Iacopo Barocci Vignola, Bartolomeo Ammannati, Giorgio Vasari

Ⓜ A Spagna, and walk through Villa Borghese

On his election to the papacy as Julius III in 1550, Giovanni del Monte immediately commissioned the building of this villa on his family estate outside the Aurelian Walls. To allow easy access from the Vatican, the site was connected to a landing stage on the Tiber by what is now the viale Valle Giulia. Del Monte was only able to enjoy its delights for five years, however, for he died in 1555, and the villa was abandoned soon afterwards. It was subsequently used as a farm, and its importance was not recognised until the nineteenth century when plans were made to convert it into an archaeological museum, an ambition only realised for the Esposizione Universale of 1911. The Villa and

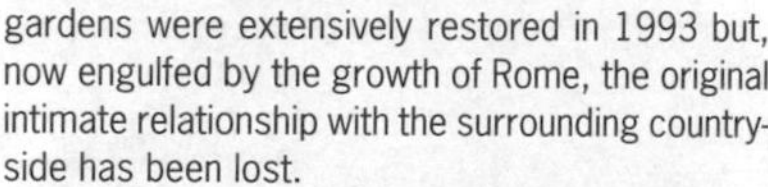

gardens were extensively restored in 1993 but, now engulfed by the growth of Rome, the original intimate relationship with the surrounding countryside has been lost.

Under the general artistic supervision of Michelangelo and supervised by Vasari but mainly designed by Vignola, the Villa itself is a modest construction of three rooms arranged lengthwise on each of two floors, presenting a rectangular façade to the approach. Its splendour is in the sequence of spaces, attributed to Ammannati, which extend along the axis of the entrance into the rising shallow valley in which the garden is set, and link the garden to the wider landscape.

These spaces are launched by the surprisingly deep concave semi-circle of the garden façade, its architecture derived from the interior scheme of the Pantheon and suggesting one wall of an outdoor 'room'. The open ends of the vaulted colonnades were originally continued by pergolas which ran along the outside of the enclosed spaces, and the first-floor windows provided views over the estate. The three linked and contrasting square gardens are separated by walls and screens. The first is contained by high walls which continue the enclosure of the villa's façade. A small opening in the far wall leads to a vaulted loggia beyond which is the delicately decorated nymphaeum, sunk two storeys below the garden and reached by steps whose semi-circular form echoes the shape of the villa's colonnade. A further loggia was added during alterations to the villa in the eighteenth century, its upper level originally reached by two internal spiral stairs. This allows access to the final walled garden which is now square but which originally extended for the full width of the estate.

Although the layout of the gardens owes much to Bramante's work on the Belvedere gardens at the Vatican, the elegant and delicate architecture is characteristic of the sophisticated Mannerist taste of the mid sixteenth century.

81Eb **Sant'Andrea della via Flaminia** 1551–54
Via Flaminia/viale Tiziano
Iacopo Barocci Vignola

Ⓜ A Flaminio

A late essay in central planning, this little oval church was designed and built while Vignola was working on the nearby Villa Giulia **80**. Its oblong plan is surmounted by an oval dome. The exterior is perhaps derived from the Pantheon, although the rectangular base has replaced the circular drum. The church was restored by Valadier in 1806, but was stripped of any context when the via Flaminia was doubled into the viale Tiziano. Its interior is rarely accessible.

82Al **Palazzo Borghese** about 1560–1613
Piazza Borghese off via di Ripetta
Iacopo Barocci Vignola, Flaminio Ponzio

The first palace on this site was constructed for Tommaso del Giglio who employed Vignola as architect. Vignola died in 1573, and the work was continued by Martino Longhi the elder for Count Cardinal Pietro Dezza. In 1596 the building was bought by Cardinal Camillo Borghese who was elected Pope Paul V in 1605. The Milanese architect Ponzio was then commissioned to extend the palace towards the Tiber to occupy the whole site, resulting in an unusual cranked palace front, and the longest in Rome. His project included both a colonnaded courtyard and a design for the corner facing the river. The plan of the building then acquired the shape of a harpsichord, and the loggia at the corner, completed in 1613–14 by Maderna after Ponzio's death, earned the nickname *tastiera del cembalo*, 'the harpsichord's keyboard'.

83Bg **Porta Pia** 1561–65, 1852–68 containing
Museo Storico dei Bersaglieri
Via Venti Settembre/piazza di Porta Pia
Michelangelo Buonarroti, Virginio Vespignani

Ⓜ B Castro Pretorio

Country side

This extraordinary work is one of Michelangelo's two last (the other was the conversion of the Baths of Diocletian **84**). His façade, which faces the city, emphasises the gate itself with the very tall feature in stone, crowned by a wildly unclassical broken pediment. The brick flanks are decorated with detached motifs including blind windows similar to those Michelangelo had designed for the attic of St

Peter's. The near incoherence of the ensemble shows the complete rejection of the canons of the Renaissance, and the gate became a stimulus for the architectural innovations of Mannerism.

Vespigniani's façade facing away from the city is a paraphrase of the Arch of Titus **7**, but with an added pediment and enlarged round-headed niches in the flanks. The housing of the Museum in the gate records the entry of Italian nationalist troops into Rome in 1870.

☞ The **British Embassy**, which lies to the south-west of the gate, was designed by Sir Basil Spence and completed in 1971. It is in the form of a palazzo raised on stilts. Its travertine-clad surfaces exhibit the then fashionable use of 45° angled projections. The department store *La Rinascente* **206** is in piazza Fiume to the north-west along Corso d'Italia.

City side

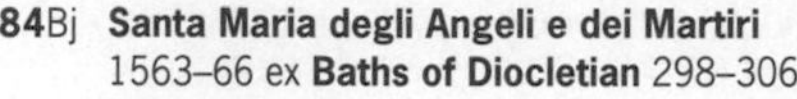

84Bj **Santa Maria degli Angeli e dei Martiri**
1563–66 ex **Baths of Diocletian** 298–306
Piazza Repubblica
Michelangelo Buonarroti, Luigi Vanvitelli

Ⓜ A Repubblica

The plan of the Baths of Diocletian, the last and largest of the Imperial baths, closely followed that of the Baths of Caracalla which were built nearly a century earlier: the agglomeration of buildings for bathing, gymnastics and assembly were set in a large rectangular walled enclosure. Their extensive ruins were subsequently always regarded with awe, and were studied and recorded by the architects of the Renaissance. Michelangelo's last work was the conversion of the ruins into a Carthusian monastery, and he used the three vaulted rectangular bays of the former *frigidarium* of the baths as its church, placing the entrance on the long axis at the south-east corner. Michelangelo died in 1564, and the work was completed by Vanvitelli, who altered the plan and moved the entrance to its present position on the short axis and on the site of the *calidarium*. His timid new façade was subsequently removed in the interests of authenticity, and the via Nazionale was deprived of even a token termination of its grand axis.

This church and the Pantheon are the only two remaining large classical interiors in Rome which still retain something of their original appearance and enclosure. But while the masonry structure and the columns which support the vault are original, the vaults themselves have lost their mosaic; the marbles which lined the walls have been stripped and replaced by paint; and the screened openings which provided connections and cross vistas to the adjacent rooms have been blocked up.

☞ The northern termination of the via Nazionale, the former Piazza dell'Esedra **154** forms a setting for the present entrance to the church. The extensive ruins of the Baths are now scattered well beyond the church. Attached to it is the Museo Nazionale Romano housed in further rooms of the Baths, while now detached is the circular church of **San Bernardo** housed in one of the circular corner pavilions of the enclosing wall. The remains of the pavilion on the opposite, south-east, corner are in via Viminale just north of the Teatro dell'Opera.

85Da **Orti Farnesiani/Farnese Gardens** 1565–77, 1601

Iacopo Barocci Vignola, Jacopo Del Duca, Girolamo Rainaldi

Ⓜ B Colosseo

In 1557 Cardinal Alessandro Farnese bought the flat land on the Palatine plateau for use as a private garden, which later became a centre for botanical studies. The cardinal was already employing Vignola to design his massive palace at Caprarola to the north of Rome, and commissioned him here to provide a monumental entrance to his new gardens. After Vignola's death in 1573, the work was continued by Del Duca.

The entrance sequence up the side of the Palatine hill from the lower via Sacra to the gardens at the top provides a rare and still coherent example in the centre of Rome of Mannerist garden design. A single axis provides a simple framework and direct views of the different parts, but the visitor's path is indirect and interrupted by events which may possess allegorical meaning. The gardens of the earlier Villa Giulia **80**, where Vignola was also co-designer, are arranged in a similar sequence, but on flat ground. At the foot of the hill, a wall was built alongside the via Sacra, with an entrance gate, now transferred to the via di San Gregorio where it provides one of the entrances to the Palatine enclosure. Beyond the site of the gate, the first landing provides a view of the bird-cages at the summit, and below these the grotto on the second landing. Steps lead from either side to another landing decorated with a fountain, and the final flights of stairs lead round the two aviaries to the top platform with its panoramic view to the north. This centres on the ruins of the Basilica of Maxentius, with the Colosseum to the right and the Colli Albani, the Alban Hills, on the horizon. The bird-cages, designed by Girolamo Rainaldi in 1601, originally had curved roofs of open iron mesh, but these are now pitched and covered with tiles.

86Aj **Santa Maria in Traspontina** 1566–87, 1668

Via della Conciliazione

Giovanni Sallustio Peruzzi

Ⓜ A Ottaviano

This run-of-the-mill sixteenth-century church was planned by Giovanni Peruzzi, son of his more famous father Baldassarre. It has a barrel-vaulted nave without aisles but lined with chapels, a domed crossing and an apse. The work was continued by Ottaviano Mascherino between 1581 and 1587, and in the following century the dome was designed by Simone Broggi in 1668. Mascherino also contributed the workmanlike, dull façade now exposed to the via della Conciliazione but formerly addressing the narrow medieval Borgo Vecchio. The fourth chapel on the left is the last work of Antonio Gheradi, but it shows little of the theatricality of his earlier chapels, such as that at Santa Maria in Trastevere **47**.

87Ap **Church of Il Gesù, (SS. Nome di Gesù)**
1568–84

Via del Plebiscito/piazza del Gesù

Iacopo Barocci Vignola

The Society of Jesus, 'the Jesuits', founded in Spain by Ignatius Loyola in 1540, first sought a design for its new church in Rome from Michelangelo. Michelangelo died in 1564, and the commission passed to Vignola. A large church was required, conforming to the new liturgical and decorative requirements of the Council of Trent for a broad nave for preaching, space for processions and an uninterrupted view of the high altar.

Vignola had previously designed two churches with centralised plans, Sant'Andrea in via Flaminia **81** and Sant'Anna dei Palafrenieri in the Vatican, but his Latin cross plan for the Jesuits' church combined Bramante's centralised arrangement of a dome surrounded by an ambulatory with a barrel-vaulted nave of three bays. (The arrangement anticipated Maderna's solution to the problem of extending and completing Michelangelo's centralised St Peter's.) The design, without aisles, and with chapels placed between the buttresses which support the vault of the nave, is a synthesis of several influences. It owes something both to Alberti's Sant'Andrea at Mantua, and perhaps to the Catalan Gothic structure of Rome's Spanish church, Santa Maria in Monserrato **68**. The original scheme of decoration was of austere stone and white painted plaster. The exuberantly Baroque fresco which covers the entire vault, *The Glorification of the Name of Jesus*, was carried out after Vignola's death between 1674 and 1679 by Giovanni Battista Gauli ('Baciccio').

For the façade, Vignola proposed the scheme of two storeys originally devised by Alberti to screen a church with aisles lower than its nave, but applied it to a very different section, and modified its style to Mannerist taste. It was completed after Vignola's death by della Porta who modified the design. The modelling is temperate, but the arrangement of its elements is uncomfortable. The three doors, all of which open into the nave, are gathered together into a narrow central composition, and the proportions of the scrolls which conceal the construction of the chapel roofs are stretched vertically rather than horizontally as in the model.

Because the church met the requirements of its times and function so satisfactorily, and because the Jesuits took the design with them on their missionary expeditions to Asia and the Americas, both plan and façade became influential and widely copied in many countries.

☞ The **Palazzo Cenci-Bolognetti** occupies the south side of the piazza in front of the church. This was enlarged and altered by Ferdinando Fuga in

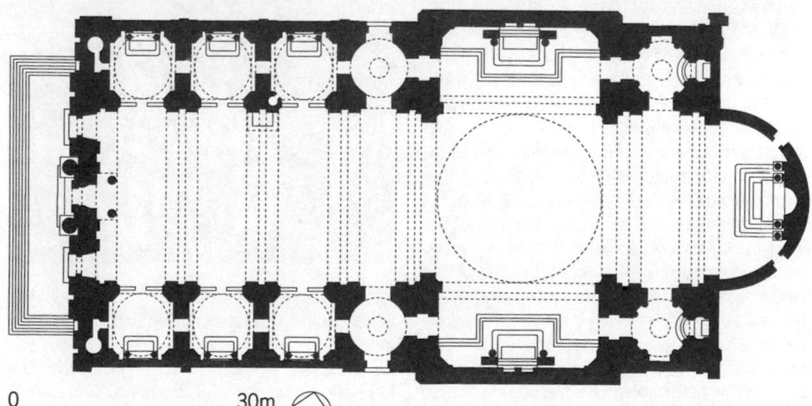

1728–30. To the north, on the other side of via del Plebiscito is the extensive **Palazzo Altieri**, started in 1650–55 by Cardinal Altieri to the designs of Giovanni Antonio De Rossi and extended and completed in 1670–76, with Mattia De Rossi, after the cardinal was elected Pope Clement X.

88Bm **Palazzo del Quirinale** 1574–1740

Piazza Quirinale

Flaminio Ponzio and Ottaviano Mascherino and others

Built on the summit of the Quirinal hill as one of the summer palaces of the popes, in 1870 the building became the residence of the Italian monarchy. It is now the official residence of the President of the Italian Republic, and its interior is inaccessible. The accommodation is arranged in two storeys round a courtyard reached from an offset ceremonial entrance, above which is a balcony for papal appearances, designed by Maderna. From this main block designed by Ponzio and Mascherino, a very long wing, the *manica lunga* or 'long sleeve', extends alongside the via del Quirinale and encloses the extensive garden, occasionally opened on public holidays.

☞ The huge homoerotic statues of Castor and Pollux, the 'Dioscuri', in the square in front of the palace are Roman copies of Greek originals. The twins and the obelisk they flank (which had earlier stood in front of the Mausoleum of Augustus) were set up by Sixtus V. The antique bowl of the fountain and the obelisk were rearranged in 1818 by Raffaello Stern. Facing the square to the right of the Palazzo del Quirinale is the Palazzo della Consultà **134**, and in via Quirinale is Bernini's Sant'Andrea al Quirinale **123**.

89Ao **Santa Maria in Vallicella** or **Chiesa Nuova (Church of the Oratorians)** 1575–1605

Corso Vittorio Emanuele

Matteo da Città di Castello, Martino Longhi the elder and others

St Philip Neri founded the Order of Oratorians, and commissioned the rebuilding of this church in 1575. St Philip's patronage was idiosyncratic: his architect was the little-known Matteo da Città di Castello who designed the first project. The work was continued under the supervision of Martino Longhi the elder who completed the body of the church and its dome in 1583. The plan occupies a simple rectangle into which are neatly fitted the barrel-vaulted nave flanked by aisles and chapels, skimpy transepts, and an apse with a chapel on either side. The architecture is formed in plaster decorated with discreet gilding. In the spirit of the harsher proposals of the Council of Trent, Saint Philip had originally intended the entire interior of the church to be painted white, but the apse and dome, and later the vaults of three of the nave's five bays were instead decorated in frescoes by Pietro da Cortona as his last ecclesiastical commission. He also painted the ceiling of the sacristy. The sumptuously decorated chapel to the left of the choir which houses the tomb of St Philip was designed in 1600–2 by Longhi's son Onorio. The large serviceable façade is the only known work of Fausto Rughesi and was completed in 1605.

90Db **Church of Madonna dei Monti** 1580–90
Via Madonna dei Monti /via dei Serpenti
Giacomo della Porta
Ⓜ B Cavour

This is a rarity: a complete and unaltered workmanlike late Mannerist church carried out while della Porta was Director of the Works of St Peter's. The plan is a small-scale variant of the plan of the Gesù **87** with a simple line of elements: the aisleless barrel-vaulted nave is flanked by chapels; the 'crossing' formed by the shallow transepts hardly warrants the large dome; and the termination of the apse is peremptory. The façade in travertine is neat and regular, and its cleaning in 1994 revealed that the central door surround is of grey marble.

☞ The little fountain in the piazza to the east of the church in via dei Serpenti was also designed by della Porta.

91Da **Santa Maria della Conciliazione**
1583 onwards
Piazza della Consolazione
Martino Longhi the elder

Longhi rebuilt the church and designed a new high altar and the lower storey of the façade. The upper storey was completed in 1826 by Pasquale Belli who working at the time on the reconstruction of San Paolo fuori le Mura **30**. The church, now magnificently cleaned, presides over a car park under the Tarpeian Rock from which Roman criminals were once thrown.

92Ao **Sant'Andrea della Valle** 1591–1665
Corso Vittorio Emanuele II/via dei Chiavari
Giacomo della Porta

While working here, della Porta was also supervising the construction of the dome of St Peter's, where with Fontana he was Director of works. The plan of this enormous church, its dome the second largest in Rome after that of St Peter's, was developed by della Porta from that of Vignola's Gesù **87**, the façade of which he had completed after Vignola's death. The architecture of the nave is treated differently, and the vertical proportions emphasised: instead of the single entablature which runs continuously round the Gesù, the pilasters here are continued to support the ribbed and panelled barrel vault. The decoration of the dome, by Giovanni Lanfranco, marked the important transition from paintings confined in frames to those which offered a painted illusion which extended over the whole, ribless, surface. (The church has achieved fame outside architectural history as the setting for the first act of Puccini's opera *Tosca*.)

The design of the façade, while employing no curves in plan, is a robust demonstration of the emerging Baroque: it is organised into two storeys whose three planes and paired columns are precisely and tectonically disposed, and the decorative flourishes like the notched triangular pediment do not destroy the order of the whole. The fountain opposite the façade of the church on the north side of the Corso Vittorio Emanuele was designed by Maderna in 1614.

93Ah **San Giacomo degli Incurabili (San Giacomo al Corso** or **in Augusta)** about 1596

Via del Corso/via A. Canova

Francesco da Volterra, Carlo Maderna

M A Spagna

Detail of façade and drum

The significance of this church lies in Volterra's use of an unambiguously oval plan surrounded by radiating chapels: it is one of the earliest examples of a form which was to become an important theme of Baroque architecture. The working out of the theme here, however, does not have the authentic authority of the Baroque, and the attempt to unify the triplets of adjacent chapels behind a triumphal arch motif was never copied. The façade to the Corso is by Carlo Maderna from a design by Giacomo della Porta. The 'incurabili' were the inhabitants of the nearby hospital which the church served.

☞ Across the Corso, diagonally opposite and to the north, is the **Church of Gesù e Maria**, of about 1675, its neat travertine façade and interior decoration by Girolamo Rainaldi.

The Baroque 1600–74

94Bj **Santa Susanna** 1597–1603
Piazza San Bernardo
Carlo Maderna
Ⓜ A Repubblica

Maderna was employed to modernise this church, founded in the fifth century and restored in the eighth and sixteenth. The interior was cleaned in 1993–95. Its important situation, at the opposite end of the via Torino from the basilica of Santa Maria Maggiore, suggests, wrongly, that the street was one of those cut through in Sixtus V's programme. Its architectural significance lies in the façade which Maderna supplied. He took the inconclusive and contradictory Mannerist scheme of church façades such as that of the Gesù **87**, and systematised it to present extensions of the classical language which suggested for the following generation the plastic experimentation which was to develop into the full Baroque.

Maderna's scheme uses pilasters, columns and wall projections to enhance the importance of the single central door. The walls of the outer single-storey bays are decorated with flat pilasters. The narrower outer bays of the church proper have pilasters at their corners, are set forward and contain shallow niches. The next bays are wider, set forward again and house deep niches. They have engaged full columns abutting those of the central bay which sets forward again to enclose the door. This occupies the full width of the bay, and is crowned with a segmental pediment below the bay's triangular one. The upper storey is treated by extending the lines of the columns of the three bays below and marking them with pilasters. The whole is crowned with a pediment into which extends a projecting layer of the face of the wall of the central bay below. The successors to this façade include, for example, those of San Luca e Santa Martina **108** where Pietro da Cortona introduced the curve into the plan, and of

Santi Vincenzo ed Anastasio **115** in which Longhi exuberantly developed the use of clustered redundant columns.

☞ The church of Santa Maria della Vittoria **101** is to the north. Directly opposite it is the Fontana dell'Acqua Felice of 1587–88, designed by Domenico Fontana. The circular church of **San Bernardo** is on the opposite side of the piazza: this is built over one of the corner pavilions of the ruins of the Baths of Diocletian, now the church of Santa Maria degli Angeli **84**.

95Da **San Giuseppe dei Falegnami** 1597–1602

off via dei Fori Imperiali

Giovanni Battista Montano

The church, built over the 'Mammertine prison' where pilgrims are told St Peter and St Paul were imprisoned, is nearly always closed. Montano was a Milanese sculptor and engraver, and this is his only work in Rome. Del Grande completed the work between 1657 and 1660. This church was, like that of San Luca e Santa Martina **108** which stands immediately to the south, stripped of its medieval surroundings in 1930–32 during clearance work for the via dei Fori Imperiali.

96Cd **Palazzo Mattei di Giove** now housing **Discoteca dello Stato, Biblioteca di Storia Moderna e Contemporanea, etc.** 1598–1611

Via dei Funari/via Caetani

Carlo Maderna

Maderna made two contributions to the development of architectural 'types'. The first, his design for the façade of Santa Susanna **94**, established a format which could be elaborated and copied by succeeding generations of architects. While the Palazzo Farnese **73** had established the type for the plan and front of the Roman palazzo, its organisation was rudimentary. In particular the relationship between the courtyard and main staircase to the important rooms on the first floor was unresolved, and it continued to be improvised in subsequent designs. At the Palazzo Mattei Maderna, helped by its position on a corner of two streets, was able to unite its two entrances. That from via dei Funari leads to the first courtyard and emerges in the centre of its arcade. The second entrance lies on the axis of this arcade and leads directly to the staircase in the corner of the plan which provides access to the *piano nobile*. The staircase itself was given architectural stucco decoration. While this arrangement was an answer to a special case, the second, axial, approach was a direct stimulus to the scenographic experiments of the Baroque planning of palaces in Rome and, later, in Germany and Austria. The exterior of the palace lies firmly within the Roman tradition, but the decoration of the courtyard with sculpture is derived from the experiments at the Villas Medici **78** and Borghese **97**.

☞ The **Fontana delle Tartarughe** ('Fountain of the Tortoises'), lies in piazza Mattei to the west past several more palaces on the north side of via dei Funari. It is one of the many designed by Giacomo della Porta and was erected in 1581–84.

97Bb **Villa** or **Palazzina Borghese**, now **Museo e Galleria Borghese** begun 1608

Villa Borghese

Flaminio Ponzio, Jan van Santen ('Giovanni Vansazio')

Ⓜ A Spagna and Villa Borghese exit

In 1608 the nephew of the Borghese Pope Paul V, Cardinal Scipione Borghese, employed the family architect Ponzio to design a country villa to be constructed on their extensive estate which lay outside the Aurelian Wall and was used as a vineyard. Ponzio was already working on designs for extending the Borghese Palace **82.** Like that of Cardinal Ferdinando de' Medici **73**, the new Borghese villa was required to house collections of paintings and antique sculpture, and to have some of the air of a public building: it was as much for the display of the collection to the public as for the pursuit of the cardinal's private connoisseurship. The form adopted by Ponzio was that of the *villa suburbana* established a century earlier by Peruzzi for the Farnesina **65**: a block with projecting wings whose exterior walls were decorated with items from the collection, and whose interior was richly ornamented with marble. Ponzio died in 1613, and the work was continued and completed by the Dutch architect Jan van Santen ('Giovanni Vansanzio').

Two cheerful *palazzine dell'Uccelliera* or aviaries are sited to the north-west of the villa. They were designed by Girolamo Rainaldi in 1617–19 and the nearer was constructed then. (The further, the palazzina della Meridiana, was not built until 1688.) The detailed layout of the garden was developed over the following two centuries, but it was first laid out as series of rectangular walled enclosures. In 1763, Prince Marcantonio IV inherited the estate and laid out the piazza di Siena or hippodrome. He also began the extensive programme of redecoration, designed by Unterberger, and of the garden pavilions and ornaments designed by Unterberger, the Aspruccis and others and described at **139**. More alterations were made in 1825–28, and parts of the garden converted to the 'English' style. In 1880 the mayor of Rome prevented a proposal to sell the estate and subdivide it for building plots. Bought by the Italian state in 1902, the land has since with the Pincio been a public park, not Rome's largest but certainly its most popular. The villa was used to house the remaining works of the original collection as the Museo and Galleria Borghese.

Palazzina dell'Uccelliera (1617–19)

☞ For the eighteenth- and nineteenth-century garden pavilions see **139**. To the north of the villa in the piazza dei Daini is the 'serbatoio idrico' or water storage tower designed in 1925 in Viennese style by Raffaele De Vico.

'Serbatoio idrico' or water storage tower, piazza dei Daini

98Cf **Aqua Paola** 1612

Via G. Garibaldi, Gianicolo

Giovanni Fontana and Flaminio Ponzio, Carlo Fontana

In order to ensure the supply to some of Rome's existing fountains, during his reign (1605–28) Paul V repaired Trajan's aqueduct which had brought water from Lake Bracciano to Rome. He caused this new fountain to be built and used stone from the Forum Transitoria. Much of the space of the façade is devoted to explaining the building programme in the large finely-lettered inscription. From the three arches, which are flanked by columns taken from the porch of old St Peter's, the water emerges into a basin added later and designed by Carlo Fontana. There is a good view to the east from the terrace in front of the fountain, and from here the enormous bulk of the Palazzo di Giustizia **151** can be appreciated.

☞ Along via Garibaldi to the east is the Tempietto at San Pietro in Montorio **62**; and to the west is the Porta San Pancrazio **144**.

99Cd **San Carlo ai Catinari** 1612–20

Piazza Cairoli/via de' Giubbonari

Rosato Rosati

The church, its plan a Greek cross with an extended apse distantly derived from Bramante's project for St Peter's, was the only work of architecture designed by Rosati, a member of the Barnabite Order who commissioned it. The severe, conservative façade was added by Giovanni Battista Soria and completed in 1638. But Rosati's larger work is eclipsed by Antonio Gheradi's much smaller Cappella di S. Cecilia to the north of the east transept. At Gheradi's earlier Cappella Avila in Santa Maria in Trastevere **47**, the viewer is invited to look forward into the chapel. Here, after the splendid sight of angels drawing back curtains from the window, the view is upwards, through one open oval dome to the opening in another. Here four angels who play musical instruments lounge on and over the balustrade, while beyond is a brightly lit rectangular salon on the ceiling of which the dove of the Holy Ghost is surrounded by plaster rays.

100 Ah **Santi Ambrogio e Carlo al Corso** 1612–19, façade 1690

Via del Corso

Onorio and Martino Longhi, Pietro da Cortona

M A Spagna

This should be one of the great works of the Baroque, but in spite of the talent involved in its construction, it remains unappealing and its interior undistinguished. Onorio Longhi's design was started in 1612, but the work was continued by his son Martino ('the younger') and only completed in 1651. Pietro da Cortona designed the fine dome with its exquisitely articulated drum, begun in 1668. It was his last work of architecture before his death in 1669. The gross façade with its gigantic columns without bases was added in 1690 to the designs of G. B. Menicucci and Mario de Canepina.

101 Bj **Santa Maria della Vittoria** 1620, façade 1625–27, Cornaro Chapel 1646

Via Venti Settembre/largo S. Susanna

Carlo Maderna

M A Repubblica

Gates of 1864

The church itself is an example of Maderna's competent proto-Baroque, and its plan and section are unremarkable. The conservatively classical and academic façade of 1625–27 is by Giovanni Battista Soria. The true Baroque lies in the chapel to the left of the high altar designed by Gian Lorenzo Bernini for the Venetian Cardinal Federico Cornaro in 1647–52. The Council of Trent imposed a rational austerity on church decoration and encouraged personal devotion to a new batch of saints. Bernini brings to the Council's programme a Spanish sensibility for a new Spanish saint. The centrepiece of the Chapel is the sculpture of Saint Teresa of Avila in a state of mystical exaltation and visited by an angel: the swooning saint hovers in her architectural frame supported on a cloud, backed by the exploding gilded rays. The pair are lit by a concealed window fitted with yellow glass. From their box in the wall to the right, the Cornaro family observe the scene. The sumptuous marbles are used both tectonically and illusionistically: red for the Cornaros' cushions, yellow for the 'silk' hangings. The whole church was cleaned in 1993 and the original and shocking sheen of its marbles restored.

Ufficio Geologico

☞ The fountain, the **Acqua Felice**, Santa Susanna **94**, the church of **San Bernardo**, all surround the crossroads. The **Ufficio Geologico** to the west has an elegant cast iron frame and was designed by Raffaele Canevari as the Museo dell' Agricultura in 1873.

102 Bm **Palazzo Chigi-Odaleschi** 1622–29, 1664–66
Piazza di SS. Apostoli
Carlo Maderna, Gian Lorenzo Bernini and others

The 'problem' of the design of the palace front may not have exercised architects of the sixteenth and seventeenth centuries as much as it did subsequent art historians. At the Palazzo Chigi, however, and taking up work started by Maderna in 1622, Bernini established a pattern for the Baroque palace which was taken up by European architects for any important or domestic building which could be shaped into the 'palazzo' format. His innovation was the introduction into what had been the exclusively horizontally divided format of, for example, the Palazzo Farnese **73**, of continuous vertical divisions in the form of giant columns or pilasters. While Michelangelo had first used the giant order for the fronts of the Capitoline palazzi **76**, Bernini used a rusticated ground floor as a base, so usefully extending the formula to at least three storeys or, with an attic, four. Bernini's original design had seven bays standing between the recessed ends of three bays. In 1745, the palace was acquired by the Odaleschi who employed Nicola Salvi and Luigi Vanvitelli to extend it: they added another seven bays to the façade.

☞ The opposite side of the street is dominated by the façade of the large church of **SS. Apostoli**, founded in 560 but largely redesigned by Carlo Fontana and his son Francesco between 1702 and 1708. Construction continued throughout the eighteenth century, and the façade of 1827 is the work of Giuseppe Valadier.

103 Dd **Santa Bibiana** façade and portico 1624
Via Giovanni Giolotti/via Cairoli
Gian Lorenzo Bernini

Ⓜ A Vittorio

Bernini was first trained and employed as a sculptor and it was as such and rather than as architect that he was chosen to design the Baldacchino of St Peter's in 1624. The façade of Santa Bibiana was his first work of outdoor architecture and a modest one, carried out when he was twenty-seven. Now engulfed by the handsome outworks of the railway station, his portico is remarkably dry, and the modelling restrained, his later exuberance only being suggested in the height of the new portico compared with the existing humble basilica, and the emphasis of the central feature of the upper storey.

☞ Pavilion in the Licinian gardens/'Temple of Minerva Medica' **25.**

104 Bi **Palazzo Barberini (Galleria Nazionale d'Arte Antica)** 1625–38

Via delle Quattro Fontane

Carlo Maderna, Francesco Borromini, Gian Lorenzo Bernini

Ⓜ A Barberini

In 1623, Maffeo Barberini of Florence was elected Pope Urban VIII, and the following year he commissioned Maderna to design a suitable Roman home on a site on one side of a ridge of the Quirinale hill. The site was open, and Maderna's plan follows that of Peruzzi's Villa Farnesina **65** rather than that of the urban palazzo type established at the Palazzo Farnese **73**. The entrance was originally from the north-east, not as now from the via dell Quattro Fontane which is on the garden side. Wings extend from the central block of three storeys to enclose the first section of the garden. The ground floor of the central block is open, occupied almost entirely by the entrance hall and stairs to the north, and towards the garden by a deep loggia (now glazed) which occupies the full width of the central seven projecting bays. The theme of loggia was continued on the upper two floors.

From Letarouilly, *Edifices de Rome*, 1840–74

Maderna died in 1629, and his chief assistant Borromini continued the supervision of the work together with Bernini until 1632. The oval staircase in the southern wing was designed by Borromini, as were the novel window surrounds, perhaps derived from Michelangelo's design for the attic of St Peter's, in the top storey of the central block and facing the garden. Bernini's individual contribution, if any, is uncertain. In 1633–39 Pietro da Cortona decorated the ceiling of the salon with frescoes, illusionistic like those of the Villa Farnesina, but far more ambitious. At the centre of the floating figures are the three bees of the Barberini arms.

The 'Baroque' iron railings and gates (illustrated) which now separate the garden from the via delle Quattro Fontane were designed by Francesco Azzuri in 1864 when the entrance was rearranged to the south. In 1949 the palace became the property of the Italian state, and one wing now houses the Galleria Nazionale d'Arte Antica.

☞ Bernini's **Fontana del Tritone** of 1642–43 stands in the centre of the piazza Barberini. Its single composition marked a decisive shift from earlier designs for fountains in which sculpture was used to decorate an architectural basin. On the north corner of the piazza at the beginning of via Vittorio Veneto stands the relocated and restored **Fontana delle Api** (*ape*, a bee) of 1644, also designed by Bernini to celebrate the Barberini.

Fontana del Tritone

105 Ap **Sant'Ignazio** 1626–85

Piazza Sant'Ignazio/via del Caravita

Orazio Grassi SJ

The second of Rome's two large Jesuit churches was started to consolidate the importance of the Order on the occasion of the canonisation in 1622 of its founder Ignatius Loyola and his colleague Francis Xavier. It is as grandiose as the earlier Gesù **87**, but its layout and detail are academic compared with its more radical predecessor. Grassi was a Jesuit mathematician, and the design with which he is credited was derived from one originally proposed by Borromini and Maderna. It was carried out in stages over a long period, and parts were designed by ad-hoc committees. The space is unified by the single order of pilasters which encircles nave, transepts and choir, below which the secondary order provides arched openings. The glory of the church lies in the painting of its vaults for which by contrast the architecture acts as a modest setting. The entire ceiling of the nave is filled with Andrea Pozzo's extraordinary frescoes which continue into the dome and apse. The fresco in the nave, the *Allegory of the Missionary Work of the Jesuits*, was painted in 1691–94. The composition, a painted architectural space continuing up and beyond the real cornice to provide a setting in which float missionary Jesuits and their converts set among clouds, is best appreciated by standing on the small disk of yellow marble set into the floor of the nave.

Piazza di Sant'Ignazio

A century after the church was started, the approach to its front, the **piazza di Sant'Ignazio**, was set up to the design of Filippo Raguzzini in 1727–28. The minuscule, delicate, yellow-painted buildings, with their convex curves (based on a composition of three ovals carved out of the blocks) and diagonal vistas, provide an elegant Rococo foil and approach to the massive façade of the church.

106 Df **San Gregorio Magno al Celio** 1629–33, 1725–34

Via di San Gregorio

Giovanni Battista Soria, Francesco Ferrari

M B Circo Massimo

The first church on this site was erected by Gregory the Great (590–604), the pope who sent the first missionary monks to England. The present façade and the court beyond were added in 1629–33 and designed by Soria, whose conservative classicism anticipated the Classical reaction to the Baroque of the following century. Between 1725 and 1730, the interior of the church was completely refitted by Ferrari, and only the antique columns of the nave arcade survive from the earlier churches.

107 Bj **San Carlo alle Quattro Fontane ('San Carlino')** 1633, façade 1667

Via delle Quattro Fontane/via Quirinale

Francesco Borromini

Ⓜ A Barberini, Repubblica

The small church and its smaller cloister are on a constricted corner site at the intersection of two of Sixtus V's new streets. They were Borromini's first important works of architecture in which the themes that dominate his later work were introduced and developed. Rome had already seen centralised oval churches such as Vignola's Sant'Anna dei Palafrenieri of 1570, but Borromini's interpretation was revolutionary. The design of the church is extraordinarily complex: while the plan can be interpreted as that of a smudged Greek cross, its generating form is an oval on the long axis of the plan, and the dome verifies this. The coffering of the dome with its pattern of interlocking crosses, diamonds and hexagons (probably derived from a mosaic at Santa Costanza) is an exercise in gratuitous geometrical virtuosity. Below the dome, however, the walls either bulge forwards to enclose niches or backwards to house the high altar and the two side chapels. The columns placed at the inflections of the walls do not follow the perimeter of the dome, and the pendentives between the arches which they support are complex, warped, surfaces. As far as is possible in architecture, a sense of movement is induced: the observing eye flickers, and the resolution of a single perception is frustrated. The minute two-storey cloister, reached from the door to the right of the high altar, is articulated by delicate convex corners supported on paired columns which reappear at the centres of the long sides.

The façade was added at the end of Borromini's life and the double curve of its plan immediately became a hallmark of the late Baroque. On each storey, four columns stand in a straight line while their entablature sways independently. The upper central cartouche nipped by the sharp cut ends of the split entablatures may not be entirely to Borromini's design.

The four fountains at the street intersection from which the church takes its name were set up in 1597 and are dedicated respectively to Rome's two rivers, the Tiber and Aniene; and to two virtues, Fidelity and Strength.

☞ Sant'Andrea al Quirinale **123** by Bernini, Palazzo Barberini **104**.

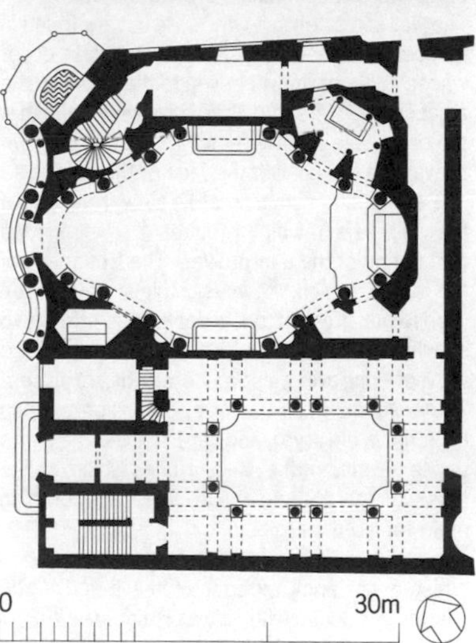

108 Da **San Luca e Santa Martina** 1635–64

Via dei Fori Imperiali

Pietro da Cortona

Pietro da Cortona was commissioned by the Accademia di San Luca to rebuild the medieval church of Santa Martina, and above this, which was reformed as the crypt, he erected the completely new church dedicated to the academy's patron saint. During the excavations for the crypt, the relics of Santa Martina were discovered, and a more grandiose programme developed into what was to become one of the first masterpieces of the High Roman Baroque, the contemporary of Borromini's façade for the Oratorians **109**. The plan is in the form of a domed Greek cross whose arms are slightly extended to form the nave and choir. The space is unified by three devices: first, the ends of the arms of the cross are rounded; second, the corners of the piers at the crossing are chamfered; and third, the sophisticated treatment of the walls below the entablature is continuous around the perimeter. The wall is treated in a way more usually found in façades: it is decorated with a Roman Ionic order whose columns are recessed to the depth of the adjacent pilasters. (An alternative reading is that the outer face of the pilasters has been brought forward to line up with the face of the columns.) The effect is to establish a Baroque 'layering' of the wall surface which requires a simultaneous perception of the alternatives. The treatment of the dome (which, however, might have been carried out after Cortona's death) also offers two simultaneous readings: the surface is enriched with coffering over which modelled ribs are placed. The Academy gave Cortona permission to build his tomb in the crypt, and here he used the same dense layering of the wall surfaces which, unlike those of the church above, were executed in multi-coloured marbles.

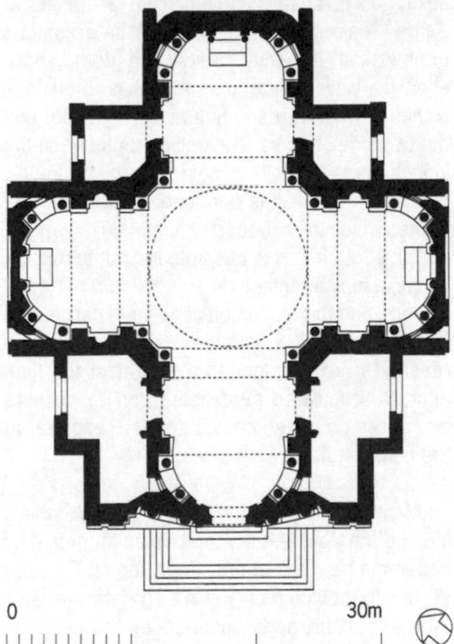

The present brick exterior of the body of the church was added when it was isolated in 1930–32 to allow archaeological excavation before the via dei Fori Imperiali was built in 1933. The original two-storey façade presents a central shallow and broken curved section framed between two rectangular parts. (The intended design included a further rectangular block on each side: these would have given a less vertical, more conventional format.) Cortona elaborated this simple framework in much the same way as he did in the interior: columns are set into the wall and back from pilasters, but here the lines of the columns run through the two storeys, unifying them. The string courses, the lower of which sets out to become the base of the pediment over the door, provide another 'layer' in the rich composition, the total depth of whose modelling is not more than two metres (six feet). The exterior of the dome and drum are less original and their features are derived from Michelangelo's late works.

☞ The church of San Giuseppe dei Falegnami **95** lies immediately to the west.

109 Ao **Oratorio di San Filippo Neri/dei Filippini** 1637–40

Piazza d'Orologio, off Corso Vittorio Emanuele II

Francesco Borromini

Borromini's successful work at San Carlo **107** led to this commission from a new religious Order for an economical building to house an oratory for musical performances, 'oratorios', and domestic accommodation for the Oratorians. It is accordingly but unusually built of fine brickwork. The architect was instructed not to use columns in order not to compete with the neighbouring church, and instead he decorated the single wide concave curve of the façade with flat giant pilasters whose clustering provides the shallow modelling. The whole is crowned with an innovative if frivolous fusion of a triangular and a segmental pediment. The façade was never intended to be seen as we can view it now: its present setting facing the inevitable small car park is the result of the clearance of surrounding buildings for the construction of the Corso Vittorio Emanuele towards the end of the nineteenth century. It would originally only have been seen in raking views like those still to be had of the later Collegio di Propaganda Fide **126**.

☞ To the east of the Oratory: the Chiesa Nova or Santa Maria in Vallicella **89**. The fountain in the form of a *terrina* or tureen had many locations before finally being placed in the piazza in front of the Oratory in 1924. It was originally commissioned by Sixtus V to stand in the Campo dei Fiori and is one of the many designed by Giacomo della Porta.

110 Ao **Sant'Ivo alla Sapienza** 1642–60

Palazzo della Sapienza, entrance off Corso del Rinascimento

Francesco Borromini

The elongated courtyard around which teaching rooms of the University, the 'Sapienza', were disposed was started in 1557 by Giacomo della Porta. Commissioned by Urban VIII (né Maffeo Barberini) and continued by Bernini's great patron Alexander VII, the University's church contains references to the coats of arms of both popes. The allegorical and symbolic programme is established by 'sapientia', 'wisdom', as the motto over the altar proposes: 'Initium Sapientiae—Timor Domini' ('Wisdom begins with the fear of the Lord'). Borromini's use of the hexagon, seen later in the columns of the porch of the Collegio di Propaganda Fide **126**, is magnified here on a grand scale. The plan is based on two equilateral triangles which are overlaid to make a six-pointed star, a symbol of wisdom, the hexagon at its centre. Semi-circular recesses are placed at the apexes of one of the triangles, one of them housing the high altar; and trapezoidal recesses are placed at those of the other. Above the continuous entablature, the dome does not have its own simple geometrical shape—here a circle would have been indicated—but it is formed by reducing the profile of the plan. The interior was later covered with frescoes, but it is now restored to its original white against which the decoration consists of sculptured references to the Temple of Solomon and the arms of Urban and Alexander: there are palms and pomegranates, and Barberini bees.

Externally, the strongly concave entrance façade, which politely continues the horizontals of della Porta's arcades, counters the irregular convexity of the drum and dome (these elements are coalesced, there being no room on the tight site to provide deep buttresses). The curious spiral of the upper stage of the dome is another symbol of wisdom and supports the flame of truth, and the orb and cross.

☞ Pantheon **16**, Palazzo Madama **114**, Piazza Navona **117.**

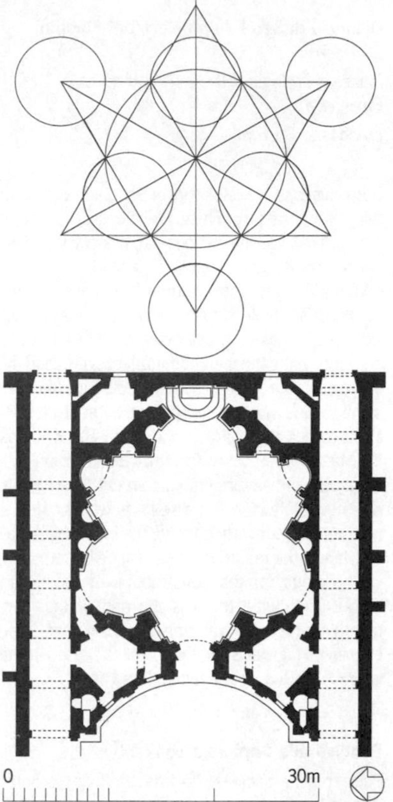

111Cc **Palazzo Falconieri** now **Accademia d'Ungheria** 1646–49

Via Giulia/via dell'Armato

Francesco Borromini

Borromini was employed to extend the palace. The façade to the via Giulia was enlarged from its previous seven bays to eleven, and its ends terminated with the unprecedented falcon-headed and breasted herms. On the garden side, wings were extended from the back towards the Tiber, and a new loggia or lookout on the roof was added, closely modelled on the bays of Palladio's design of 1549 for the recladding of the 'Basilica' at Vicenza. Finally, Borromini painted the ceilings of twelve of the more important rooms.

☞ Next to the palazzo on via Giulia and to the south is the church of **Santa Maria dell'Orazione e della Morte** of 1733–37. It was Ferdinando Fuga's first design for a Roman church.

112 Dh **Basilica of San Giovanni in Laterano** (312, 1220–32), 1646–49, façade 1732–36

Piazza di Porta San Giovanni

Francesco Borromini (nave) and others

Ⓜ A San Giovanni

Established on land donated by Constantine in 312–13, against the Aurelian wall and as distant as possible from the centres of civil power, the earliest basilica of San Giovanni was the first official Christian place of worship in Rome and the seat of its bishop. That building has been obliterated by subsequent churches, and from Constantine's time only parts of the nearby **Baptistery** or San Giovanni in Fonte now remain. This building now has an octagonal plan, although it may originally have been circular. Eight columns dating from the period of the first restoration in the reign of Sixtus III (432–40) surround the font. The building became the basis for one of the type of the Christian baptistery and was frequently subsequently copied, but any reminiscence here of the Constantine period is now prevented by the seventeenth-century frescoes which cover most of the surfaces.

The present plan of the church retains the form of a fourth-century basilica with nave, aisles, transepts and apse, but the church has been repeatedly repaired and rebuilt after fires, sackings and earthquakes. The cloister, off the south transept, was added in 1220–36, and carried out by members of the Vassalletti family of sculptors. It is a fine example of the style of the Cosmati workshop applied three-dimensionally, particularly to the exquisite pairs of twisted columns and the frieze. The sumptuous nave of 1646–49 is the work of Borromini who, perhaps seeking a robust structure which would withstand earthquakes or the occasional sacking, substituted piers for the earlier columns of the nave and thereby deprived it of its transparent basilican character. He had further planned a vault to span the nave, but there was neither time nor money for this and the present flat ceiling was erected. In alterations carried out

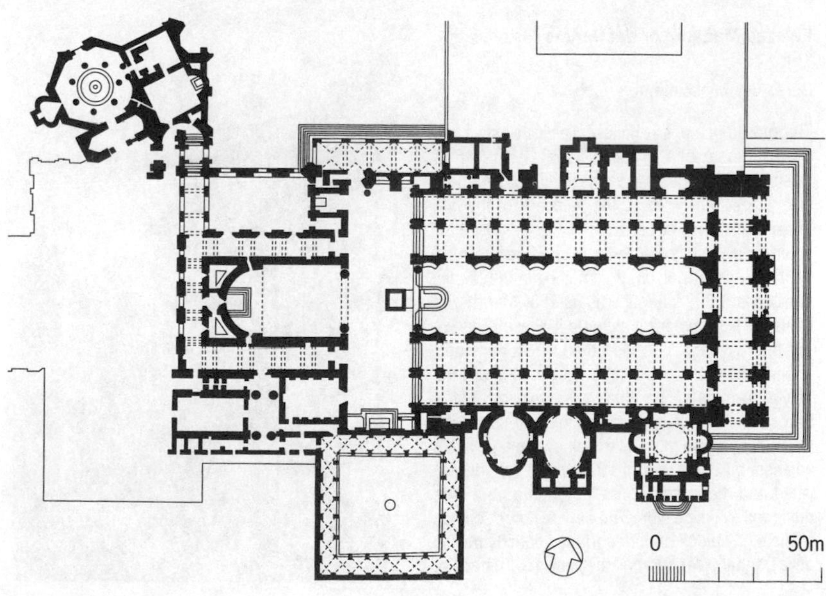

between 1874 and 1886 by Virgilio Vespignani, the apse was extended and the altar and ciborium were rebuilt: the present mosaics in the apse are copies of the originals.

Borromini had also designed a new west front but this was not built. The façade of 1732–36, now magnificently presiding over a car park, was designed by Alessandro Galilei who won the competition sponsored by Clement XII in 1732. It was required to form a conspicuous and fitting climax to the pilgrims' route up the via Appia, to shelter them in its vestibule, and to provide a balcony for papal benedictions. Its enormous scale and use of the giant order, derived from the central section of Maderna's façade for St Peter's and from Michelangelo's palaces at the Campidoglio, and the statues which are essential to the silhouette, look back to the origins of the Baroque. But in spite the Baroque plasticity of its depth, the whole is dryer and more Classical than its models. Galilei also designed the very severe Cappella Corsini (1733–52), the first chapel off the south aisle, for his patron Clement XII, who confirmed his classical taste in selecting for his tomb which stands in it the Roman sarcophagus which is supported on four columns from the portico of the Pantheon.

☞ North of the basilica, the **Lateran Palace** was reconstructed in 1586 to the designs of Domenico Fontana. Intended as a summer palace for the popes who since their return from Avignon had used the Vatican as headquarters, it was Fontana's largest papal commission, but it lacks distinction, and the Quirinal palace became preferred. Constructed at the same time and opposite the basilica, the **Scala Santa** was also designed by Domenico Fontana. This curious contribution to the taxonomy of building types has an uneconomical percentage of circulation to usable space of 100: five flights of stairs run side by side. The central flight of stairs was imported from Jerusalem by Constantine's mother St Helena in the belief that they came from Pontius Pilate's palace and that Jesus had walked up them. The **Porta San Giovanni** to the south of the basilica was constructed in the Aurelian Wall in 1574 by Michelangelo's former assistant Jacopo Del Duca to replace the earlier Roman gate to the west, the **Porta Asinaria**, which was fully excavated in 1955.

Porta San Giovanni and Porta Asinaria beyond

113 Ao **Palazzo Madama** or **del Senato** restored 1642

Corso del Rinascimento

The importance of this building lies in its use: it has been the seat of the Italian Senate since 1871 when a new chamber was inserted, designed by Luigi Gabet. The core of the palace is of the late fifteenth century, but in 1503 it was restored for count Ferdinando II de' Medici, later Pope Leo x and Raphael's great patron. It remained in the Medici family until 1537 when it was used by Margherita d'Austria from whom it derives it present name. The massive façade to the Corso di Risorgimento, added in 1642, follows the horizontally divided astylar formula of the Palazzo Farnese **73**, but is Baroque in its details. As all large institutions tend to do, the Senate gradually took over the palace's adjacent buildings, and in 1930 these were demolished and their uses consolidated in a new wing designed by Felice Nori. The Senate now occupies a whole city block bounded to the south by the via della Doghana Vecchia and the piazza S. Eustachio.

114 Ap **Palazzo di Montecitorio 1** now housing **Chamber of Deputies** 1650 and 1902–18

Piazza Montecitorio

Gian Lorenzo Bernini and others

Bernini designed only two palaces, this for the Ludovisi family; the other was the Palazzo Chigi-Odaleschi **102**. Supplying one of his less satisfactory ideas, he articulated the huge, very long, but otherwise unremarkable, façade of the palace by setting back its wings at a slight angle. Since 1871, the palace has housed the Chamber of Deputies. Between 1902 and 1918 the palace was extended to the north and a new entrance provided. Ernesto Basile's palazzo façade which faces the piazza del Parlamento is clamped between two towers, and Floreale decoration applied sparingly.

115 Bm **Santi Vincenzo ed Anastasio** façade 1646–57

Via del Lavatore/via di S. Vincenzo

Martino Longhi the younger

M A Barberini

Longhi took on the building of the body of the church from his father, but Pietro da Cortona completed the high altar, apse and dome. It is, however, the façade commissioned by Cardinal Luigi Alessandro Omodei in which two of the Baroque's characteristic themes of mass and 'movement' are powerfully presented, now mostly to the backs of the crowds which swirl in front of the Trevi Fountain. Artfully placed columns dominate its two storeys. On the lower storey, a bay at either side is flanked by a single recessed outer column and a pair of widely spaced columns. The central door is flanked by a pair of columns. From edge to centre, each column is placed forward of its neighbour, confusing a straightforward interpretation of exactly how each supports the entablature above. For the second storey, the triple columns of the central bay are repeated, and each pair carries one of three pediments, two triangular and an inner segmental; while below only the central two pairs carry segmental ones. The fine carving of the details of the façade was revealed by the cleaning of 1992–93.

116Al **San Rocco** 1646–80, façade 1834

Via di Ripetta

Giovanni Antonio De Rossi, façade: Giuseppe Valadier

This is one of the two churches formerly facing the quay of the Ripetta which were exposed by clearance and rearranging of the area round the Mausoleum of Augustus in the Fascist period. The original church with a Latin-cross plan and domed crossing was reordered early in his career by Giovanni Antonio De Rossi. Valadier's façade of 1834 is one of his last works, and shows that he had left the mainstream of European neoclassicism for an academic reworking of the Palladian church front with its scheme of superimposed temple fronts. The lower order is Ionic with pilasters, the taller Corinthian and with three-quarter round columns on very high bases.

☞ The church to the south is that of **San Girolamo degli Schiavoni**, commissioned by Sixtus V and reconstructed to the designs of Martino Longhi the elder in 1588–91, his last work. To the north is the building housing the Ara Pacis **10**.

117Ao **Fontana dei Quattro Fiumi (Fountain of the Four Rivers)** 1647–51

Piazza Navona

Gian Lorenzo Bernini

Classical Rome had many large architecturally defined open spaces, and these were usually associated with an important religious or commercial building. The squatters of medieval Rome built over most of them and quarried the buildings. The survival of what is now the open piazza Navona is an accident: it lies over and preserves the shape of the former racing track or Stadium of Domitian completed in AD 86. The stadium's original northern entrance has been excavated: its stone arch can be seen preserved under a later building on the south side of the piazza di Tor Sanguigna. At first

lined with houses which incorporated some of the original structure of the seating tiers, the piazza later became a prime site for monumental buildings, the grandest of which is now the church of Sant'Agnese **118** on the west side and started in 1652. The **Palazzo Doria Pamphili** of 1644–50 lies immediately to its south; like the church it was designed by Carlo Rainaldi with his father Girolamo, and supervised by Borromini. The flat-fronted church on the east side is that of **Nostra Signora del Sacro Cuore**, originally constructed in about 1450 to designs by Bernardo Rossellino, but subsequently much altered. Since the eighteenth century the piazza has been a place for the fashionable *passeggiata*, its Roman crowds always augmented by tourists and pilgrims. Closed to wheeled traffic, the piazza is on Sundays free even of the noisy motor scooters which infest the rest of Rome's 'pedestrian areas'. The best terrazza is that of the *Tre Scalini*.

The Fontana dei Quattro Fiumi which now occupies the centre of the square was like the palace commissioned by Pope Innocent X, né Pamphili. It was not intended merely as a magnificent urban decoration. Every one of Bernini's sculptural works has an associated literary programme, the *concetto* or 'concept', and here it is the message of the Catholic church triumphant, ruling the world. At the base the large statues of the world's four rivers, Danube, Ganges, Nile and Plate, are seated on rocks from which their waters flow, and are surrounded by emblems of their continents. The rocky setting rises behind them to support the obelisk, symbol of the sun, which Innocent had moved from its original setting in the Circus of Maxentius, and which was originally crowned with his symbol of a dove. Two other fountains at the ends of the piazza are overshadowed by this display. That to the south, its statue of *Il Moro* now replaced by a cast, was also designed by Bernini in 1652–54, while to the north the basin containing Neptune struggling with a sea monster was erected in the nineteenth century.

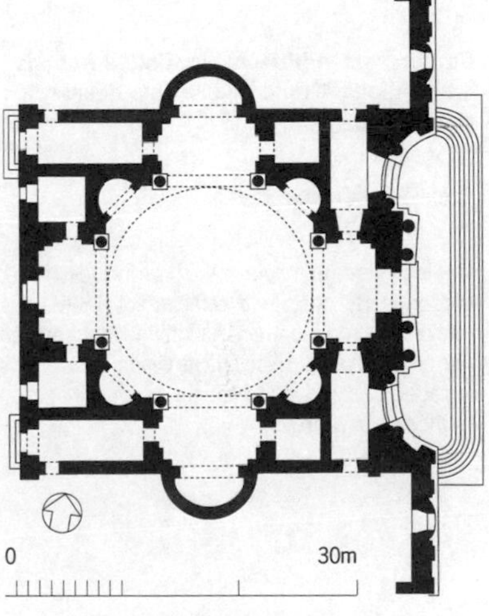

118 Ao **Sant'Agnese in Agone** or **in Piazza Navona**
1652–66

Piazza Navona

Carlo and Girolamo Rainaldi, Francesco Borromini, Gian Lorenzo Bernini

The Rainaldis' plan for this church was not based on the fashionable oval of the time, but on a circle enclosed in an octagon from which the very large dome springs. What characterises it as Baroque, however, is the extension with deep chapels of this primary space *sideways* to produce a long axis parallel to the façade. While the arrangement approximates to the transversely-placed oval which became one of the most copied Baroque plans, it may also have been determined by the restricted depth of the site bounded by the piazza Navona and the via del'Anima to the west. The façade with its twin flanking towers, a Northern Italian usage, was started by Borromini in 1653 and subsequently modified by Carlo Rainaldi. Its shallow central recess exposes the drum of the dome which rises directly from it to provide with the towers a remarkable density of architectural events.

119 Bi **Sant'Andrea delle Fratte** 1653–65

Via Capo le Case off via Due Macelli

Dome and campanile by Francesco Borromini

M A Barberini

Begun in 1605 by Gaspare Guerra, the body of the church is unremarkable, although it contains two of Bernini's sculptures of angels made originally for the Ponte Sant'Angelo **17** in 1668–71. The dome and campanile were added by Bernini, and completely restored in 1992–94. (They are best seen from via Capo le Case beyond via Due Macelli.) Externally, the dome is supported by four sharply projecting buttresses and every profile of its plan is restlessly curved. The first stage of the campanile, a drum supported on paired columns, is conventionally classical, but above this is a wild plastic invention finally crowned by the gilded coronet of Borromini's patron, the marchese Paolo del Bufalo. The neoclassical west-facing façade was supplied by Giuseppe Valadier in 1826.

120 An **Carceri Nuove (Prison)** now **United Nations Interregional Crime and Justice Research Institute** 1652–55, 1828

Via Giulia

Antonio Del Grande

This is the only example of the type included here, and an early one. In a refacing of 1828, this palazzo for imprisonment had its façade crowned with an Egyptian cornice and its window surrounds replaced. It contrives to appear much higher than its mere four storeys.

121Bm **Galleria, Palazzo Colonna** 1654–1703

Entrance at via della Pilotta 17

Antonio Del Grande

The Palazzo Colonna was erected in the fifteenth century by Oddone Colonna, later Pope Martin V. Subsequently expanded, it now occupies a site larger than that of the Palazzo Farnese. Its accommodation is arranged around two courtyards, and is connected by bridges from the first floor to the garden, called the Villa Colonna, set on the slope of the Quirinale hill. The Gallery, commissioned in 1654 by Girolamo i Colonna to house the family's picture collection, occupies the first floor of one wing. Designed by Del Grande, a former assistant of Borromini's, but completed after his death in 1671 by Girolamo Fontana, it was one of the secular splendours of Roman Baroque, and takes the form of a long high salon with a barrel-vaulted ceiling, the 'Sala della Colonna Bellica' approached through square ante-chambers at either end. The rooms are separated by screens of free-standing columns. The whole is sumptuously decorated with marble and mirrors, and the walls are covered with the paintings of the collection. The vaulted ceiling which glorifies the bellicose Colonnas and in particular, in the central panel, the role played by Marcantonio II at the Battle of Lepanto (1571), was painted in the late 1670s by Giovanni Battista Coli and Filippo Gherardi assisted by Giovanni Paolo Schor. Further rooms of the painting galleries extend in another wing at right angles to the main gallery.

122 Ao **Santa Maria della Pace** 1656–57

Vicolo della Pace

(Donato Bramante), Pietro da Cortona

The body of the church was constructed in the fifteenth century but its distinction lies in two later additions, the first the cloister designed by Bramante in 1504. This work, one of the few examples of High Renaissance architecture in Rome, was carried out at the same time as he was working on the Tempietto **62**. There Bramante was able to realise the object but not its setting, here he built a limpid square space of four bays a side. The lower storey is arcaded and vaulted, the upper trabeated and the pitch of its columns doubled, a feature sometimes found in medieval cloisters and some classical Roman work but rarely copied subsequently. Vasari particularly disapproved of the columns lying over the centres of the arches below.

One hundred and fifty years after Bramante's work, the second addition provided a substantial new frontispiece and, as important, a new setting for the front of the church. Cortona's new façade extends beyond the church itself to cross the narrow streets on either side thus providing a concave screen from which the porch and upper storey project. Houses were demolished to provide a better view of the ensemble. The straight lines of the notched pediment preside over a compendium of characteristically Baroque usages, of turbulent masses and curves. The upper storey, with its bulging central surface and massed columns, is developed from Cortona's previous church, SS. Luca e Martina **108**, and here too the travertine stone is cut so that its grain makes symmetrical patterns. But here he added another element: the half-oval porch whose curve counters that of the concave screen, and whose depth beyond the paired columns further adds a surprising chiaroscuro.

☞ At the corner of vicolo della Pace and via di **Santa Maria dell'Anima** is the church of the same name. This is the German national church in Rome, but its façade was designed by the Italian Andrea Sansovino supervising Giuliano da Sangallo's project of 1511.

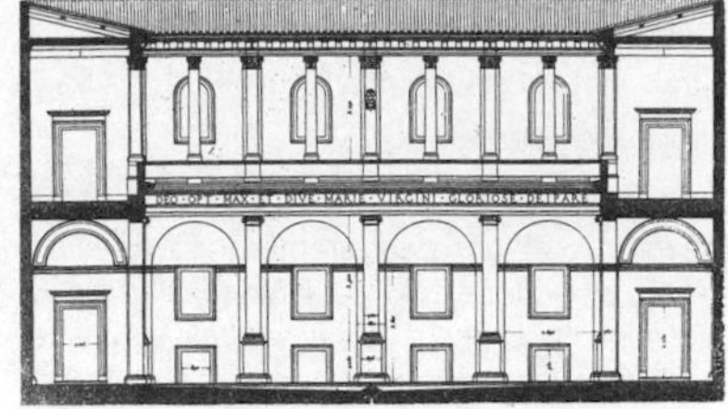

Section through cloister, from Letarouilly

123 Bm **Sant'Andrea al Quirinale** 1658–70
Via Quirinale
Gian Lorenzo Bernini

If Borromini's earlier San Carlo **107** represents the idiosyncratic and restless Baroque, this only slightly larger church is the perfection of Bernini's more Classical development. The plan is very straightforward: an oval domed space placed lengthwise is surrounded by chapels whose walls buttress the dome. The comparative lack of architectural importance given to the altar, and the delicate pink marble of the pilasters suggest a salon as much as a church. The religious message, however, is supplied in the sculptured figure of St Andrew flying above the altar. The simple forms of the exterior are generated by the interior: the top of the wall of the chapels carries the same entablature as the interior, while above this the drum of the dome is surrounded by the buttresses above the chapel walls and their tops support the set-forward entablature round its springing. The elements of the projecting porch are assembled with academic precision.

☞ The Palazzo del Quirinale **88** lies to the south; San Carlo alle Quattro Fontane **107** and Palazzo Barberini **104** to the north.

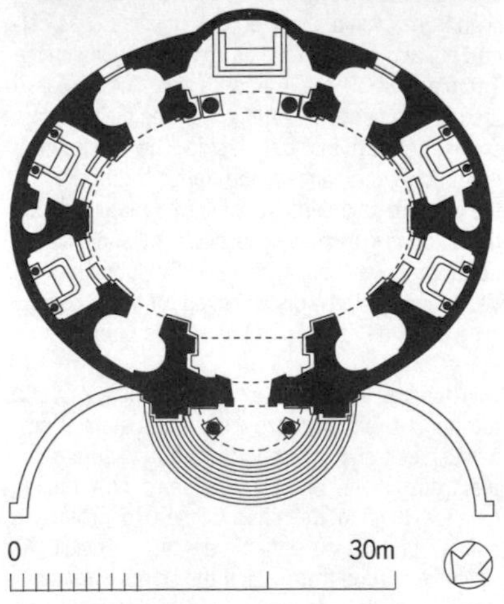

124 Ap **Santa Maria in Via Lata** façade 1658–62
Via del Corso
Pietro da Cortona

Ⓜ A Spagna

This is the last of Pietro da Cortona's great church façades, completed seven years before his death in 1669. The portico was built over the rooms of a sixth- or seventh-century Christian diaconate, and its remains were preserved as a crypt. On the narrow via del Corso, there was very little room for the curved manoeuvres of the façades of, for example, Santa Maria della Pace or San Luca e Santa Martina. Instead, the modelling here is supplied by the densely packed columns and pilasters of the central part; by the depth of the barrel-vaulted portico; and by the crowning feature of the second storey: the broken entablature spanned by an arch which frames the deep opening. The composition is capped by the triangular pediment with its agitated lower cornice. (The removal of traffic dirt, undertaken as part of the 'Roma capitale' programme may be a revelation or, since the sun rarely strikes the façade to provide chiaroscuro, it may not.)

☞ The church of San Marcello **70** is on the opposite side of the via del Corso.

125 Cd **Santa Maria in Campitelli** 1662–67
Piazza Campitelli
Carlo Rainaldi

Rainaldi was first commissioned to renovate an existing medieval structure, but then in 1658 he was asked to prepare a design for a new church. The first project which had an oval plan was not taken up, but in 1662 building work started on the final design. Its plan produces picturesque effects but is muddled. A very wide nave with deep recesses at its centre is all that remains of the original centralised oval, and this is linked by a narrow neck to the brightly lit domed sanctuary. The type is characteristic of churches in northern Italy and is rarely found in Rome. Some unity is restored to the staccato arrangement of the plan by the detached Corinthian columns which stand at all the projecting corners. The design of the façade is bold but also staccato, (its chiaroscuro enhanced by black dirt from Rome's traffic), and the bold projections from the wall plane are emphasised by the chunky entablature of the detached columns. While the lower storey is sober, the cornice of the upper is both corrugated and interrupted by the Baroque device of a crowning segmental pediment set in a triangular one.

☞ The piazza is almost entirely lined with small palaces. Numbers 2 and 3, the **palazzo Albertoni-Spinola** started in 1580, and the **palazzo Capizzuchi-Gaspari** of about 1600, were both designed by Giacomo della Porta and completed or extended by Girolamo Rainaldi. The restored fountain at the southern end of the piazza is also by della Porta.

126 Bi **Collegio di Propaganda Fide**, façade and chapel 1662

Via Gregoriana, off southern corner of Piazza di Spagna

Francesco Borromini

M A Spagna

The College, an extension of the Congregazione di Propaganda Fide in piazza di Spagna, was founded by Urban VIII to train missionaries. Its chapel is visitable only with special permission, so the façade alone serves as introduction to Borromini's last large work. We do not know if its design was intended to be understood only from the oblique views that the narrow street affords, or whether the spectator ought to reconstruct a 'flat' picture of it like that now obtained of the Oratory of San Filippo **109**. A giant order with sketchy capitals supports the heavy cornice above the central seven bays in which the entrance is signalled by a segmental recess echoed in the cornice of the attic. The entrance itself is protected by a novel porch whose pediment takes up a double curve generated by the angled columns which support it. These columns, perhaps following Michelangelo's experiments at the Laurentian Library in Florence, are tapered towards their bottoms, and of hexagonal section. The use of the hexagon was a Baroque innovation: see for example the plan of Borromini's Sant'Ivo **110**.

☞ Borromini's tower and lantern of Sant'Andrea della Fratte **119**.

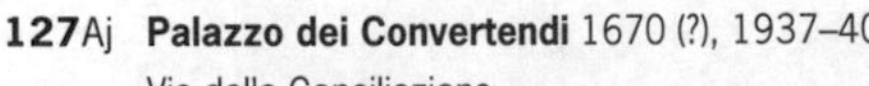

127 Aj **Palazzo dei Convertendi** 1670 (?), 1937–40

Via della Conciliazione

The palazzo was rebuilt to house part of the Propaganda Fide when the Via della Conciliazione was constructed, and redesigned by Clemente Busiri Vici. The central three bays are a reconstruction of one of the so-called 'Houses of Raphael'.

Classicism and neoclassicism 1675–1869

128 Al **Santa Maria in Campo Marzio** 1676–86
Piazza Santa Maria in Campo Marzio/via della Stelletta
Giovanni Antonio De Rossi

De Rossi's late work was often considered old-fashioned by his contemporaries, and this example supports their view. Approached via a small courtyard whose decoration is on the verge of Rococo delicacy, and a portico, the church has a conventional Greek-cross plan, but its oval dome has no drum and is supported directly on pendentives.

.29 Ap **Santa Maria Maddalena** 1676–99, 1733
Piazza Maddalena
Giovanni Antonio De Rossi and others

Carlo Fontana was responsible for the original design, but it was continued by De Rossi. The architects of the Roman Baroque experimented not only with plan forms like the oval, but with others which were the result of combining various geometrical figures. Rainaldi's earlier plan for Santa Maria in Campitelli **125** was one such; here is another in which the basic figure of the Latin cross has been distorted by using a very elongated octagon for the body of the nave. This renders the nave self sufficient, and any architect would have had great difficulty in satisfactorily connecting it to the crossing and apse. On the west wall a fine sculptural torrent threatens to engulf the organ. The exuberant façade, added nearly a century after work started and freely borrowing from Borromini's work, was designed by G. C. Quadri and continued by G. Sardi. It presents a single convex curve with a tripartite composition with a single motif applied to each of its bays, all crowned by the doubly-curved split pediment.

130 Ao **Santi Pantaleo e Giuseppe Calasanzio** 1681–89

Piazza San Pantaleo, Corso Vittorio Emanuele

Giovanni Antonio De Rossi, Giuseppe Valadier

De Rossi reconstructed the interior of the church in 1681–89. Giuseppe Valadier provided the neat, reticently modelled, neoclassical façade in 1806.

☞ The Palazzo Braschi **140** is to the east; the Piccola Farnesina **71** to the south.

131 Be **Scalinata di Trinità dei Monti ('Spanish Steps')** 1721–25

Piazza di Spagna/Santa Trinità dei Monti

Francesco De Sanctis

Ⓜ A Spagna

Very little building took place in Rome in the eighteenth century compared with the activity of the seventeenth: the popes commissioned few buildings, and those that they did were works of public engineering such as these Steps and the Trevi Fountain **133**. Unlike similar enterprises of the early Baroque, these rarely had a *concetto* or programme, and were designed to be used or enjoyed. Sixtus V's via Sistina had connected with the road to the Pincio along the top of the hill, though it had been separated from the via Condotti cut through the medieval quarter below, and its extension westwards to the Tiber, thence to St Peter's. The Spanish Steps monumentally supplied the connection. Their architect De Sanctis, otherwise only known for his water-colours and the façade of SS. Trinità dei Pellegrini, provided a magnificent and unprecedented High Baroque composition, its flights of stairs alternately separating and joining, concave and convex.

☞ At the foot of the Steps, the **Fontana della Barcaccia**, the fountain in the form of a leaking boat, was designed by Pietro Bernini (Gian Lorenzo's father) in 1628. The **Palazzo di Spagna** on the south side of the piazza, was the former residence of the Spanish Ambassador, from which the piazza, the Steps and Metro station take their name. The Collegio di Propaganda da Fide **126** lies to the south, and the church of All Saints **150** to the north.

132 Ap **Teatro Argentina** 1730, façade 1826

Largo Argentina, west side

Façade, Pietro Holl

The first theatre on this site was erected in 1730, designed by the aristocratic autodidact Girolamo Theodoli. Like most theatres built in the eighteenth century, this one has had a difficult history. The present appearance of the building is due largely to Holl's comely neoclassical façade of 1826, and in the interior, to the complete reordering carried out by Giulio Sterbini and his collaborators between 1967 and 1971.

133Bm **Fontana di Trevi** 1732–62
Via della Stamperia/via delle Muratte
Nicola Salvi

Ⓜ A Barberini

In 1732, Clement XII held a competition for the replacement of the fountain, attributed to Alberti, which stood on the site. Like the fountains in the piazza di Spagna and piazza Navona, it had been fed from the waters of the Acqua Vergine built by Agrippa. Salvi's design covers one entire wall of the Palazzo Poli which had been completed in 1730. It combines Late Baroque magnificence and charm, and has since its inauguration justly been one of Rome's chief attractions for citizens, tourists and film crews. The façade of the palace is relegated to the three bays on either side of the centrepiece, their entablature broken by the segmental hoods of the windows of the upper storey. The fountain emerges from a triumphal arch, its central niche occupied by Neptune. Accompanied by tritons, he leads a team of sea horses out over naturalistically sculpted rocks which had previously only been seen in the decoration of gardens. The rocks, cracking at the corners and interfering with the architecture, extend to form a crumbly base for the palace. The figures in the niches on either side show Abundance on the left and Health to the right, while the panels above show on the left Agrippa discussing the plan for the aqueduct, and on the right the legendary Virgin of the aqueduct's name revealing the source to a group of Roman soldiers. The four statues on the projecting entablature are of the seasons, and the whole is topped with the huge arms of Clement XII's family, the Florentine Corsini. In modern times the Fountain has been celebrated in two films: *Roman Holiday* of 1953, and *La Dolce Vita* of 1960 in which Anita Ekberg memorably waded through its waters at night to taunt Marcello Mastroianni.

☞ The church in the eastern corner of the square is that of SS. Vincenzo ed Anastasio **115**. In piazza Crociferi to the west, the little church of **Santa Maria in Trivio** was reconstructed in 1573–75 by Jacopo Del Duca, one of Michelangelo's assistants and few followers.

134 Bm **Palazzo della Consulta** now **Corte Costituzionale** façade 1739

Piazza del Quirinale

Ferdinando Fuga

Built as the supreme court of the Papal States, the palace now houses the Constitutional Supreme Court of the Italian Republic. It is one of Fuga's two palace façades in Rome, the other is the Cenci-Bolognetti. The design, while derived distantly from that of Bernini's façade for the Palazzo Chigi-Odaleschi **102**, is flatter and more regular, and divided into two storeys, the lower incorporating a mezzanine. The autonomy of the flanks is emphasised by their separate central entrances. The simplicity of the design encouraged subsequent imitation.

☞ Palazzo Quirinale **88.**

135 Ee **Santa Croce in Gerusalemme** (1144) remodelled 1743

Piazza di Santa Croce in Gerusalemme, south of Porta Maggiore

M A San Giovanni

The first basilica was rebuilt on its original plan in 1144, and the campanile is from that date. The building was substantially modernised in neoclassical taste in 1743 by Domenico Gregorini and Pietro Passalacqua who added piers between alternate pairs of the columns of the nave, which remain visible, and applied a new giant order to these elements. They also added the delicate, structurally daring baldacchino, the sideways-placed oval vestibule and the new, vigorously modelled façade. Reached from the left transept, the Chapel of the True Cross, reconstructed in 1930 by F. di Fausto, is lined with fine marble and contains timber, and relics relating to the crucifixion including a nameplate, nails, and thorns. These were brought to Rome by Constantine's mother Saint Helena.

☞ The Porta Maggiore **12** lies to the north at the end of via Eleniana.

136 Bc **Villa Albani** now **Torlonia** 1746–63

Via Salaria/via Adda

Carlo Marchionni

There are two Villas Torlonia: this is the earlier; the second **141** lies about a kilometre to the east alongside via Nomentana. The public park containing the house has been closed for several years for restoration. Marchionni was employed by the dilettante architect Cardinal Alessandro Albani to reconstruct an existing house on the site to contain his collection of antique sculpture. This was carried out in a feeble Late Baroque. In 1763, the German art historian J. J. Winckelmann, who was cataloguing the sculpture collection, was consulted about the provision of garden ornaments and, were the park accessible, these would be found to include the romantic neoclassical Greek temples attached to the villa and the strange collage, the Tempietto Diruto, a synthetic ruin assembled from antique fragments.

137 Al **Caffè Greco** 1760

Via Condotti 86 (north side)

Ⓜ A Spagna

Stylish and expensive, but not intimidating, the café, once the haunt of the Roman and visiting artists and intellectuals who inhabited the district to the east, now regards itself as an institution and brand name marketing opportunity. It has a very long, deep plan consisting of a double row of interconnecting rooms each with a different type of ceiling or vault. In its most recent re-decoration its walls were covered in red, gold and sage green damask, over which the extraordinary collection of pictures was re-hung.

138 Cl **Santa Maria del Priorato** or **dell' Aventinense** 1764–65

Piazza dei Cavalieri di Malta

Gian Battista Piranesi

Ⓜ B Piramide and a long uphill walk

Described by Mario Praz as 'romantic, morbid and hallucinated', Piranesi as a theoretician contributed to the collapse of the Classical consensus from which eclecticism and neoclassicism were to emerge, but as architect he built little. His masterpiece, the priory church which he remodelled is visitable only with special permission, so that the decorated wall and gate which enclose the forecourt of the priory serve as the only visible evidence of his work in Rome. The gate is the less unconventional of the two, with a crisp pediment and cornice, although much of its supporting entablature and the remaining tectonic elements are reduced to panels. Look through the gate's keyhole. The wall which faces it, decorated as a collage of obelisks, stelae and panels, looks wilfully picturesque, and its ambiguous composition is of either five or three bays.

☞ In via Santa Sabina, the **Church of Sant'Alessio** ex **San Bonifacio** was modernised inside and out by Tommaso De Marchis 1750–70. Further along the same street to the north, is a small park with a fine view north-west over the Tiber and Trastevere towards St Peter's. The Basilica of Santa Sabina **32** lies beyond the park.

Chiesetta di Piazza di Siena

Entrance gates

139Ba **Villa Borghese, garden buildings**
1785–92, 1818–28

Antonio and Mario Asprucci,
Christoph Unterberger and others

M A Spagna, Villa Borghese exit

The present park gets its name from the Palazzina on the eastern side of the estate which was started in 1608 for the Borghese family. It was designed by Flaminio Ponzio. The family assembled a fine collection of paintings and sculpture and this, now the Museo and Galleria Borghese **97**, was always open to the public. In 1902, the City bought the property and its gardens which together with the Pincio terrace are among Rome's larger public gardens which are heavily used, especially at the weekend.

In the second half of the eighteenth century the family employed the Scottish landscape painter Jacob More to redesign the garden to the west and south-west of the palazzina, and his layout was subsequently decorated in two phases with neoclassical gates, temples and fountains, and a church. The father and son Antonio and Mario Asprucci contributed the **Temple of Aesculapius** which stands on an artifical island in the lake, and in 1787 Mario designed the **Chiesetta di Piazza di Siena**, a remarkably severe neoclassical work whose porch of unfluted Doric columns and bare entablature first brought Greek architecture back to Rome after an interval of nearly two thousand years.

The second phase took place in the ten years after 1818 when Luigi Canina built the very bare **Triumphal Arch** near the lake and at the top of via Esculapio at its junction with via M. Letizia; the **Fountain of Esculapius** whose rocks and fountain provided a setting for an ancient statue; and the **Gates** which give access to the park from Piazzale Flaminio at the

Temple of Aesculapius

Triumphal Arch

foot of the hill. Canina completed his portfolio of the Romantic Classical types with the **Egyptian propylea** (1827), now used as a bus stop, on either side of via Fiorello Guardia.

Egyptian propylaea

140 Ao **Palazzo Braschi: Museo di Roma** 1792
Corso Vittorio Emanuele
Cosimo Morelli

The palazzo which since 1930 has housed the museum illustrating the history of Rome is the only work in the city designed by the Ticinese Cosimo Morelli. In 1804 he was replaced as architect by Valadier who completed the building and designed the chapel on the first floor.

☞ The church immediately to the east is San Pantaleo **130**. The 'Piccola Farnesina' **71**, now also a museum, is on the south side of the Corso Vittorio Emanuele.

141 Bd **Villa Torlonia** 1802–42
Entrance from via Nomentana
Giuseppe Valadier and others

Ⓜ A Bologna

This the later of two Villas Torlonia; the earlier **136** lies about a kilometre to the west. The grounds in which the villa stands are now an accessible but wild, unmaintained public park, originally Count Torlonia's vineyard. In 1829, Valadier was commissioned to reconstruct an existing building of the 1800s, but the history of subsequent changes is unclear, and he may have designed the wide portico to the front of the house, or its author may have been Antonio Sarti. The projecting semicircular Grecian wings at the sides are almost certainly Valadier's work. The villa has been disused since 1943 when it was vacated by its last resident Benito Mussolini whose state and family residence it had been since 1929. The grounds contain the ruins of the various garden structures in states of unpicturesque decay.

☞ The flats in viale di Villa Massimo of 1934, **188**, and the Provincial Medical Association headquarters, 1966–73, **215**, are to the north-east of the entrance to the Villa, both north off via Alessandro Torlonia.

142 Ah **Giardino del Pincio** 1806–14,
Casina Valadier 1813–17, **Loggiata** 1816–20
Viale Trinità del Monte/viale del Muro Torto
Giuseppe Valadier

Ⓜ A Flaminio

The Pincio hill has been occupied by gardens since the time of the Roman Republic, but was first laid out as a public park by Valadier at the beginning of the nineteenth century, since when it has been a fashionable resort. The terrace provides a fine view, especially at sunset, over the piazza del Popolo **75** (also laid out by Valadier) towards the dome of St Peter's. Behind this is a densely planted formal garden, its paths lined with white marble busts of famous Italians. On the highest, open, terrace, the **Casina Valadier**, built as a residence, now houses a restaurant whose present apparatus of blinds and signs unfortunately obscures the original. Here Valadier's neoclassical practice aligns very closely with that of his Berlin contemporary Schinkel in its blocky composition placed on a podium, the use of the free-standing granite columns which encircle the podium, and the careful use of many different materials. But the cut-off Doric columns which support the terrace are notably eccentric, and perhaps look back to Valadier's hero Piranesi.

143 Ap **Teatro Valle** 1819–22
Via del Teatro Valle
Giuseppe Valadier

Valadier redesigned and rearranged the existing theatre and designed the new façade to the street. Two flat wings enclose an Ionic colonnade of the sort that was *de rigueur* for European public buildings of the time: see, for example, Berlin's Altes Museum, or London's British Museum, both started in 1823. The colonnade is set over a rusticated base punctured by frequent arched doorways for the use of the audience.

☞ At the north end of the street, the church spire with its spiral termination is that of Sant'Ivo, **110**.

144 Cf **Porta San Pancrazio** 1857
Via Garibaldi/via San Pancrazio
Virginio Vespignani

While Vespignani later became well known for the design of churches, notably his completion of the rebuilding of San Paolo fuori le Mura and its quadriportico **30**, his early career was founded on the work of repairing the fortifications of Rome after the occupation by French forces in 1849. He redesigned one of the gates in the Aurelian Wall, the country side of the Porta Pia **83**, and this one in the wall originally constructed on the instructions of Urban VIII in the 1620s for the defence of Trastevere and with it the southern flank of the Vatican. As was customary in the architecture of gates, the city and country faces are quite different. The approach to the city is commanded by a tough neoclassical design, its fine orange brick framed by stone quoins and voussoirs. The city side is a more conventional paraphrase of a Roman triumphal arch carried out in cheap rendering in imitation of stone.

145 Cg **Manifattura dei Tabacchi** 1859–63
Piazza Mastai, Trastevere
Antonio Sarti

This is one of only two of Rome's remaining buildings which record its scant industrial history. Both celebrate Roman habits: the one, the Peroni brewery **165**, drinking; the other, smoking. As the inscription 'PIUS IX PM OFFICINAM NICOTIANIS...' makes clear, the processing of tobacco carried out in this building was a papal monopoly. Of the original factory, only Sarti's façade to the offices of the administration survives to celebrate what was then a gentlemanly recreation in conventional sub-Palladian but un-Roman respectability. The remaining buildings were reconstructed in 1927, and then rebuilt as offices in 1955.

Ministero delle Finanze, 146

Capital of Italy 1870–1921

146 Bjk **Ministero delle Finanze/Ministry of Finance**
1870–77 (illustrated opposite)
Via di Venti Settembre/via Cernaia
Raffaele Canevari, Martinori Martinozzi, Francesco Pieroni
M A Repubblica

The capital of unified Italy urgently required accommodation for the apparatus of the new government. Some of this was found in palaces and appropriated religious institutions, the rest in hurriedly started new buildings. One of the first of these was the gigantic new building occupying a block 300 by 125 metres (984 feet by 410 feet), for the Ministry of Finance. The offices are arranged round three courtyards and the articulation of the façades reflects this tripartite division. The style, loosely based on Michelangelo's Palazzo dei Senatori, is respectable and dull.

147 Bn **St Paul's American Episcopal Church**
1872–76
Via Nazionale/via Napoli
George Edmund Street
M A Repubblica

Of Street's two churches in Rome built while he was working in London on the Gothic Royal Courts of Justice this, the first, was surprisingly for the Americans who lived in or were visiting the city. (His second was the Anglican All Saints **150**.) It was the first non-Catholic church to be built in Rome following the fall of the Papal States. Its architecture has nothing to do with Rome, but rather with the striped Gothic of Verona's San Zeno, and English craft was imported to decorate the neat, dry interior. Burne-Jones designed the very fine mosaics in the apse, and the encaustic floor tiles are by William Morris' firm. The mosaics on the façade are, however, of American provenance, designed by George Breck, the contemporary Director of the American Academy in Rome.

148 Bn **Palazzo dell'Esposizione** 1878–82
Via Nazionale
Pio Piacentini

Ⓜ A Repubblica

After the financial affairs of the new Italy had been housed in their Ministry **146**, it was the turn of trade and culture to acquire a palace on the via Nazionale, the street which it was intended to line with the monuments of the state. Eventually, however, only this palace and Koch's Banca d'Italia **153** were built.

One of Piacentini's first buildings, its façade was perhaps derived from von Klenze's Munich Glyptothek of 1816: conventional classical architecture is used for the modified triumphal arch of the open porch, which is framed by the simply trabeated wide blind wings of the rooflit exhibition halls. Note the Palladian statues on their parapets. The interior has been modernised several times.

☞ To the north of the Palace, and sunk well below the level of via Nazionale is the church of **San Vitale**, characterised only by its age.

149 Bn **Teatro dell'Opera** 1878–80
Via Firenze/via Viminale
Achille Sfondrini

Ⓜ Termini

The construction of what is one of Italy's finest opera houses was not carried out by the state, but by a speculative builder, and the result is one of the less grandiose monuments of the 1870s. It was bought by the city of Rome in 1926 when the whole was modernised by Marcello Piacentini. Further alterations were carried out in 1960.

150 Ah **All Saints** 1880–1937

Via del Babuino 154/via di Gesù e Maria

George Edmund Street, A. E. Street

M A Spagna

Street's second and last church in Rome was commissioned by the Anglican Society for the Propagation of the Gospel and the Anglican Bishop of Gibraltar. It was set in the district which in the eighteenth century had become the favourite for visiting foreign artists and intellectuals. Unfinished when Street died in 1881, it was completed by his son who modified the design and redesigned the spire. The site planning is Street's, however, and the placing of the nave parallel to the side street, the via di Gesù e Maria, generates with the tower the picturesque corrugated façade to via del Babuino. Unlike Street's earlier All Saints **150**, the style here is not even Italian but an Early English Gothic carried out in pink brick with travertine dressings.

151 Ak **Palazzo di Giustizia** 1880–1911

Lungotevere Castello/piazza Cavour

Guglielmo Calderini

M A Lepanto

The inclination of the new Italian state to be represented by increasingly gigantic buildings started with the Ministry of Finance **146**, continued with these Law Courts, and culminated in the excess of the Monument to Vittorio Emanuele II **155**. Calderini was the winner of a two-stage competition for the design. He provided a mainly two-storey building on a near square plan of 170 by 150 metres (558 by 492 feet), perforated by courtyards and with a raised central portion. He avoided towers, domes or pediments and concentrated his architectural effects mainly in the intensely modelled façades, entirely of travertine, their motifs drawn from sources such as Piranesi and Assyrian architecture. When completed, the building was attacked and disliked, and earned the nickname 'Palazzaccio': the 'horrible' or 'nasty' palace.

The building's foundations in the marshy land next to the Tiber proved unsatisfactory, and it has been evacuated and now stands empty.

152 Al **Galleria Sciarra** 1883
Via Minghetti/piazza dell'Oratorio
Giulio De Angelis, paintings by G. Cellini, 1887
Ⓜ A Barberini

Rome's first 'arcade' was an atrium of six storeys with a glass roof and housed in one of several contemporary buildings in which the cast iron frame was introduced. The architectural detail is unremarkable, but the gallery's glory is its (restored) decoration. *Every* surface of the atrium is painted with panels showing scenes of late nineteenth-century everyday and ceremonial life.

☞ To the north at via delle Muratte 25, another building with a cast iron façade, also by De Angelis.

153 Bm **Banca d'Italia (Bank of Italy)** 1885–94
Via Nazionale 183
Gaetano Koch
Ⓜ B Cavour

Koch won the commission for his first large official building in competition with Pio Piacentini. The building was an up-to-date ofice block, equipped with lifts, electricity, central heating and telephones. Planned around two courtyards, its architecture takes the palazzo recipe and extends it over twenty-three bays and three enormous 'storeys' (the lower two have mezzanines) using a style more Florentine than Roman.

☞ On the opposite side of the via Nazionale, the **Magazzini Piatti** of about 1890 are now occupied by Renault. The former shop has a cast iron frame exhibited in its delicate façade. In the via Ventiquattro Maggio to the south-west is the little church of **San Silvestro al Quirinale**, originally of 1580–85, but partially rebuilt and with a new façade to the designs of Andrea Busiri Vici in 1873–77 when the via Nazionale was established at a level much higher than its surroundings. In via Mazzarino to the south is the church of **Sant'Agata dei Goti**, approached through a court. Founded in 462, it retains some ancient material, but it was modernised in 1632 by Domenico Castelli, and the façade was provided by Francesco Ferrari in 1730.

Magazzini Piatti

154 Bj **Piazza della Repubblica** ex **Pallazzi della Piazza dell'Esedra** 1885–94

Gaetano Koch

M A Repubblica

Contemporary with his building for the Banca d'Italia **153** and his work at the piazza Vittorio Emanuele **155**, Koch provided this termination to the north end of the most important of the new streets in Rome undertaken after 1870. His task was to arrange the awkward traffic intersection caused by the orientation of the via Nazionale towards the remains of the Baths of Diocletian rather than the Stazione Termini. He used a circle generated in part by the remains of the exedra of the Baths' *calidarium*, around which the carriages flowed. At its centre is the large Naiad fountain of 1901–14 by Guerrieri and Mario Rutelli. On two quadrants of the circle, the buildings provide Rome's second colonnaded pavement, a northern Italian usage and one subsequently rarely copied. Although never one for bombast, Koch's architecture here follows contemporary French practice such as that of Garnier rather than that of his favourite *cinquecento*.

155 Da **Vittorio Emanuele II monument** 1885–1911

Piazza Vittorio Emanuele

Count Giuseppe Sacconi, Gaetano Koch and others

Vittorio Emanuele, first king of the united Italy, died in 1878. Plans were immediately made for a monument to celebrate his reign, and an architectural competition held for a site at the end of the axis of the Corso and near the Capitol. This was inconclusive, and a second competition was won by Sacconi for a monument which would be a symbol of the new age and house a statue of the late monarch. Work started in 1885 but was incomplete when Sacconi died in 1905, and his design was continued and completed with modifications by a committee of distinguished architects including Koch, Pio Piacentini and Manfredo Manfredi. The result is the enormous pile of white marble topped by a shallow columned exedra which dwarfs the statue. Its form is an inflated paraphrase of the Temple of Fortune on the hillside at Praenestina, without a central feature but with the emphasis transferred to the porticoed wings in the fashionable manner of the time. (See, for example, the later Galleria Nazionale d'Arte Moderna formerly the Palazzo delle Belle Arti **167** of 1911.)

156Dc **Palazzo Brancaccio** housing **Istituto Italiano per il Medio ed Estremo Oriente** and **Museo Nazionale di Arte Orientale** 1892–96

Via Merulana 248/viale del Monte Oppio

Luca Carimini

M A Vittorio

At the time of writing, the palace has been under reconstruction for several years. Originally begun for the Americans Mr and Mrs Henry Field, it now houses institutions of the state. The design is noteworthy only for its size, and for its accommodation to the sloping site: the garden at the back is one storey higher than the street. Carimini's earlier modest architectural ideas could not encompass the enormous size of this enterprise which was only realised after his death in 1890.

157Ap **Palazzo Pacelli** now **Albergo Tiziano** 1888

Corso Vittorio Emanuele II 110

Gaetano Koch

An example of the many elegant, well-mannered blocks with which the prolific Koch equipped Rome when he was not involved in much larger enterprises. The client here was Cardinal Pacelli, later Pope Pius XII. The quiet good taste of its softly curved façade would be enhanced by redecoration (1994), and the removal of the tatty canopy.

158 Bj **Palazzo Margherita** ex **Piombino** now **United States Embassy** 1886–92

Via Vittorio Veneto/via Bissolati

Gaetano Koch

Ⓜ A Barberini

By far Koch's largest residential building, this palace was the consequence of his aristocratic client Prince Piombino's speculation in Rome's building boom of the 1880s. Since 1926, when its last occupant Queen Margherita died, it has been the United States Embassy. Its plan is in the form of a 'T' containing a suite of interconnecting rooms on the first floor facing the street, with an atrium and the main staircase in the part projecting into the garden. The long façade of thirteen bays is modelled on that of the Palazzo Farnese **73**, constructed of pink brick framed by pillow-shaped quoins, and surmounted by a cornice decorated with birds.

☞ To the west, on via Liguria, the church of **Sant'Isodoro** with a façade of 1704; to the south, on via San Nicola da Tolentino, that of **San Nicola**, under reconstruction in 1995.

159 Cd **Tempio Israelitico (synagogue)** 1889–1904

Lungotevere dei Cenci 1/via del Tempio

Luigi Costa and Osvaldo Armanni

A large area of the former Ghetto was cleared in the 1880s. The medieval buildings were replaced by four large blocks between the via Portico d'Ottavio and the Lungotevere. One of these blocks was reserved for a new synagogue which contributed to the series of non-Catholic places of worship with which Rome became equipped after becoming a secular capital. The plan is a Greek cross with shallow arms, the central space roofed with a very large high dome covered in the aluminium which was then in vogue. While the general arrangement is Classical, the details are not but combine features from Assyrian and Babylonian architecture. The interior has frescoes by Bruschi and Brugnoli.

160 Af **San Gioacchino** 1890–96

Via Pompeo Magno, near piazza dei Quiriti, Prati di Castelli

Raffaele Ignami, Lorenzo De Rossi

Ⓜ A Lepanto

The area to the west of the Tiber between viale delle Milizie and via Cola di Rienzo was rapidly developed in the 1870s and 1880s, the piazza dei Quiriti at its centre. This large, lavishly decorated church was built to serve the new inhabitants. Its plan is a Latin cross, its crossing marked with a pointed dome covered in the then fashionable aluminium and decorated inside with stars. To the street it presents a narthex crowned by an unsatisfactory attic.

161BI **Policlinico** 1886–1903

Viale del Policlinico

Giulio Podesti

Ⓜ B Policlinico

Most earlier hospitals in Rome had been attached to or had been part of religious institutions, although some, like that of San Gallicano in Trastevere of the 1720s, had been built for the purpose. The Policlinico, however, was constructed as a large modern and secular teaching hospital. It was laid out according to the ideas propagated by Florence Nightingale and others in two ranges of parallel pavilions housing specialised functions in those nearer the street, general wards behind. These were set in gardens and all connected together by a network of cast iron galleries of two storeys. The elegance of the layout has been obscured by subsequent additions and alterations: for an indication of how the galleries must have appeared, look over the wall of the earlier Ospedale militare del Celio in piazza Celimontana, of 1885.

☞ In 1975, the **Biblioteca Nazionale Centrale Vittorio Emanuele II**, the National Library and with 2,300,000 volumes the largest in Italy, was built on the site of the Castro Pretorio to the west of the Policlinico. While large in the tradition of institutions in Rome, the monumental impulse was lacking: its buildings are undistinguished, and its entrance worthy of a suburban petrol station.

162AI **Maggazini ('Palazzo') Boccioni** now ***La Rinascente*** 1886–99

Via del Corso/piazza Colonna

Giulio De Angelis

Ⓜ A Spagna

The first purpose-built example in Rome of one of the quintessential building types of the nineteenth century, the department store, has a structural frame of one of that century's characteristic materials, cast iron. Like De Angelis' earlier Galleria Sciarra **152**, the sales floors, now much altered, are planned around a glazed court which survives. The exterior, however, is less sure than the other façades where he used the same material, and the sharp horizontal division into two, the lower half mainly glazed, the upper with more masonry, appears clumsy.

☞ Other cast-iron buildings by De Angelis include the Galleria Sciarra **152**; **flats** at via delle Muratte 25, and the **offices** of 1887 at via Due Macelli 9.

163 Bh **Villino Aletti** now part of **Scuola Svizzera**
1900–2

Via Marcello Malpighi 14

Giuseppe Sommaruga

M B Castro Pretorio

This very large, very tall villa is the only example of the Milanese Sommaruga's work in Rome. Less agitated than his northern work, the house, however, has a wilfully asymmetrical 'L' shaped plan crowned with a tower and loggia over the entrance at the crook of the 'L'. The window openings are variously and innovatively treated.

164 Dm **Housing for ICP: Istituto Case Popolari**
1907–14

San Saba district: viale Giotto, piazza Bernini, via Maderno, via Piranesi

Quadrio Pirani and Giovanni Belluci

M B Piramide

In the 1920s Pirani designed the large suburb at Aniene which, with that at Garbatella **173**, was one of the two garden cities developed outside Rome. This earlier very large scheme is developed at much higher densities than the proponents of the garden city movement suggested, and its layout is much tougher and more urban. The site was a strip of steeply sloping land between the Aurelian Wall and the hilltop of Santa Saba. At the foot of the slope and facing the Wall is a long line of four-and five-storey blocks which follow the cranks of the wall and the via Giotto. At the top of the hill, a road parallel to the lower is lined with semi-detached flats, two-storey to the street but with a lower storey exposed to the slope. Between these two rows a third row of three-storey dwellings perches precariously on the slope. Circulation is achieved by regular broad flights of stairs which rise from viale Giotto to via Maderno.

The architectural language is particular, tough and consistent: all the dwellings have rugged stone bases. The walls above are of rubble, rendered and framed by quoins or pilasters and window hoods of red brick. The brick is laid carefully and often decoratively, and occasionally that of the pilasters is extended in random ragged steps across the rendering, a remarkable usage which anticipates the language and landscape metaphors of Alvar Aalto.

☞ To the north-west, the church of **Santa Saba**, the present building of the tenth century, restored in 1943. The parish hall in piazza Bernini was completed in 1956 and designed by Maurizio Constantini of Studio Pasarelli.

165 Bg ex **Peroni brewery** from 1907

Piazza Alessandria/via Bergamo/via Mantova/ via Nizza

Gustavo Giovannoni

Giovannoni was an important member and one of the chief theorists of the influential Roman society *Associazione artistica fra i cultori di architettura* (see Introduction), and was later involved in the planning of the garden suburb at Garbatella **173**, and a surprising architect for the design of an industrial installation. He provided a rich frontispiece to the piazza Alessandria, in exquisitely crafted brickwork topped by alpine gables and a wooden look-out tower. To the sides, the works extended in more severe regular bays with deeply overhanging northern Italian eaves. Later extended to fill the entire block, but abandoned in 1971, the factory was gentrified for use as offices and shops in 1992–94.

☞ Flats of 1940–41 designed by Adalberto Libera in via Messina **194**.

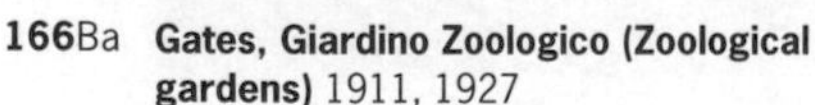

166 Ba **Gates, Giardino Zoologico (Zoological gardens)** 1911, 1927

Via del Giardino Zoologico

Armando Brasini and Giulio Barluzzi, Raffaele De Vico

M A Flaminio, and walk through Villa Borghese

The Zoo's main gates designed by Brasini and Barluzzi are a delightful classical joke, rare in Rome. The elephants which so captivated the sculptors and painters of the Baroque reappear here in the keystones of the entrance arches. Much of De Vico's practice was in landscape design and his cheerful spiral gateposts to the left of the present main entrance were part of a larger scheme of 1927 for re-arranging the layout of the Zoo.

☞ The large **serbatoio idrico** (water tower) to the north east of the Zoo in the centre of the piazzale dei Daini was also designed by De Vico 1923–24. Partly disguised as a Viennese garden pavilion, it actually regulates the waters of the Acqua Marcia.

167 Ad **Galleria Nazionale d'Arte Moderna** ex **Palazzo delle Belle Arti** 1911, enlarged 1933, 1965–88

Viale delle Belle Arti

Cesare Bazzani

Ⓜ A Flaminio

Built for the international exposition of 1911 which celebrated fifty years of the Kingdom of Italy this, with his Ministero dell'Educazione Nazionale **170**, is one of two contemporary huge official buildings which Bazzani designed. The design of the façade follows that of Piacentini's Palazzo dell'Esposizione **148** where the blind wings of the exhibition halls flank an intense architectural event, but the central motif here is a colonnade of paired columns held between broad piers. The details show the passing influence of the *floreale* style rarely represented in Rome: the classical architecture has been overlaid with lions' heads, ribbons and festoons, and the piers are emphasised at the expense of the centre by their crowns of women holding wreaths aloft. The building, its interior modernised in 1933 and again between1965 and 1988 when R. De Stefano and others refitted the galleries, now contains the state's collection of nineteenth- and twentieth-century Italian painting and sculpture, and houses temporary exhibitions.

☞ The **British School in Rome** lies to the northwest of the Galleria on via A. Gramsci. Its imposing front, modelled on the upper storey of the portico of St Paul's Cathedral, London, was designed by Sir Edwin Lutyens (1869–1944), for the British presence at the 1911 exposition. The present building's stone façade replaced the original temporary wooden structure.

168 Eb **Ponte del Risorgimento** 1911

Piazzale delle Belle Arti/piazza Monte Grappa

François Hennebique

Ⓜ A Flaminio, Lepanto

The bridge was built as part of the works for the 1911 exhibition. Its job was to connect the newly arranged area of valle Giulia, with the Palazzo delle Belle Arti at its centre, with the newly developed housing areas beyond the Tiber to the west where some model dwellings had been constructed in 1909. Hennebique was a French engineer already famous for his development and promotion of the new building material of reinforced concrete, and the bridge has a simple single span, extraordinarily slim at its centre. The scant applied decoration is limited to incised panelling and the scrolls which occasionally support the residually classical (concrete) balusters.

169 Ap **Galleria Colonna** 1910–22

Piazza Colonna

Dario Carbone

Ⓜ A Spagna

The site of Rome's only true arcade was cleared in 1889, and the first proposal was for a garden which would have connected with the open space of the piazza Colonna across the Corso. Many schemes for arcaded shopping were proposed, but the site stood open until 1914 when work started on the present building. The two arms of the arcade open discreetly off the central entrance on the axis of the piazza and under a new colonnade to emerge at the far corners of the block. The arcades themselves are unremarkable, of wide square section and lit through lay-lights in the flat ceilings.

170 Cg **Ministero della Pubblica Istruzione** ex **Ministero dell'Educazione Nazionale** 1913–28

Viale Trastevere/viale Glorioso/via E. Morosini

Cesare Bazzani

Education was housed later than the other new agencies of the Italian kingdom but in time to receive one of Bassani's enormous buildings (the other was the Galleria Nazionale d'Arte Moderna 1911 **167**). Planned around five courtyards, the building presents to viale Trastevere a travertine and brick façade which is 140 metres (460 feet) long, its emphasis on the projecting central bays and entrance for which Bassani appropriated Michelangelo's scheme for the wings of the Campidoglio, but then deranged its giant order and added Floreale decoration of sculptured swags and women.

☞ To the east, in via G. Induno, the **Gioventù Italiana** is a brave *moderne* composition painted red and yellow: the former headquarters of the Fascist youth organisation *Gioventù Italiana del Littorio*, offices and a cinema.

Former Gioventù Italiana del'Littorio

171 Bd **Flats, residential quarter 'Dora'** 1919–24
Via Po off viale Regina Margherita
Gino Coppedè

Coppedè's very particular talent was employed here to startling effect in the design of several large housing blocks. Two of these are connected across the via Po by a huge arch which leads diagonally to the small piazza Mincio, its fountain by Coppedè. The usual tag for the decorative style is 'Floreale', but the overscaled incessant decoration, particularly that of the often redundant brackets which support the frequent projections, and the enlarged keystones, is both 'animale' and vegetal. The yellow house on the opposite side of the piazza at via Aterno 3, is also by Coppedè. Here, in more lyrical medievalising mode, he decorated the exterior with frescoes celebrating the arts and poetry of Florence, the city of his birth.

Fountain, piazza Mincio and house, via Aterno 3

172 Bn **Palazzo del Viminale (Ministry of the Interior)** 1920
Piazzale del Viminale/via A. De Pretis
Manfredo Manfredi

Ⓜ A Repubblica

Another gigantic but late building for a ministry for the Italian state. Its designer had worked earlier on the gigantic Monument to Vittorio Emanuele II **155**. The piazza which it faces was reformed after his death but to Manfredi's design in 1931 when the fountain was also installed.

☞ The church of **Santa Pudenziana** is in via Urbana off via Agostino Depretis to the east. This was built over a Roman thermal hall, and though one of the oldest-established churches in Rome has had its original character destroyed by restorations and alterations.

173Eg **Garbatella neighbourhood** 1921–30

Piazza S. Eurosia, piazza Damiano Sauli

Plan by Gustavo Giovannoni and Marcello Piacentini, housing by Innocenzo Sabbatini, Pietro Aschieri, Mario De Renzi and others

M B Garbatella

Piazza S. Eurosia

The neighbourhood of Garbatella was with that at Aniene (to the north-east of central Rome) one of two garden suburbs promoted by the *Associazione artistica fra i cultori di architettura* whose role is described in the Introduction. It was intended to serve the workers of a planned industrial estate nearby. While this was never built, Garbatella was started. Its layout of winding streets lined with picturesquely arranged housing in various styles returns to a suburban tradition going back to Nash's Park Village in London. Since its inception, Garbatella has suffered less alteration than Aniene, and it was developed over a decade by the ICP 'Istituto Case Popolari' with a variety of housing types.

Two-storey semi-detached houses

The first dwellings were constructed from 1921 around the Piazza S. Eurosia where the first example of a very specific building type, the *suburbana*, was built. Two classicised symmetrical blocks step down and back from a junction of three streets, their formal unity suggested by the shallow concave curves of their gable ends, and physically by the bridge connecting them across the central road. The street leading diagonally to the left from these buildings is lined with picturesquely arranged two-storey semi-detached houses in a folkloristic, 'characteristic' style. It leads towards the planned centre of the suburb, the formally arranged piazza Damiano Sauli where the school occupies the important position on the axis.

***Suburbana*, piazza Michele da Carbonara**

Via della Sette Chiese which leads west out of piazza S. Eurosia, is lined with model houses by De Renzi, built from 1929, and beyond this is a street of villas by Guglielmotti, the via G. Ansaldo. At the northern edge of the scheme are several blocks developed in 1927 not with houses but with increasingly large examples of the *suburbana* type, smaller around piazza Michele da Carbonara, the most grandiose at the junction of the circon–vallazione Ostiense and piazza Eugenio Biffi. These buildings, by Sabbatini, are highest at the centre of the block and step down and out towards the corners which are occupied by loggias and balconies. Their forms were a genuine and interesting alternative both to the corridor street and the free-standing housing block which was being considered at the same time elsewhere in Europe, and whose absentmindedly rectangular successors of the 1960s now surround the original settlement.

***Suburbana*, piazza Eugenio Biffi**

The Fascist era 1922–43

174 Ag **Flats** 1926–29

Lungotevere Arnaldo da Brescia 9

Giuseppe Capponi with engineers Pier Luigi Nervi and Nebbiosi

Ⓜ A Flaminio

In his very short career Capponi (1893–1936) completed only two works in Rome: this block of flats in the 'palazzina' format, and the later Istituto Botanica at the Città Universitaria **184**. His training had been as interior designer and decorator, and while the building as a whole exhibits an extremely stripped classicism, the Baroque convex curves of the attic storey countered by the convex of the entrance canopy suggest the influence of the *moderne* style encouraged by the International Exhibition of Decorative Arts held in Paris in 1925. The travertine cladding is disposed decoratively, set with its grain both horizontal and vertical and, on the attic, on the diagonal. It is not clear why a simple block of flats should require the services of so eminent an engineer as Nervi, or what was his particular contribution.

☞ The **Ponte Pietro Nenni**, the bridge over the Tiber which carries both road traffic and Line A of the Metropolitana railway on two elegant 'Y'-shaped piers, was designed by Luigi Moretti and built in 1965–67. Further upstream and on the east bank, **Lo Scalo do Pinedo**, the elaborate flights of steps down to the Tiber's quay, were constructed in about 1926 to celebrate an aviator, and supply one of the few examples of works to the Tiber's embankments later than those first carried out in the 1870s.

175 Ee **Flats for ICP: Istituto per le Case Popolari** 1926–30
Via della Lega Lombarda/via Arduino
Innocenzo Sabbatini

Built at around the same time as Sabbatini's 'suburbana' flats at Garbatella **173**, these are not as radical in form, being planned round a small courtyard and with their outer walls parallel to the street. They do, however, share the same characteristic stepping down of the two splayed wings, which collide at an angle and provide broad balconies to the flats at the ends of the block. The style is a simple, repetitive, calm stripped classicism, the façades of stucco panels and with pronounced string courses.

☞ To the south and on the corner of via della Lega Lombarda and via Tiburtina is the ruined **Cinema Jolly** of the 1930s, developed at the same time as the small block of flats designed by Mario Marchi to its west, and showing a brave neo-Baroque curve to its acute corner.

176 Eb **Foro Italico** ex **Foro Mussolini** 1927–35
Piazza del Foro Italico and surroundings
Enrico Del Debbio and others

Town planners of the Fascist era had two proposals for reforming the city: one was for monumental new roads, the other for 'centres', *città*, which gathered together a group of similar functions in one monumentally-disposed area. The Città Universitaria **184**, and the Foro Italico built to serve and celebrate physical sport, are examples of the second. The very different styles of the various structures demonstrate the extreme architectural pluralism which the Fascist regime was capable of sponsoring and that individual architects such as Del Debbio were capable of providing.

The history of the construction of the 'forum' is complicated, but its final layout on a fine site against the tree-covered Monte della Farnesina was designed in two phases by Del Debbio. It is best understood by an approach from the Tiber to the east. (The bridge which now provides the approach from the east, the Ponte Duca d'Aosta **189**, was built in 1939 after most of the buildings of the complex were completed.) The gold-tipped obelisk of 1932 by Constantino Constantini celebrates ten years of Mussolini as Duce. It marks the beginning of the monumental avenue lined with severe stone blocks. These record the Fascist 'struggle' and flank a beautifully executed pavement of neo-Roman black and white mosaic. The avenue terminates in a circular piazza, its centre occupied by the fountain in the form of an abstract stone sphere designed in 1932 by Mario Paniconi

Monumental avenue

Sphere fountain

Accademia di Educazione Fisica

Stadio dei Marmi

and Giulio Pediconi. On either side of the avenue to the north and south lie the two buildings of the **Accademia di Educazione Fisica** by Del Debbio, both carried out in the regime's cheerfully kitsch decorative style. The **Stadio dei Marmi** ('Stadium of Marbles') of 1928–35, entirely constructed of marble, is also by Del Debbio. It is cleverly sunk into the ground, but its effect is reduced by its surrounding sixty larger than life size statues of overdeveloped male athletes. These aspire to heroism but achieve a breathtaking vulgarity. To the west of this stadium lies the **Stadio Olimpico** planned in 1930 and designed by Del Debbio. It was eventually constructed for the Olympic games of 1960, and its present suspended canopy roof was added in 1990 when Italy hosted the World Cup football competition.

Stadio Olimpico

To the south of the piazza lie the unmonumentalised tennis courts and swimming pools arranged on either side of the viale delle Olimpiadi whose southern end originally provided another entrance into the Forum. This entrance is flanked to the north by the stone-clad **Casa delle Armi**, formerly the **Accademia di Scherma** (Fencing School) of 1935–36. A modern and Rationalist precocious masterpiece by Luigi Moretti, sadly it was severely altered in its conversion into a barracks for the Carabinieri, and is surrounded by the ugly apparatus of security. Opposite this on the other side of the road and also clad in stone is the **Forestiera Sud** by Del Debbio and now converted into a youth hostel.

Former Accademia di Scherma

Former Palazzo del Littorio

☞ To the north facing piazzale della Farnesina, is the enormous office building: the former **Palazzo del Littorio** or Party Headquarters, now the Ministero Affari Esteri, (Foreign Office), designed by Vittorio Ballio Morpurgo, Enrico Del Debbio and Arnaldo Foschini. Started in 1933, work was interrupted by World War II, and it was only completed in 1950. To the east, the Ponte Duca d'Aosta **189** extended the approach to the Forum eastwards across the Tiber.

177 Ac **Ministero Difesa Marina (Ministry of Marine)** (1914), 1928

Piazza della Marina/lungotevere della Marina

Giulio Magni

M A Flaminio

A late addition to Rome's stock of gigantic Ministries, this is the largest building Magni ever designed. He spent his early years in Romania and his later practice in Rome had been restricted mainly to public housing and villas. The building has two façades: one towards the piazza della Marina and set back beyond a garden, the other facing the Tiber.

178 Da **Via dei Fori Imperiali** ex **via dell'Impero, via del Teatro di Marcello** ex **via del Mare** 1926–32

Cesare Valle, A. Muñoz

M B Colosseo

Rome's Fascist local government, installed in 1926, made many amendments to the Piano Regolatore of 1909. These were confused in their intentions towards the historic centre: some parts were to be demolished, some were to be cleared to make settings for ancient monuments, and others cut through for new roads. The two monumental roads which now start at the piazza Venezia and divide in front of the Vittorio Emanuele Monument were designed to do all three. The via del Mare (now via del Teatro di Marcello) provided a direct connection to EUR and Ostia on the coast beyond. The via dei Fori Imperiali connecting the monument to the Colosseum (and extended beyond as the via dei Trionfi) was designed to provide a ceremonial avenue of the sort that other European capitals already had and on which evidence of the Fascist 'struggle' could be paraded. The route cut diagonally across the Imperial Fora rendering the plans of their ruins unintelligible. Churches like San Giuseppe dei Falegnami **95** and San Luca e Santa Martina **108** were stripped of their surroundings. Cesare Valle designed much of the new work, such as the wall and fountain which now front the Colosseo station of the Metropolitana, the setting for the maps next to the Basilica of Constantine on the south side, and the setting for the partial restoration of the temple of Venus and Rome. The new landscaping works and the standard benches and railings were all robustly detailed and have stood the onslaught of the tourists who now struggle up and down the road.

A plan for a monumental 'Danteum' to be sited opposite on the north side of the road did not progress beyond a competition. New offices for the **Comune di Roma** were built in the via del Mare: they are housed in the brick building to the south of Santa Nicola in Carcere **50** and were also designed by Cesare Valle with Ignazio Guidi and completed in 1939. In the planning doldrums through which Rome went in the 1970s, suggestions were made to demolish the via dei Fori Imperiali and rebuild at least one of the Fora, but the road remains, although its outworks are being eroded by the continuing excavations in the Forum.

179 Ag **Flats: palazzina 'De Salvi'** 1929–31

Piazza della Libertà 20/
lungotevere Michelangelo

Pietro Aschieri

M A Lepanto

This modest block of flats is included here because Aschieri went on to make significant contributions to the monumental public building programme of the 1930s in, for example, the Istituto Romano dei Ciechi di Guerra **180**, the Istituto di Chimica at the Città Universitaria **184**, and the Museo della Civiltà Romana at EUR **191**. The five-storey block presents an uneasy mixture of *moderne* usages such as the broadly splayed surrounds to the windows, and more straightforwardly modern elements like the cantilevered balconies.

☞ Note the house at via dei Gracchi 340 in a wild mixture of Moorish, Art Nouveau and Secession styles.

180 Ec **Istituto Romano dei Ciechi di Guerra (Institute for the Blind)** now **LUISS: Libera Universitaria Internazionale degli Studi Sociali** 1930

Via Parenzo 5–13/via Bolzano

Pietro Aschieri

The institute and workshop for blind war veterans occupied a large site on a corner. In 1994 it was drastically altered and restored to house LUISS. While much has been gained, including the handsome and plausible external colour scheme in three un-Roman greys, several features of the original building, including a single-storey curved wing which connected the two wings which enclose the street corner, have been removed: what remains is a building which Aschieri *might* have designed, but which he did not.

The plan of the large building is as complex and sophisticated as any of those produced by, for example, Le Corbusier at this period. Its bold curves may, however, be derived as much from the Roman Baroque as from international modernism. On the corner, two four-storey wings embrace a convex curve of workshops now exposed. These have Aschieri's characteristic and idiosyncratic window treatment of broad splayed surrounds which are here separated by full height convex panels. Along via Bolzano, beyond this corner lies the second part of the plan, an open court, the ends of whose enclosing wings contain the fully glazed staircases. The main entrance is placed in one of these wings, reached by a busily detailed flight of stairs. The building does not apparently make any particular accommodation to its intended original users: the blind.

☞ Santa Costanza **27**, Sant'Agnese fuori le mura **28.**

181Ee **Flats 'casa convenzionata'** 1931
via Catania 21/viale Lucca
Pietro Aschieri

M B Bologna

Sadly in need of repair, this large symmetrically planned block, more Art Deco than modern, only shows evidence of its architect's attention in the diagonal projections of the balconies, and in the splayed reveals to the entrance: a characteristic Aschieri motif.

182Ec **Flats 'casa convenzionata'** 1931–37
Viale XXI Aprile 27–29/via Barracco
Mario De Renzi

M B Bologna

Piacentini's plan for Rome of 1930 had introduced a new category of housing development more dense than the *fabbricato*, the *intensivo* which could be up to 35 metres (115 feet) high, or of about twelve storeys. This is one of the first examples of the new type, 'E A XI F' ('from the eleventh year of the Fascist era') as its inscription tells us, fortunately by one of the better architects of the period and more coherent than many of its contemporaries. The flats are planned around two courtyards, and the canyon-like spaces which result are relieved by the glazed projecting half landings of the staircase towers. The site slopes slightly to the east, and the planning at ground level exploits this, showing considerable ingenuity in providing separate circulation arrangements for pedestrians and delivery vehicles. The block played a notable role, along with Marcello Mastroianni and Sophia Loren, in Ettore Scola's film *Una giornata particolare* of 1977.

☞ The **Jordanian Embassy** on the opposite side of viale XXI Aprile in via Marchi presents a delirious vision from the 1960s, the walls projected from its curly plan forms are clad in cheerfully decorative mosaic.

183 Bi **Flats, Casa Nicoletti** 1931–32
Via San Basilio 53
Adalberto Libera
Ⓜ A Barberini

Libera's first building in Rome was this remodelling of a nineteenth-century house. His alterations combine delicacy and bluntness: the regular fenestration of the original was disrupted by providing its traditionally shaped full-height windows with projecting travertine frames, and with nautical balconies in the end bays. The bar at street level acquired a travertine facing.

184 Ee **Città Universitaria** started 1932
Viale delle Scienze
Marcello Piacentini and other architects
Ⓜ B Policlinico

Until this campus was completed, the University of Rome had occupied the Palazzo della Sapienza (containing Sant'Ivo **110**) and an *ad hoc* collection of buildings in the historic centre. The present site now houses departments of the natural sciences, medicine and the history of medicine, pharmacology, law, literature and philosophy. The new Città, intended to be the biggest university campus in the world, was one of a number of such centres planned during the Fascist regime. These included the Città dello Sport, started in 1928 as the Foro Mussolini and now the Foro Italico **176**; the Città del Cinema, now Cinecittà; and a Città Militare. Mussolini's brief to Piacentini, who was responsible for the plan and the co-ordination of the various architects commissioned for the first stage of building, was for a layout which would demonstrate 'the highest and most modern possibilities of Italian construction'. Piacentini's plan proposed a main axis running east-west. This was initiated with a monumental entrance from viale delle Scienze, flanked by the faculties of the natural sciences, and terminated by the Rettorato (the Rectorate). The pool in front of the rectorate marks a cross axis along which avenues extend to be terminated in rhetorical buildings devoted to the faculties of Mineralogy to the west and Mathematics to the east. The planning proposal was then exhausted, and further subsequent buildings have been added more or less casually on either side of and beyond the two axes. Later, at EUR **191**, Piacentini devised a way of providing sites for more buildings: he increased the number of cross axes. Although working with architects who included some from the Rationalist group, Piacentini himself was determined to evolve an appropriate modern or

'Mediterranean' style. He avoided both international modernist forms such as *pilotis* and continuous windows, and the arches and oversized trabeation of the *stile littorio*, and the materials he and his colleagues chose are Roman: travertine for the Rectorate and other significant buildings, and brown or yellow brick for the more mundane.

The **Ingresso monumentale** of 1932 and by Arnaldo Foschini, provides a stark portico of piers flanked by solid walls of yellow brick pierced by simple inset fountains. Beyond this, the axis is flanked with the four simple brick-clad faculties of **Igiene** (Hygiene) and **Fisica** (Physics) by Giuseppe Pagano on the left; and **Ortopedia** and **Chimica** (Chemistry) by Pietro Aschieri to the right. Piacentini's **Rettorato** (Rectorate) is another simple blocky composition distinguished from its neighbours by its travertine cladding now weathered to a blinding white; by the very large areas of blank wall in the upper parts of the central block; and by the simple but vertically elongated porch, all that remains of Piacentini's original proposal for a tower in this position. The statue of Minerva, Roman goddess of wisdom, presides over a monumental pool surrounded by the clutter of academics' cars.

Ingresso monumentale

At the western end of the cross axis lies the **Istituto di Mineralogia** of 1932–36 by Giovanni Michelucci. Its two entrances are placed at the ends to provide book ends for the mannered arrangement of small openings in the large expanse of sheer stone. Opposite this, at the eastern end of the avenue is one of Gio Ponti's first works, the **Istituto di Matematica (h)**, the upper half of whose façade again presents an expanse of blind stone cladding interrupted by a monumental entrance, but whose curved back suggests a more playful knowledge of international modernism. This brand of modernism appears more forthrightly in the former **Istituto di Botanica e Farmacologia**, now **Genetica** of 1934 by Giuseppe Capponi, whose curved and largely glazed walls provide an alternative to flat expanses of stone. At one corner of the campus to the south-west, at the junction of viale delle Scienze and viale dell'Universitaria, lies the **Dopolavoro universitario**, the 'after hours' social building, by Gaetano Minucci. Formerly one of the showpieces of suave modern architecture, it has been destroyed by subsequent alterations and additions. The university church of **Divina Sapienza** was completed in 1948. Its oval plan and cupola suggest Baroque pretensions, but the whole sadly demonstrates that satisfactory stripped classicism needs as large a budget as the clothed kind.

Istituto di Mineralogia

Istituto di Matematica

☞ The Policlinico **161** lies to the north, and the very large but very undistinguished **Ministero dell'Aeronautica** of 1931 by Roberto Marino is to the west on viale P. Gobetti and viale Pretoriano.

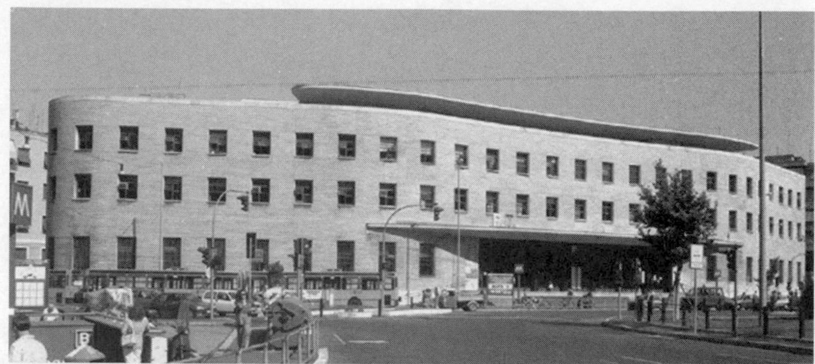

185 Ee **Ufficio Postale (Post Office)** 1932–33 Piazza Bologna

Mario Ridolfi and Mario Fagiolo

M B Bologna

Serving the Nomentano quarter, this was the first to be completed of the four new 'postal centres' to serve the new outlying districts of Rome for whose design a competition was held in 1932. Ridolfi and Fagiolo's design responds to the newly laid out piazza Bologna by using an inflected ellipse for the plan form: the sliding surface of this shape makes it very difficult to perceive that the building is actually aligned on the axis of the street leading out of the piazza on the opposite side. The *stile Littorio* is absent: as 'rationalists', the architects also perhaps intended to suggest the modernity of the postal service. While the smooth exterior of narrow travertine strips separated by pronounced joints has weathered well, the internal rooflit hall has been considerably altered.

See also: De Renzi and Libera's Post Office **187** of 1933–34 in the via della Marmorata, and Samonà's in via Taranto **186.**

186 Dh **Ufficio Postale (Post Office)** 1932–33

Via Taranto/via La Spezia

Giuseppe Samonà

M A San Giovanni

Two of the post offices of the programme of four had sites on which free-standing buildings could be placed. Samonà's site occupies one corner between existing buildings, and the design is much more conventional, the axis of symmetry of its plan bisecting the angle between the streets. The public hall is laid out around this axis and signalled to the streets by two very large windows interrupted only by columns covered in dark green marble. Above these, and separating them at the corner are areas of travertine cladding punctured by neat square windows for the offices, and rectangular ones for the stairs. The corner itself is negotiated with a convex curve. The back of the building facing the service yard is clad in beautifully laid yellow brick.

See also the contemporary Post Offices in via Marmorata **187**, and Piazza Bologna **185**.

187 Cp **Ufficio Postale (Post Office)** 1933–34
Via della Marmorata 4/porta San Paolo
Mario De Renzi and Adalberto Libera

Ⓜ B Piramide

De Renzi and Libera were among the winners in the competition held in 1932 for the design of four new 'postal centres' to serve the new outlying districts of Rome. Their building is a rationalist masterpiece, hardly affected by the influence of the more official *stile Littorio*. It is, however, far from being a straightforward example of international modern architecture: previously De Renzi and Libera had separately worked in very different styles, and the proximity to the site of the Aurelian Wall and the Pyramid of Gaius Celstius **11** may have been responsible for the introduction of ambiguously classical usages. The arrangement of the plan is simple: a U-shaped block of offices of three storeys surrounds the single-storey public postal hall. The various functions of the interior are suggested on the exterior, clad entirely in white limestone, by particular patterns and shapes of windows. This simple modern proposal is, however, elaborated by the presence of the frankly classical portico or stoa which extends across the front of the building; and the slight elevation of the building's ground floor above the level of the street is reconciled by a stepped ramp like that at the Campidoglio. This ramp was originally flanked by ornamental pools, now filled in, from which the bases of the two flagpoles emerged.

☞ Pyramid of Gaius Celstius **11**, Porta San Paolo.

188 Ee **Flats** 1934
Viale di Villa Massimo 39
Mario Ridolfi with Wolfgang Frankl

Ⓜ B Bologna

As Ridolfi's earlier Post Office at piazza Bologna **185** had shown, he was capable of surprising curvilinear extensions to the formal vocabulary of modern architecture. Here, however, designing a semi-suburban 'palazzina', he achieves an almost Swiss orthogonal calm and severity. The façade of the small block delicately balances horizontal and vertical elements with a classicist taste contradicted only by the placing of the open balconies towards the corners. The hints of classical influence are furthered in the travertine-faced wall to the street. See also and compare Luigi Piccinati's twin 'villas' of artists' studios **192** of 1938.

189 Eb **Bridge, Ponte Duca d'Aosta** 1936–39

Piazza Lauro de Bosis/via Filippo Brunelleschi

Vincenzo Fasolo, design; Antonio Martionelli, execution

This final link between the Foro Italico **176** and the east bank of the Tiber was part of the plan for the Forum, but was last to be built. A handsome single span clad in stone, it is distinguished by the widening of the pavements at its abutments, and by the square piers at its approaches which are decorated with bloodthirsty sculptures of fighting.

190 Aj **Via della Conciliazione** 1937

Marcello Piacentini, Attilio Spaccarelli and others

M A Ottaviano

Bernini's piazza and colonnade in front of St Peter's **63** were completed 1667, and for the nearly three centuries following were approached from the east through the narrow streets of the medieval Borgo district. In 1929, the Lateran Accords were signed reconciling and regularising relationships between the Italian state and the Catholic Church. In what proved to be the last of the Fascist regime's new monumental roads, this new road intended to symbolise the Accords was cut through the Borgo between the piazza to the west and the Tiber to the east. In the process, some existing important buildings were exposed and given new settings; others were demolished and rebuilt in new positions. Some new buildings for state insurance companies were built to consolidate the south-eastern end. The resulting broad approach to St Peter's added nothing to the appreciation of its façade or its composition. It deprived Bernini's space of its Baroque characteristic of surprise, and provided a boring street whose spatial quality is defined largely by Piacentini's dull oversized stone lamp posts in the form of obelisks. The connection between the road and the piazza, the architecturally insignificant piazza Pio XII, designed by Giorgio Calza Bini, was completed in 1950.

☞ The palazzo Torlonia **60** and the church of Santa Maria in Traspontina **86** are on the north side of the street; the palazzo Rovere/Penitenzieri, now the Hotel Columbus, is on the south.

191Eg **EUR (Esposizione Universale di Roma)**
started 1937

Marcello Piacentini and others

M B Marconi, EUR Fermi, EUR Palasport

The idea for an international exhibition like that held in Chicago of 1933, and those planned for Paris in 1937 and New York in 1939, first emerged in Rome in the mid 1930s. It was to take place in 1941, and its theme was to be *XXVII Secoli di Civilità* (the 'Twenty-seven Centuries of Civilisation' since the traditional founding of Rome). The site, halfway between Rome and Ostia, was chosen to further Mussolini's vision of 'Roma al mare'; to provide for Rome's expansion by connecting her with her former seaport. The first plans considered the whole urban region, suggesting new railways, roads, 'centres' and zones for various uses. The Metropolitana linking Stazione Termini to the site was built (now Line B) and extended north and south from its original ends. Italy's first *autostrada* or motorway was constructed to run between EUR and Ostia.

Piacentini's first plan for the exhibition prepared in 1937 allocated a site of 400 hectares (988 acres). The principles of the layout were simple and similar to those he had employed at the earlier Città Universitaria **184**. A very wide avenue, now part of the via Cristoforo Colombo, connected Rome to the site and formed the main axis on which several large spaces were located. Regularly spaced cross axes were extended from these spaces, and important buildings placed at their ends. Competitions were held for the design of the various pavilions, and Piacentini, while encouraging the rationalist architects, also ensured that the majority of buildings were designed in his favourite *stile Littorio*. These were to be carried out in various traditional and robust and characteristically Roman materials: limestone, tufa and marble. Building started in 1937, but the outbreak of war led first to the postponement of the opening of the exhibition to 1942, the twentieth anniversary of the Fascist revolution, and then to its abandonment. The buildings of the original exhibition are described below in the order in which they were constructed.

The site remained untouched through the war and up to the mid 1950s when work began to complete some of the buildings and to develop other sites: Rome had accidentally acquired the nucleus of a modern ex-urban business centre which other European capitals were considering building from scratch (for example Paris' La Défense or London's Docklands). Much of the infrastructure of roads and landscaping had been installed and, with the latter now wonderfully matured and some housing scattered through the scheme, EUR has become a satisfactory suburb for business and living, a fine and civilised alternative to the noise, dirt and congestion of central Rome. The permanent materials of the earlier buildings will probably ensure that they will outlive the more flimsily constructed office buildings of the 1960s. The north-south axis was finally terminated in 1960 when the site on top of the hill was used as the location for the Palazzo dello Sport **211**, one of several buildings which were erected in 1960 for the Olympic Games.

The first building to be completed housed the offices of the exhibition organisation, the L-shaped **Palazzo degli uffici dell'Ente Autonomo (a)** at piazza Konrad Adenauer of 1937–38 by Gaetano Minucci. It established the pattern of solid walls clad in limestone and punctured by severe regular openings. Facing piazza J. F. Kennedy, the **Palazzo dei Ricevimenti e dei Congressi (b),** the large hall now used for exhibitions, was the one prominent building which represented rationalist modern architecture. Started in 1937, work was abandoned in 1943, and it was completed in 1952. The building lies off the main axis but connected to it by a fine arcaded street. Designed by Adalberto Libera to an unashamedly modern formal programme, the cubic central hall roofed with a shallow dome rises out of a pure rectangle, its plan

(a) Palazzo dell'Ente Autonomo

(b) Palazzo dei Ricevimenti

a double square, containing supporting uses. The full widths of its ends form gigantic columned porches in front of fully glazed screens. That the proposal is not entirely 'rational' is suggested by the fact that the height of the dome is intentionally exactly the same as that of the Pantheon.

Facing this palace at the opposite end of the handsomely landscaped viale della Civiltà e Lavoro is the exhibition's other 'flagship' building, the **Palazzo della Civilità Italica (c)** (now del Lavoro), of 1939, completed in 1952, by Giovanni Guerrini, Ernesto B. La Padula and Mario Romano. This stands on the highest point of the site, and was intended to be visible from Rome. The repeated arches of its façades are the clearest manifestation of the *stile Littorio*: the arches literally represent Roman civilisation, their number suggest its endurance, the (flaccid) sculptures which decorate the lower openings its art.

(c) Palazzo della Civilità Italica (now del Lavoro)

The twin **Palazzi INA and INPS (d)** which face each other across the main axis originally formed the first piazza on this axis and introduced the exhibition. Now offices for government agencies, they were started in 1939 and completed in time for the exhibition. Their forms are simple, their materials robust, and the light masonry frames which compose the façades of the exedras avoid the crushing bombast of their less well executed companions. They were designed by Giovanni Muzio, Mario Paniconi and Giulio Pediconi.

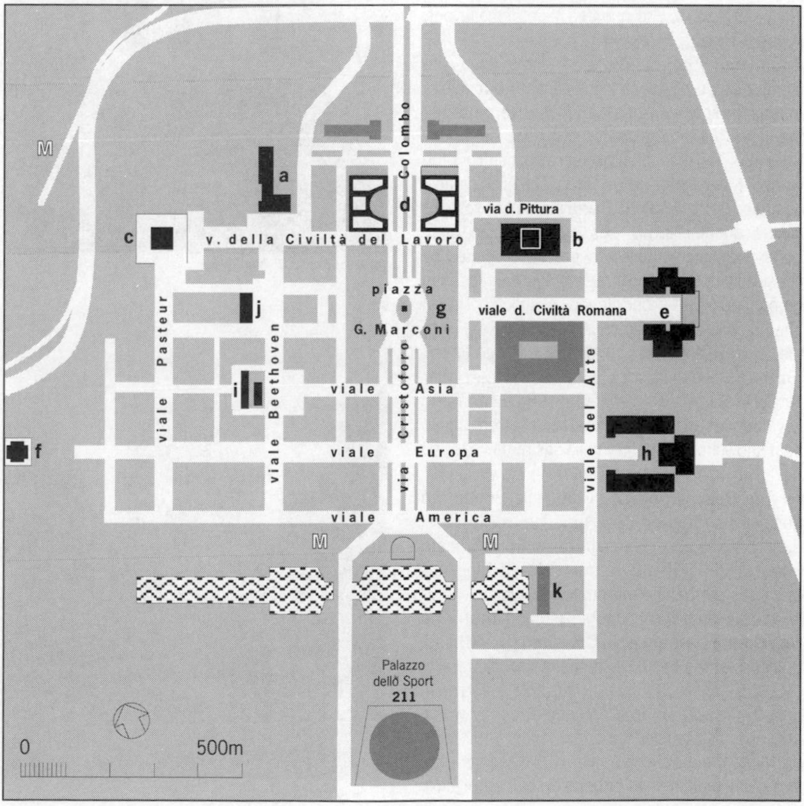

The architecture of the contemporary and extraordinary **Museo della Civilità Romana (e)** by Pietro Ascheri, D. Bernardini and Cesare Pascoletti (193941) is one of the more extreme examples of an attempt to intimidate, but its would-be alarming notched entrance lined with monstrous unfluted columns has lost any power it might once have had to shock or crush. The museum contains very little original material and houses a collection of didactically displayed plaster casts of Roman artefacts and architectural fragments under constant rearrangement. Its glory is the **Modello plastico**: the large model of Rome as it appeared at the beginning of the fourth century which gives a vivid indication of a city with at least half its surface devoted to monumental architecture, and which enables some sense to be made of the ruins which now litter the centre of Rome.

(d) Palazzi INA and INPS

Other buildings under construction when the exhibition was abandoned and subsequently completed include the church of **Santi Pietro e Paolo (f)** on the very edge of the site, a feeble effort at stripped Baroque notable only for its size: its dome is nearly as large that of St Peter's. The central space and intended heart of the layout, now the **Piazza Marconi (g)**, measures 290 by 130 metres (950 by 426 feet), and is lined with ineffectual buildings and colonnades that fail to master the space which is in any case interrupted by the incessant through traffic of the via Cristoforo Colombo. The monumental stela at its centre is the work of the sculptor Arturo Dazzi. The building now occupied by the **Archivio Centrale dello Stato (h)** closes another cross axis presenting an open courtyard (now occupied by cars) surrounded by fine buildings of two and three storeys, their façades composed of well-proportioned columned screens. The Archivio was designed by Mario De Renzi with the Milanese architects Luigi Figini and Gino Pollini. (On the next but one block to the north is the former Alitalia tower of 1967, refaced in 1994 for IBM. The new façades are designed by Gino Valle from Udine, best known for his factory buildings of the 1960s.)

(e) Museo della Civilità Romana

☞ The **Post Office (i)** in the viale Beethoven designed by the Milanese practice BBPR (G. L. Banfi, L. Belgioioso, Enrico Peressutti and Ernesto Rogers) in 1939–40: a four storey block of offices is set behind the public hall which is clad in marble and has a double pitched roof. The **Sede della Democrazia Cristiana (j)**, the headquarters of the former Christian Democrat Party of 1955–58, is by Saverio Muratori at Piazzale Luigi Sturzo 2: an amazingly inept essay which attempts to combine monumentality with forms perhaps intended as populist. To the north, the two office buildings on either side of the northern

(f) Santi Pietro e Paolo

(h) Archivio Centrale dello Stato

entry to EUR were designed in 1963–65 by Vittorio Ballio Morpurgo (in via dell'Agricoltura to the west), and Luigi Moretti for **Esso Standard Italiana** (in via dell'Industria to the east). Their flimsy aluminium and glass curtain walls were an understandable but regrettable reaction to the masonry cladding of the earlier buildings nearby. The office slab for the state corporation **ENI (k)** which stands to the west of the landscaped lake to the south of EUR was designed by M. Bacigalupo and U. Ratti in 1961–62. The Palazzo dello Sport **211** is on the crest of the hill to the south.

(i) Post Office

(j) Former Sede della Democrazia Cristiana

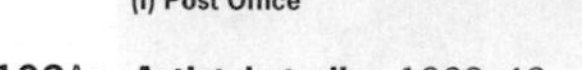

192 Ac **Artists' studios** 1938–43

Via G. Nicotera 22–4

Luigi Piccinato

M A Lepanto

With Ridolfi's earlier flats in viale di Villa Massimo **188** and De Renzi's Palazzina Furmanik **193**, these studios provide the third example of extreme international modernism in Rome which, apart from their various materials, were unaffected by local conventions. The studios are stacked up in two simple blocks separated and served by the central lift and stairs. The stone tiles (now detaching themselves) which clad the ends of the crosswalls were part of the original design.

☞ On the corner of via G. Nicotera at numbers 1–3, Marcello Piacentini's first building, the small block of flats, the **Villino Allegri** 1914–17, a manifesto of his beliefs at that time in an eclectic modernism derived from vernacular forms.

193 Eb **Flats, Palazzina Furmanik** 1938–42
Lungotevere Flaminio 18
Mario De Renzi

M A Flaminio, then tram along via Flaminia

Earlier in the 1930s De Renzi had been co-designer with Libera of the Post Office in via Marmorata **187** and with others of the Archivio dello Stato at EUR **191**. These works had employed some of the usages of his more bombastic contemporaries, but as sole designer of this block of flats he achieved a masterpiece of simplicity, a pure product of twentieth-century modernism. To the Tiber the block presents a severe façade of five storeys from each of which projects a continuous deep balcony. The whole building is consistently clad in render scored in squares and framed by travertine.

☞ The church of Sant'Andrea in via Flaminia **81** is to the east, a block away from the Tiber.

194 Bg **Flats** 1940–41
Via Messina 13–19
Adalberto Libera

M B Castro Pretorio

The format of this simple neat block of flats is that of neither the *palazzina* nor the *intensivo*. Its cornice line follows that of its nineteenth-century neighbours, the proportions of whose windows are adopted for the central section. Only the cantilevered balconies which frame at the ends suggest that this is the work of a modernist architect.

☞ The former Peroni brewery **165.**

The first Republic 1944 to the present

195 Eg **Mausoleo delle Fosse Ardeatine** 1947–51

Via Ardeantina

Nello Aprile, Gino Calcaprina, Aldo Cardelli, Mario Fiorentino and Giuseppe Perugini

In 1944, in reprisal for the killing of thirty-two German soldiers by the Italian Resistance, German forces shot sixty-six military and 257 civilian Italians and buried their bodies in one of the caves at this spot. This is their memorial, the sombre outcome of one of the first architectural competitions to be held in Italy after World War II. The first and second prize winners combined themselves into a single group to work up the design. Inside an enclosure defined by a wall of cyclopean masonry, a path leads first through the re-excavated caves and terminates in a partly underground mausoleum. Here the 323 graves are laid out in rows and sheltered by a massive concrete roof supported and lifted just above the ground on six squat columns. Except for the possibility that the roof might be regarded from the outside as a gigantic sepulchral slab, the architectural language is entirely abstract; only the figurative sculpture at the entrance, by Mirko Basadella and Francesco Coccia, explicitly suggests grief.

196 Eb **Flats** 1947–49

Via dei Monti Parioli 15

Bruno Zevi, Silvio Radiconcini, Luigi Piccinato

Ⓜ A Flaminio

This ordinary block of flats in the palazzina format is included as one of the few works to be co-credited to the distinguished architect, theorist and historian Bruno Zevi.

☞ The single house the Casa del Maresciallo **210**, is further up the street at the corner of via Bartolomeo Ammannati. The 'Girasole' flats **197** are to the east on viale Bruno Buozzi.

197 Eb **Flats, Casa del Girasole** 1947–50

Viale Bruno Buozzi 64/ via G. Schiaparelli

Luigi Moretti

Forty-five years after the completion of this palazzina, it is hard to recreate the furore which resulted from the completion and publication of Moretti's first post-war work: one which radically questioned the orthodoxy of both pre-war European and regional Italian modernisms, and which set the architect on his subsequent career as architectural chameleon. The format of the palazzina was undone by the gash in the main façade which indicated and provided the entrance and which ventilated the centre of the block. The two pitched gables on either side of the gash cheekily suggested a classical 'split pediment'. The assumption that the surface of a building should be contained within a prismatic form was challenged by the deliberate extensions of parts of the flimsy skin of mosaic beyond the main volume of the façade. The building was provided with a base of enigmatically distressed 'antique' masonry. Moretti's design can now be seen as part of a general attempt by many progressive Italian architects practising immediately after World War II to find an architectural style which could not be associated with the work of the 1920s and 1930s. One of the detailed techniques was to introduce small angled inflections in the plans, structure and surface of buildings. These are seen here both in the 'pediment' and in the projecting windows towards the back of the building. (*Girasole* is Italian for 'sunflower'.)

198 Bo **Stazione Termini** 1947–50

Piazza dei Cinquecento

Leo Calini and Eugenio Montuori with Annibale Vitellozzi, M. Castellazzi, V. Fatigati and A. Pintonello

M Termini

Rome's first central railway station was completed in 1874, and its replacement was started as part of the programme of infrastructure improvements in the late 1930s. The platforms and the 200 metre (656 feet) long north and south flanks with their bare stacked arches, designed by Angiolo Mazzoni, were completed in 1938, but further work was interrupted by World War II. A competition for its completion was held after the war and won by a group of well-established architects whose mature design provided Rome with one of its few authentic large examples of international modern architecture.

There are three parallel elements: the office building with its enigmatic pattern of glazed slots which extends across the full width of the piazza dei Cinquecento; between this and the platforms runs the magnificent calm concourse lit from the high clerestory above the platforms. This space contributes to Europe's limited stock of skilfully designed covered public spaces. The entrance and ticket hall with its great cantilevered canopy is placed artfully off-centre in front of the office building. The restaurants to the north extend into the forecourt from which they are separated by the remains of a stretch of the Servian Wall **1** whose foundations can be seen in the basement.

When built, the station was viewed as an example of the role which modern design could play in providing efficient and luxurious standards in public buildings. Nearly half a century after its construction, its forms and materials still seem appropriate, but the design does not receive additions and alterations kindly, and it is drifting towards the seediness to which many European railway stations have succumbed: the whole ensemble is in urgent need of cleaning and restoration, and the arrangements for traffic in the piazza Cinquecento are now inadequate.

199 Bb **Upper floor addition** to **Villino Alatri** 1948-49

Via Paisello 38/via Carissimi

Mario Ridolfi, Wolfgang Frankl and Mario Fiorentino

The addition consists of three floors of new accommodation placed on top of the earlier two-storey house designed by V. Morpurgo in 1928. The new work is separated from the old by a thin continuous concrete plate which projects beyond the original perimeter to provide a second base. The new flats have a delicate reinforced concrete structural frame, and their balconies are wittily placed above Morpurgo's earlier loggia. The quirky projecting planters to the new balconies suggest that this was not an essay in orthodox modernism.

200 Ee **Housing, Quartiere INA-Casa, Tiburtino**
1949–54

Via Tiburtina 1020, and between via Diego Angeli and via Lucatelli

Team co-ordinated by Mario Ridolfi and Ludovico Quaroni and including: Carlo Aymonino, C. Chiarini, Mario Fiorentino, Federico Gorio, M. Lanza, Sergio Lenci, P. M. Lugli, C. Melograni, G. C. Menichetti, G. Rinaldi and Michele Valori

M B Pietralata

After World War II and in the absence of a plan, Rome was allowed to expand chaotically on its periphery. While most of the new housing was provided by speculators, some was carried out by autonomous state agencies like INA-Casa. With the precedent of the Garbatella neighbourhood **173** of thirty years earlier, here the architects too planned an entire 'quarter', its housing arranged around a nucleus with a church, some shops and a street market. The highest buildings, towers of six storeys, are placed along the via Tiburtina. The gently winding streets leading from the main road are lined with a variety of types of housing including terraces and linked blocks of flats of four storeys grouped loosely round entrance courts.

The scheme was an attempt to furnish alternatives in layout, form and detail to those of the speculators, to some of the architects own earlier work, and to the orthodox modern architecture of northern Europe. The knowingly chamfered corners, shallow pitched roofs, artfully irregular window patterns and gold-anodised window frames with folding green shutters are combined with direct quotations of regional vernacular building such as the loggias which crown the towers. The cantilevered balconies with their tapered sections derive from international modernism. In the 1990s the scheme was repaired and repainted in sparkling grey, yellow and pale sienna. Although highly regarded at the time, the scheme had little direct influence on subsequent housing patterns elsewhere in Rome, and it has itself subsequently been surrounded by housing of the sort to which it was intended to stand as example and reproach.

201Ec Housing district for INA-Casa, viale Etiopia

1950–54

Via Tripolitania 195, 211/via Galla Sidama/via Adua/viale Etiopia

Mario Ridolfi and Wolfgang Frankl, Mario Fiorentino, Henriette Huber

The earlier housing layout at via Tiburtino **200** had first proposed residential towers as an alternative to the street-bound and lumpy format of the *intensivo* block. The development of this residential quarter by INA gave various architects the opportunity to experiment further with the form (as the Milanese were a little later to use it in the design of offices such as the Pirelli building). Ridolfi and Frankl's slabs which lie between viale Tripolitana and via Etiopia are of nine storeys, no higher than an *intensivo*, but much less bulky, and the delicate chamfers of their plan forms enhance the slimness. Their mansard roofs were generally reintroduced into Italy at about this time and replaced the more folkloristic pitched roofs of, for example, the towers at via Tiburtina. The brutality of the deliberately 'poor' exposed reinforced concrete structural frame is offset by the tiled decoration of the panels under the windows for which fourteen different patterns were specially produced. The only problem with the arrangement is the one general to developments of this kind, and one that becomes particularly acute in Italy, where shared or semi-public space is usually enclosed in a gated courtyard: what is the use and status of the ground on which the isolated blocks stand?

The later blocks on viale Etiopia 2–8 at its junction with piazza Addis Abeba, whose plans step out and in and which nearly touch each other, were designed by Fiorentino with Huber in 1957–60. The two slabs side by side in viale Etiopia and via Galla e Sidama and via Adua and via Tripolitania which follow the same general form as Ridolfi and Frankl's but angled to the street were designed by Fiorentino.

202Eh Housing, Quartiere Tuscolano, for INA-Casa

1952–55

Between largo Spartaco and via Selinunte, and via Cartagine and via del Quadrato

Mario De Renzi, Saverio Muratori, Lucio Cambellotti, Giuseppe Perugini, Dante Tassotti and Luigi Vagnetti

Ⓜ A Numido Quadrato

The rectangular site for the housing development is bounded by roads, and subdivided by a central street, the via Segesta. The area was further subdivided, and various architects developed particular sites with different housing forms which do not together make a unified scheme. Facing largo Spartaco, a long cranked block of seven storeys provides an apparently defensive wall against an invisible malign force lying to the north-east. Its exposed reinforced concrete frame is filled with 'poor' brick panels, and the gold-anodised aluminium window frames which were so strangely fashionable in the housing of the 1950s.

To the south and west of this block, cranked three- and four-storey terraces are laid out on either side of via Segesta, and those on the south-east terminate against a row of ten-storey towers with irregular cruciform plans and cantilevered unprotected balconies, clichés of international modernism probably unsuitable in Rome's climate.

As a model development, the quarter is less successful than some earlier schemes such as

that at Tiburtino **200**. The layout seems to be determined as much by the inclinations of individual architects as by a unified plastic or organisational vision, and the problems caused by too much unassigned semi-public space were not considered. It is, however, well maintained, and there are no obvious signs of decay or social collapse.

☞ To the west of this housing lies Adalberto Libera's experimental **'Unità di abitazione orizzontale'** of 1950–54, its single entrance at via Selinunte 49 marked by a concrete arch. An early example of what later become known in Britain as 'high density, low rise' housing, the two hundred single-storey dwellings which enclose their own patios are laid out along pedestrian streets. The scheme, which was never subsequently copied, is now poorly maintained and has the air of a besieged camp for temporary occupants. To the south-west in what remains open country, are some of the arches of the Roman aqueduct the **Acqua Felice**.

203 Do **Flats, Palazzina Mancioli** 1953

Via Lusitania 29

Mario Ridolfi and Wolfgang Frankl

Ⓜ A Re di Roma

In their search for an appropriate post-war style, Ridolfi and Frankl were able to experiment in designing a large number of palazzine. This essay is simply planned, its four storeys rising above a square travertine base from which it is separated by a projecting redundant 'beam'. The block is capped with rendered mansards of smudgy profile, and the windows are equipped with little projecting hoods.

204 Eb **Stadio Flaminio** 1957–60 and **Palazzetto dello Sport** 1956–58

Viale Tiziano, piazza Apollodoro

Pier Luigi Nervi, Antonio Nervi and A. Vitellozzi

Ⓜ A Flaminio and tram along via Flaminia

These two structures were among those built for the various sporting activities of the Olympic games held in Rome in 1960. The Stadio Flaminio to the south has raked seating protected by a canopy. Their structures are good examples of the virtuoso engineering in concrete for which Italian engineers generally and Nervi in particular were famous. Nervi's particular forte was in the profiling of concrete sections to suggest how the forces were transmitted through and along them, here shown in the doubly-tapered stiffening beams of both seats and canopy. Considerable skill was required of the carpenters who constructed the moulds for some of the curved sections. The Palazzo dello Sport which housed indoor sports such as basketball and gymnastics has a circular plan, and its roof of crossing concrete ribs is carried externally by a ring of thirty-six delicate 'Y'-shaped leaning supports, modern equivalents of the Gothic flying buttress. The insignificant external architecture is restricted to the perimeter wall of orange Roman brick separated from the structure above by a continuous clerestory.

☞ The former Olympic village **205** is to the north. In 1994, the office of Renzo Piano won a competition to design three concert halls between viale P. de Coubertin, the southern end of the elevated motorway, the corso di Francia, and the Villa Glori.

205 Eb **Villagio Olimpico/Olympic village** 1957–60

North and south of viale xvii Olimpiade between viale Tiziano and via Argentina

Adalberto Libera, Luigi Moretti, Vittorio Cafiero, Amedeo Luccichenti and Vincenzo Monaco

Ⓜ A Flaminio and tram along via Flaminia

The athletes of the twenty-seventh Olympic games held in Rome in 1960 were accommodated in this 'village' which was subsequently used as public housing. The village is laid out in long parallel blocks, mostly of five storeys, lifted off the ground and supported on 'pilotis' of delicately profiled concrete. The materials are uniform: an exposed reinforced concrete frame, and panels of dull orange brick. The slight and irregular cranking of the plans of the blocks prevents the spaces between them becoming canyon-like, and the modernist proposal of buildings lifted off the ground to allow the landscape to flow under them has been more than fulfilled by the subsequent growth of the original planting. Less satisfactory is the lack of a discernible difference between the fronts and backs of the blocks: they are exactly like housing 'ships' floating in a green 'sea'.

☞ The Stadio Flaminio and Palazzetto dello Sport **205** lie to the south. The motorway, the **Corso di Francia** was built in 1959–60 to connect the Foro Italico to the west with the Stadio Flaminio to the south. Where it passes through the village it is carried on a viaduct whose angled and profiled legs were characteristic of the work of its engineers Pier Luigi Nervi and Annibale Vitellozzi.

206 Bg **Rinascente department store** 1957–62

Piazza Fiume

Franco Albini and Franca Helg

Ⓜ B Castro Pretorio

Much of the building activity in Rome after World War II was concerned with housing: there were few new public or commercial buildings. The Rinascente department store chain commissioned the Milanese architect Albini for this store, and its completion brought a northern sophistication to Rome's less quirky architectural scene. The main difficulty in designing the façades of such a store is that windows are not required except at street level, and some suitable way of treating large areas of blind surface must be found. Albini here provided a complex answer in materials which have weathered unusually well. First, he exhibited parts of the delicate steel structure, emphasising the horizontal edges of the floors and the beams on which these are placed. Against this horizontality, the walls of carefully textured and coloured concrete are corrugated to house an irregular arrangement of air supply and extract ducts. The whole is topped with a fretted cornice. The only windows are provided on the south end, where they look out over the piazza, and on the side away from the street. The surprisingly small interior spaces are now generally unremarkable, but the sophisticated detailing of the escape staircase at the north end with its pointed-oval plan is worth inspecting.

207 **Leonardo da Vinci Airport** 1952–57
Fiumicino
Riccardo Morandi, Vincenzo Monaco, A. Zavitteri and Amedeo Luccichenti

After World War II, Rome equipped itself with two large buildings devoted to transport, the Stazione Termini **198** and this airport. The designs for both emphasise their engineering structures, here in Morandi's corrugated reinforced concrete roof which originally covered the whole terminal and which was cantilevered to provide a shelter for passengers arriving by road. Morandi also designed the structures of the two nearby large sheds, the Alitalia hangar and the maintenance centre for jumbo jets. The approach to the original terminal is now obscured by the railway station and the access from it, and the originally sparse finishes of the workmanlike interior have been overwhelmed by the standardised decoration of the international shopping mall.

208 Bn **Offices** 1958–59
Via Torino 6/via Cesare Balbo 3
Adalberto Libera, Leo Calini and Eugenio Montuori

M A Repubblica

The first of Libera's realised commercial buildings showed him aware of the developing use of the metal curtain wall in the United States. The office building, on a steeply sloping site in Rome's historic centre, has a trapezoidal plan in which a central core of services planned inside hexagonal forms is surrounded by general office space. (The hexagons arise from the angle of sixty degrees with which via Torino meets via Balbo, and this angle appears again in the free-standing roof structure.) It is clad with a curtain wall of aluminium sections which hold enamelled and laminated steel panels. Possibly heroic in 1958, this cladding now looks shabby and provisional.

209 Ee **Cinema Maestoso** 1958
Via Appia Nuova 416
Riccardo Morandi

M A Furio Camillo

Before television became ubiquitous in Italy, cinemas supplied the mechanical entertainment for the population of the new extensions to Rome. Morandi's early career was occupied almost exclusively in helping to meet the need. The Maestoso is included here as an example of his work and because it is one of the few which has not been demolished or converted. Like only the more important earlier palazzi, its façade is set back from the street. Its height is determined by the envelope of an *intensivo*, and the flats of this type are loaded on top of the front of the cinema proper.

210 Eb **House, Casa del Maresciallo** 1958

Via dei Monti Parioli 21/via Bartolomeo Ammannati

Federico Gorio

M A Flaminio

A highly wrought single-family house was partly converted from an existing rural building, given new window openings and tentative discontinuous string courses.

☞ Flats at via dei Monto Parioli 15, **196**; the 'Girasole' flats **197** are to the east on viale Bruno Buozzi.

211 Eg **Palazzo dello Sport** 1958–60

Via Cristoforo Colombo 42, south of EUR

Pier Luigi Nervi and Marcello Piacentini

M B EUR Palasport

The new buildings to house the various events of the Olympic Games held in Rome in 1960 were distributed on three sites: to the north at the refurbished Foro Italico **176**; south of the Ponte Milvio; and on a prominent site on the ridge south of EUR. For the last, Piacentini had proposed placing two sports buildings to complement the business, administrative and residential uses already partly developed there. (The other building was the nearby Velodromo.) Piacentini's first design was for a circular building containing an oval arena, the whole clad in a very late version of his robust masonry architecture. At some stage in the subsequent collaboration with the engineer Nervi to consider the design of the shallow domed roof, the masonry disappeared and was replaced by the present bland glazed and tiled exterior. The interior is inaccessible except when an event is being staged, but examples of Nervi's structurally acrobatic stairs and the complex ribbed structure supporting the seating can be seen through the glass from the outside.

212 Ec **Flats** 1961

Via Arbia 21

Carlo and Maurizio Aymonino, and Alessandro and Baldo De Rossi

The Trieste district, the land between via Salaria and Corso Trieste, was developed in the 1960s, laid out on a rectangular grid of streets and zoned for 'palazzine'. This block of flats was one of the first: photographs of the newly completed building show it standing isolated. Its multiple authors accepted the palazzina format of three flats per floor, and resolved on a stylistic exercise. The surfaces of the two main façades are slightly disrupted by very slight planar shifts to make ambiguous the relationship between the supporting reinforced concrete structure and its covering of square orange tiles. The result has geological associations, and Alvar Aalto's work may have been influential.

213 Ea **Flats, Palazzina San Maurizio** 1962–65

Via Romeo Romei 39

Luigi Moretti

A remote palazzina on a hillside is given a particular character by the bulging curves of some of the balustrades of its living-rooms and balconies, with a different arrangement on each floor. The effect is vulgar, and the views which the palazzina commanded have been destroyed by the terrible bulk further down the slope of the Città Giudiziaria built to replace the terrible bulk of the Palazzo di Giustizia **151**.

214 Bf **Offices and flats/edificio polifunzionale** 1963–65

Via Campania 59/via Romagna

Vincenzo, Fausto and Lucio Pasarelli with engineers P. Cercato and M. Constantini

M A Spagna and Villa Borghese exit

Most of Rome's buildings had traditionally been 'polyfunctional'. A palace might contain a dwelling for its sponsors on the first floor, shops or workshops on the ground floor, and before the modern 'office' was introduced 'work' or business might have been carried out anywhere in the building. Here, on a trapezoidal site just inside the Aurelian Wall, is a very literal essay in the exposition of three different uses arranged on the same site. Occupying the whole site, three floors of offices clad in a curtain wall of brown glass surmount a ground floor now mostly devoted to car parking. Above this are four storeys of flats planned in a rectangular block whose short side is parallel to via Campania and whose long side is at an angle to via Romagna. The flats have a random profile and their external materials are 'domestic': bands of concrete and panels of brown tile. The proposal has its attractions as an academic exercise, but the effect on the street is no improvement over a real roof addition. (Compare Ridolfi's Villino Alatri **199** of 1949.) The site simply looks overdeveloped.

215 Ee **Provincial Medical Association headquarters** 1966–73

Via Giovanni Battista De Rossi 12/via Bosio

Piero Sartogo, Carlo Fegiz and Domenico Gimigliano

Ⓜ B Bologna

This building is included as a small but very intense instance of the fully-fledged 'brutalism' of which Rome has few examples. It is not clear why the various functions of this office building should have been dismembered and reassembled, some of them two storeys below ground level, into a picturesque composition built mainly of raw reinforced concrete. The flying offices with their 'control tower' windows are particularly baffling.

☞ On the opposite side of the road at via Giovanni Battista De Rossi 9 is the **Palazzina Zaccardi** of 1950, two blocks of flats which meet on a corner and were designed together by Mario Ridolfi.

216 Ag **Offices, Banco Popolare di Milano** 1974

Piazzale Flaminio

Luigi Moretti and C. Zacutti

Ⓜ A Flaminio

Moretti developed his penchant for curved plan forms in the 1960s: see for example the Palazzina San Maurizio **213**. Here two diminutive and otherwise unremarkable bank office buildings linked on a podium are given an extravagant crown of curved white baffles on the roof. The fussy detailing of the roof balustrade also betrays the modishness of the sixties.

217 **Stations for the Metropolitana Line B** 1977–94

Studio Transit Design: Giovanni Ascarelli and others

Ⓜ B San Paolo to Laurentina, Castro Pretorio to Rebibbia

Station 'Marconi'

Rome's first underground railway system was started in 1938 to link the Stazione Termini to EUR and Ostia. Built by the 'cut and cover' method with shallow excavations, there was ample room for large spacious stations roofed with vaults, and their passages lined with travertine. The public areas of Line A, developed in the 1970s and 1980s were disappointingly under-designed, and had cramped circulation and poor, ugly finishes. The extensions north (1977–90) and south (from 1984) to the original line, now 'B', were far more satisfactory, with uncluttered platforms and clear graphics, even if the gain in convenience has excluded a more specifically Roman character. Transit Design are architects, planners and industrial designers, based in Rome but with an international practice.

Selected bibliography

Anthony Blunt, *Baroque and Rococo Architecture and Decoration* (Granada, London, 1978)

Jean Castex, *De architectuur van renaissance, barok en classicisme* (Paris, 1990; SUN, Nijmegen, 1993)

Richard A. Etlin, *Modernism in Italian Architecture, 1890–1940* (MIT Press, Cambridge, Mass; London, 1991)

Irene de Guttry, *Guida di Roma Moderna dal 1870 ad oggi* (de Luca editore, Rome, 1978)

Henry-Russell Hitchcock, *Architecture: Nineteenth and Twentieth Centuries* (Pelican History of Art, Yale, 1987)

Emil Kaufman, *Architecture in the Age of Reason* (Dover, Harvard, 1955, 1968)

Richard Krautheimer, *Rome Profile of a City, 312–1308* (Princeton University Press, New Jersey, 1980)

Peter Murray, *Architecture of the Renaissance* (Harry N. Abrams Inc, New York, 1971)

Sergio Polano, with Marco Mulazzani, *Guida all'architettura italiana del novecento* (Electa, Milan, 1991)

Steenbergen, Smienk, van der Ree, *Italian Villas and Gardens* (Thoth, Amsterdam, 1992)

Vittorio Sgarbi, *Dizionario dei monumenti Italiani e loro autori, Roma* (Bompiani, Milan, 1991)

Wylie Sypher, *Four Stages of Renaissance Style: Transformations in Art and Literature 1400–1700* (Anchor/Doubleday, Garden City N.Y., 1956)

J. B. Ward-Perkins, *Roman Imperial Architecture* (Pelican History of Art, Penguin, 2nd ed., 1981)

John White, *Art and Architecture in Italy 1250–1400* (Pelican History of Art, Penguin, 1966, 1987)

Rudolph Wittkower, *Art and Architecture in Italy 1600–1750* (Pelican History of Art, Penguin, 1982)

Fiction

Robert Graves, *I Claudius, Claudius the God,* ([1934], Penguin, 1986)

Alan Massie, *Augustus* (Sceptre, London, 1987)

Marguerite Yourcenar, *Memoirs of Hadrian* (Penguin, 1951, 1982)

Gore Vidal, *Julian* (Panther, 1962, 1976)

Illustration credits

The photographs are by the author with the exception of **1**, **56**, **93**, **137**, **156**, **165**, **172**, **190** and **217** which are by Miles Lanham and Graham Southgate; and **67** which is by Matthew Saunders.

The drawings on pages 99 and 112 are from Letarouilly, *Edifices de Rome*, Paris, 1840–57.

Index

References to entries are in bold type e.g. **24**
References to items within entries are in plain type: 33
References to page numbers are in italics: *55*

Churches are indexed under the prefix, 'San', 'Santa', 'Santi', Sant'; *or* 'Basilica of...'

Index

Index

Index

Map A north-west

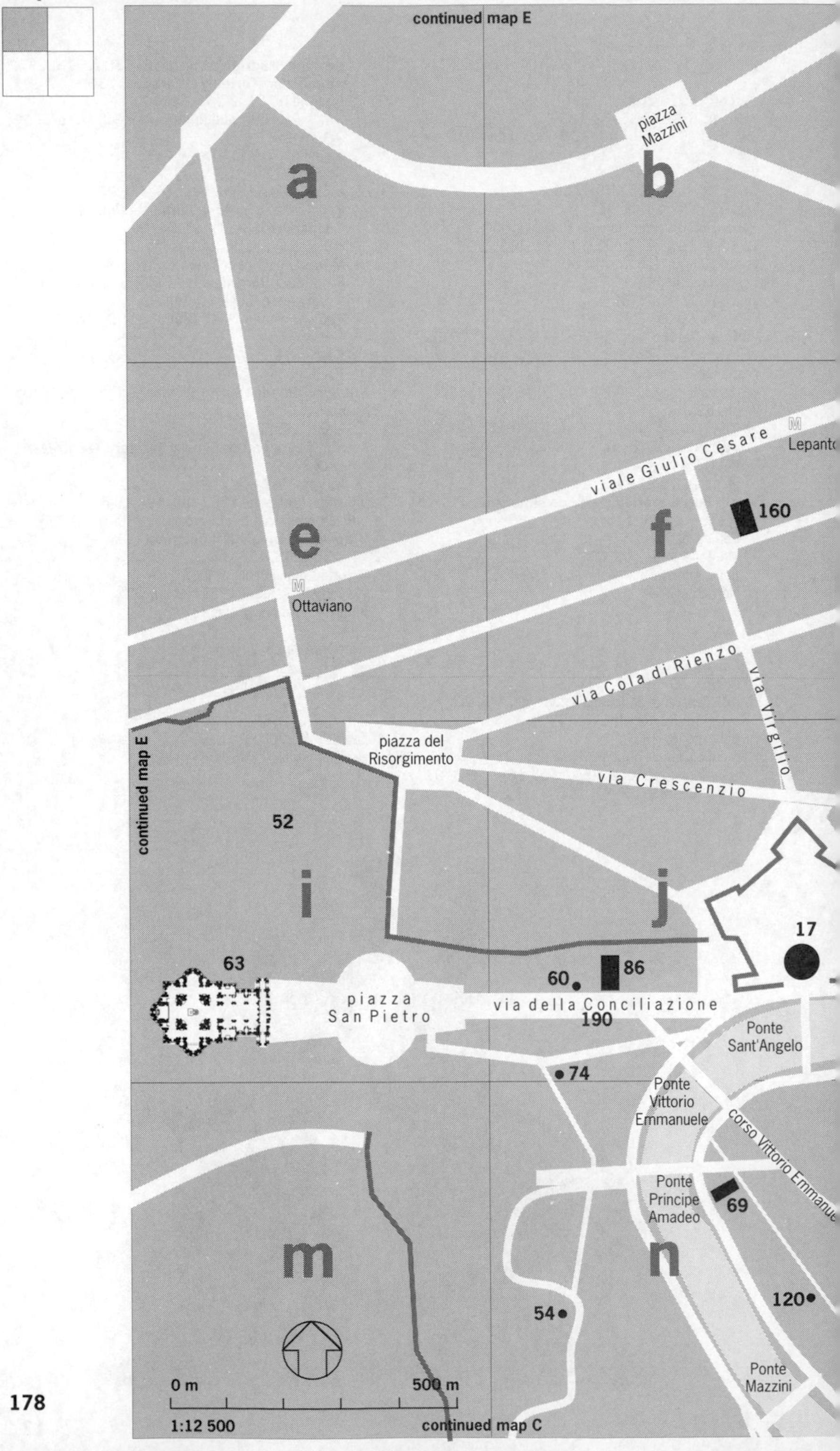

continued map E

piazza Mazzini

a

b

viale Giulio Cesare

Lepanto

160

e

f

Ottaviano

via Cola di Rienzo

via Virgilio

continued map E

piazza del Risorgimento

via Crescenzio

52

i

j

17

63

60

86

piazza San Pietro

via della Conciliazione

190

Ponte Sant'Angelo

74

Ponte Vittorio Emmanuele

corso Vittorio Emmanuele

Ponte Principe Amadeo

69

m

n

120

54

Ponte Mazzini

0 m

500 m

1:12 500

continued map C

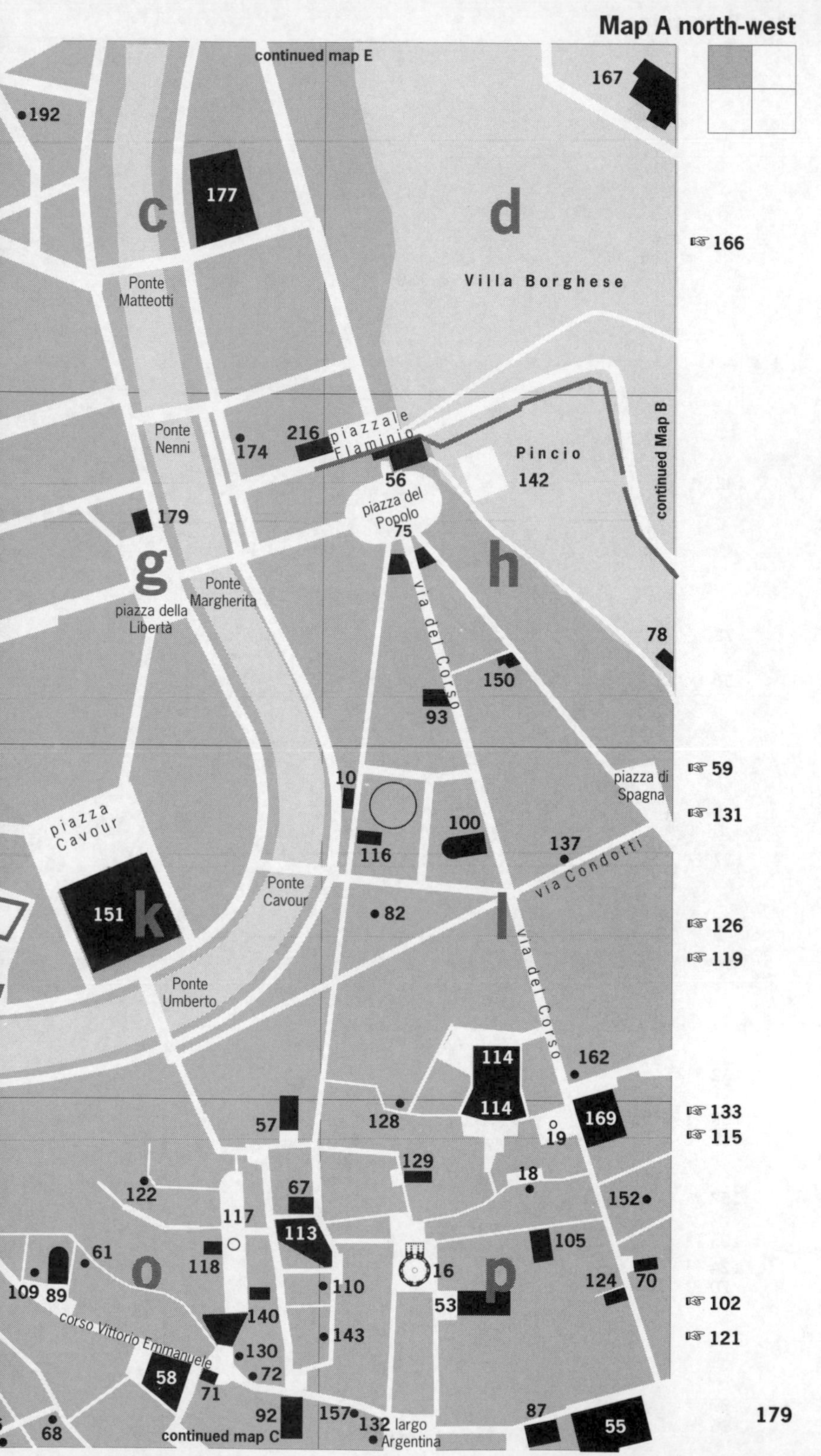

☞ 166
☞ 59
☞ 131
☞ 126
☞ 119
☞ 133
☞ 115
☞ 102
☞ 121

Map B north-east

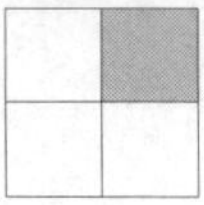

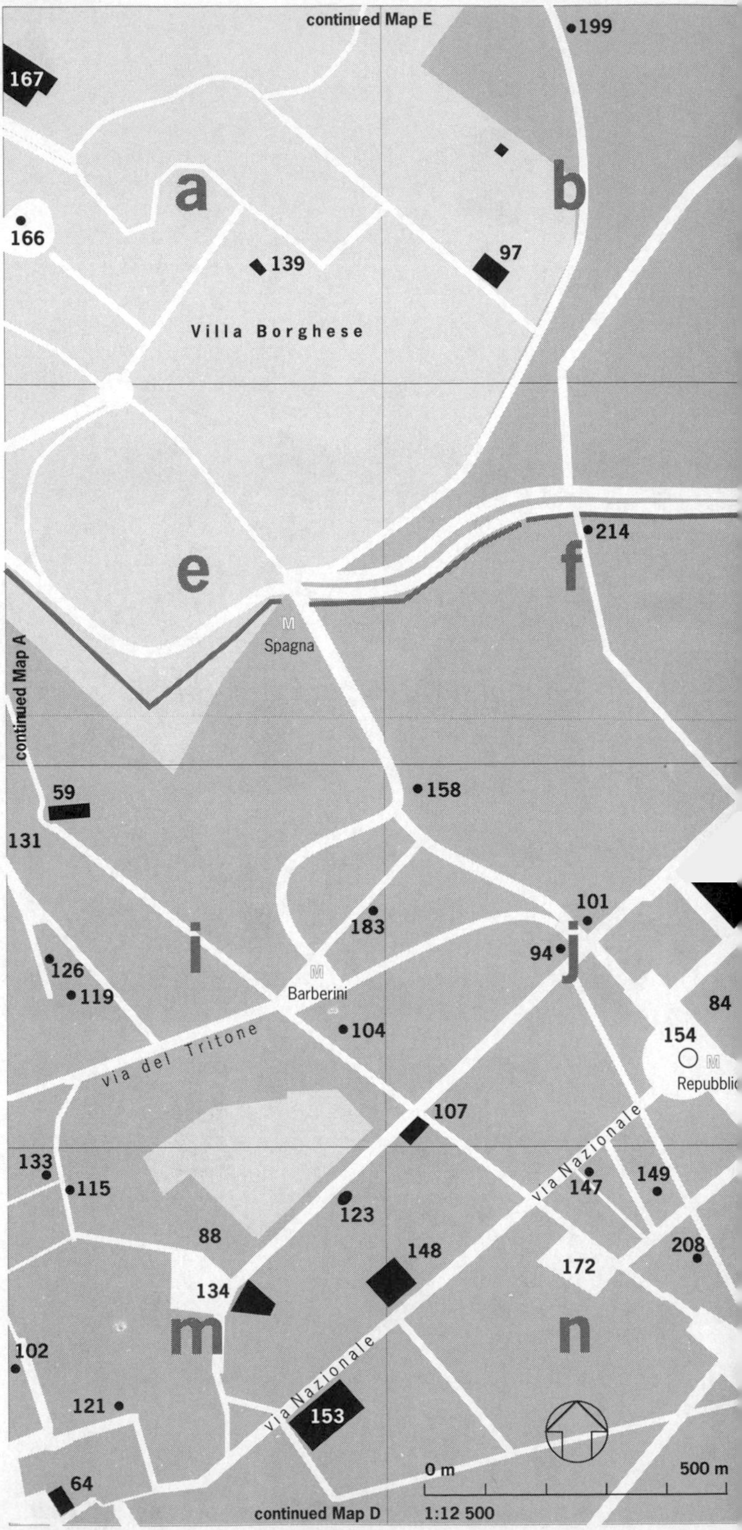

142
78
150
137
162
169
19
152
105
124
70
87
55

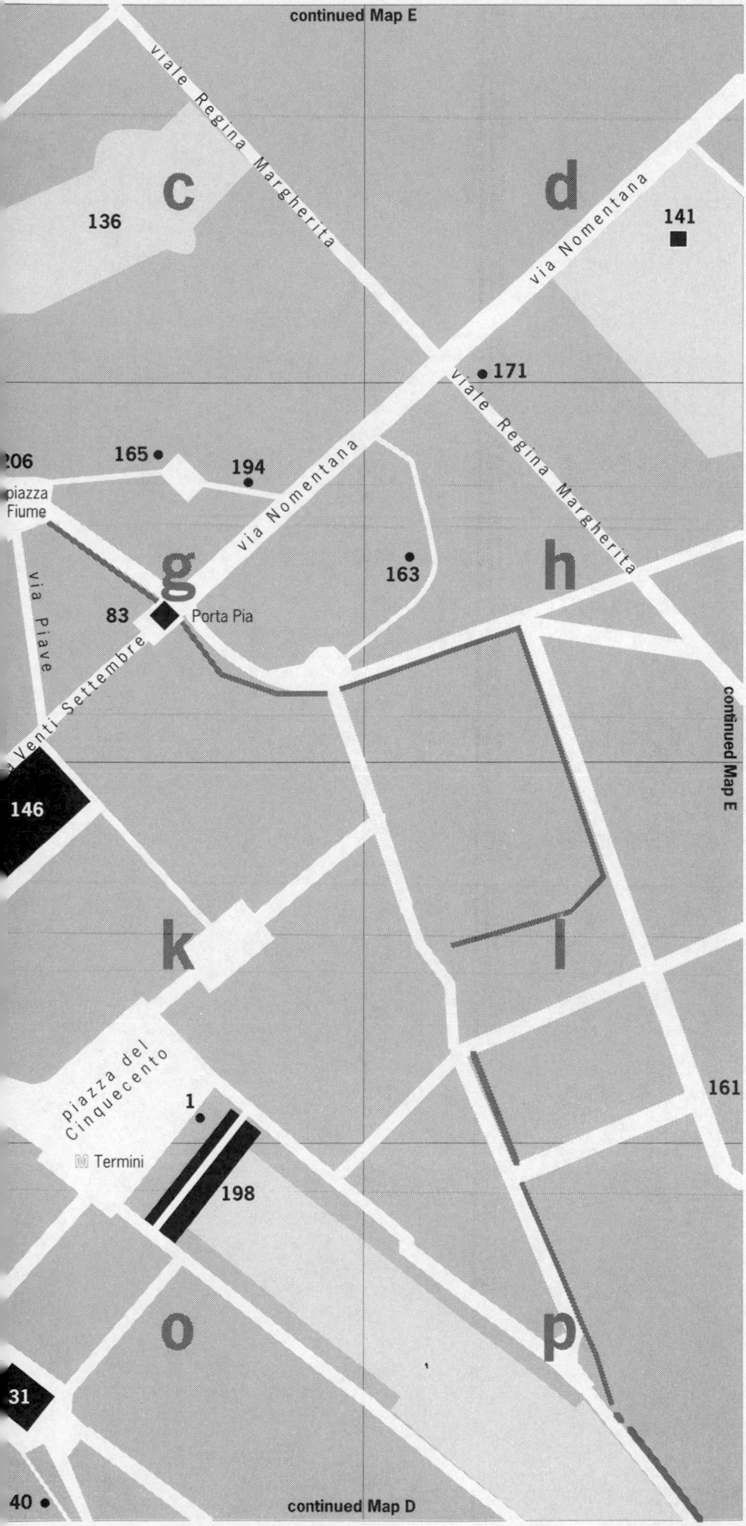

continued Map E

viale Regina Margherita

c

d

136

141

via Nomentana

171

206

165

194

piazza Fiume

g

h

163

83

Porta Pia

via Piave

via Venti Settembre

146

continued Map E

k

l

piazza del Cinquecento

1

Termini

161

198

o

p

31

40

continued Map D

Map C south west

continued Map B

a

b

Porta San Pancrazio

144

98

62

e

f

Villa Doria Pamphilii

continued Map E

i

j

Viale di Traste

m

n

0 m

500 m

1:12 500

continued Map E

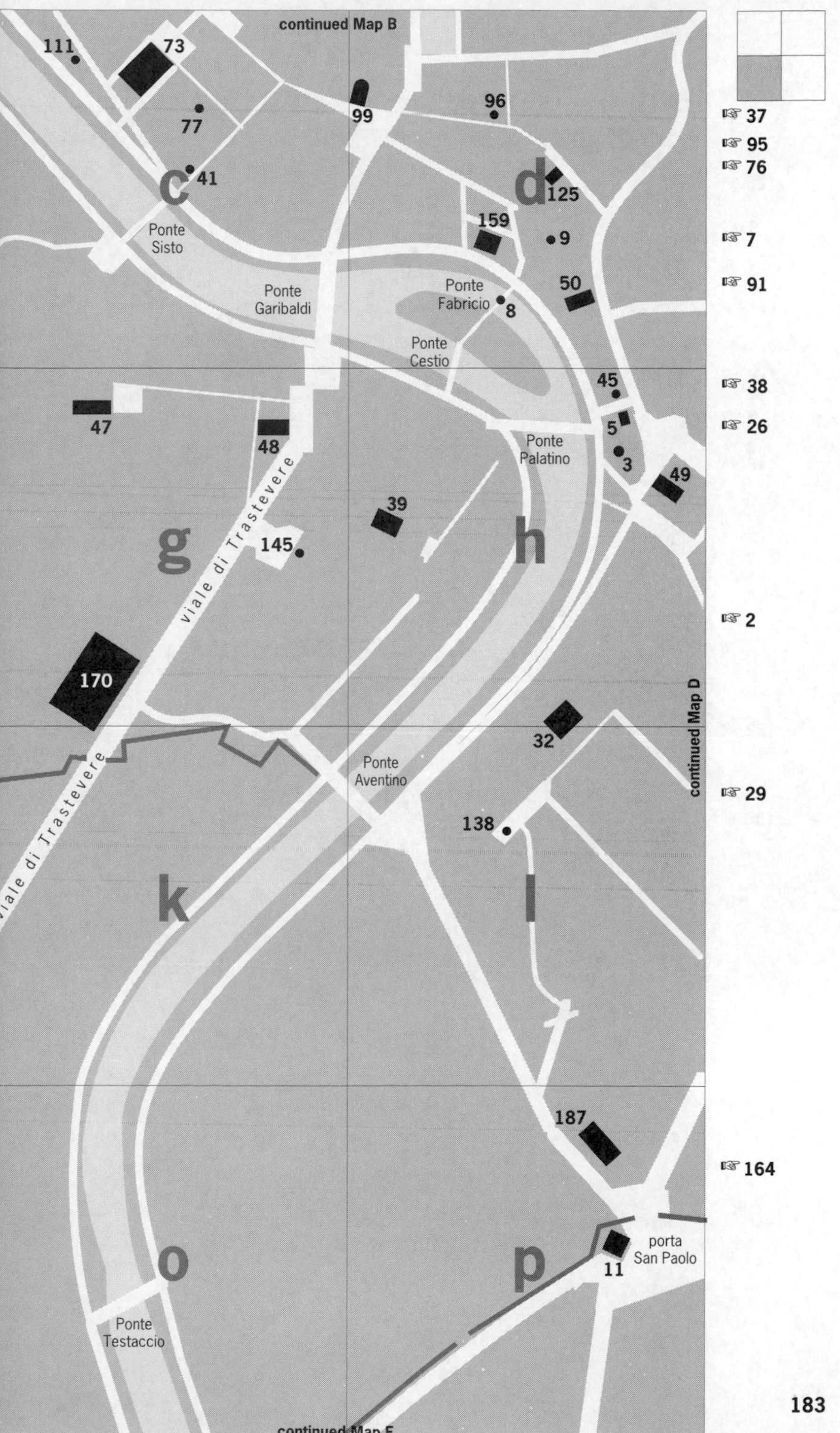
continued Map B
111
73
77
41
99
96
c
d
125
159
9
Ponte
Sisto
Ponte
Garibaldi
Ponte
Fabricio
8
50
Ponte
Cestio
45
47
48
5
3
Ponte
Palatino
49
viale di Trastevere
39
g
145
h
170
continued Map D
32
Ponte
Aventino
138
viale di Trastevere
k
l
187
porta
San Paolo
11
o
p
Ponte
Testaccio
continued Map E
☞ 37
☞ 95
☞ 76
☞ 7
☞ 91
☞ 38
☞ 26
☞ 2
☞ 29
☞ 164

Map D south east

continued Map B

155
14
90
via dei Monti
via Cavour
178
37
33
95
108
76
a
b
Foro Romano
7
35
91
23
51
85
via dei Fori Imperiali
via Labicana
13
38
Palatino
6
24
26
42
via Celimontana
via Claudia
viale di San Gregorio
e
f
44
2
via del Circo Massimo
106
34
continued Map C
via delle Terme di Caracalla
29
viale Aventino
i
j
20
164
viale Giotto
m
n
Porta Ardeatin

0 m 500 m
1:12 500

continued Map E

125
9
50
45
5
3
49
32
138
187
11

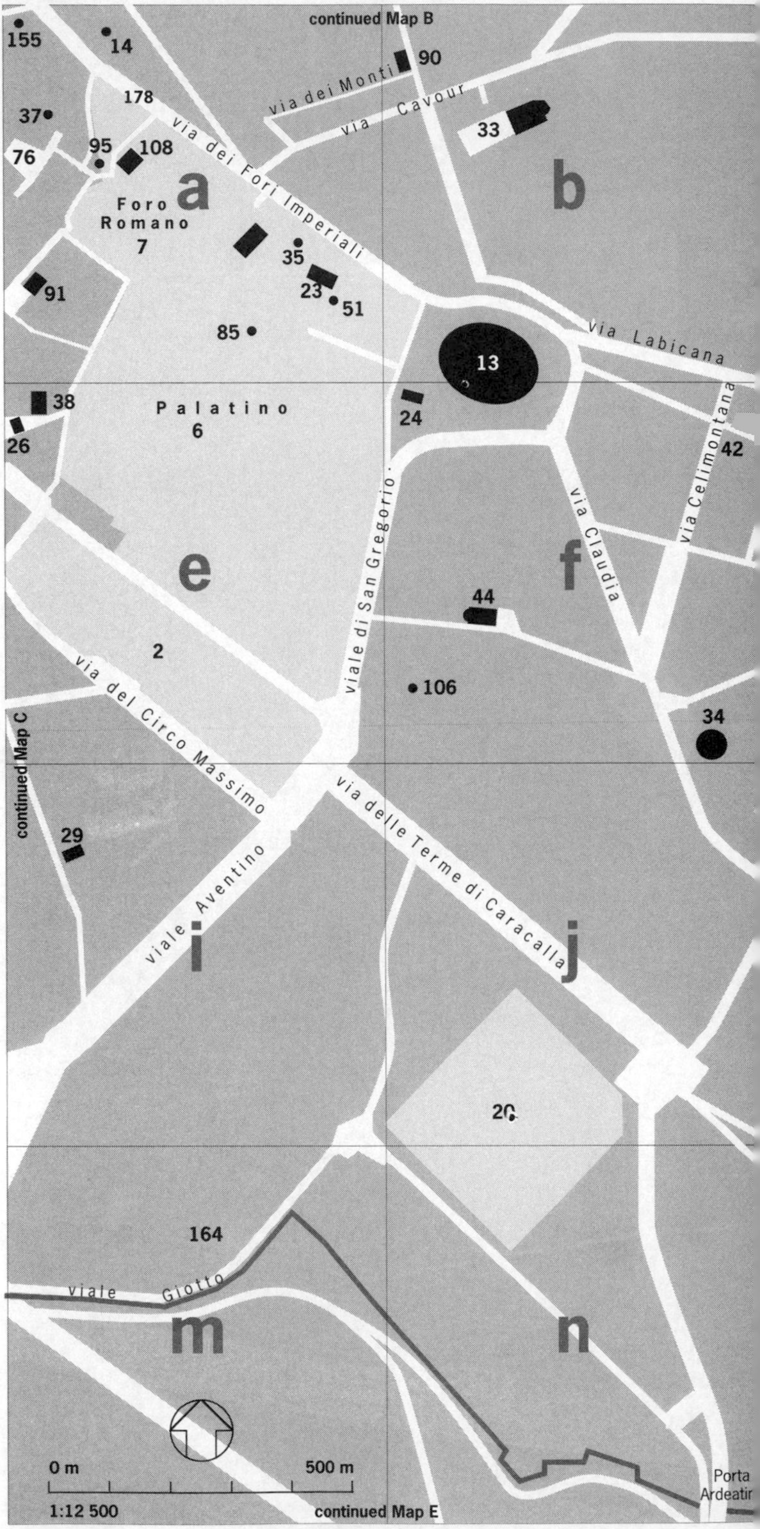

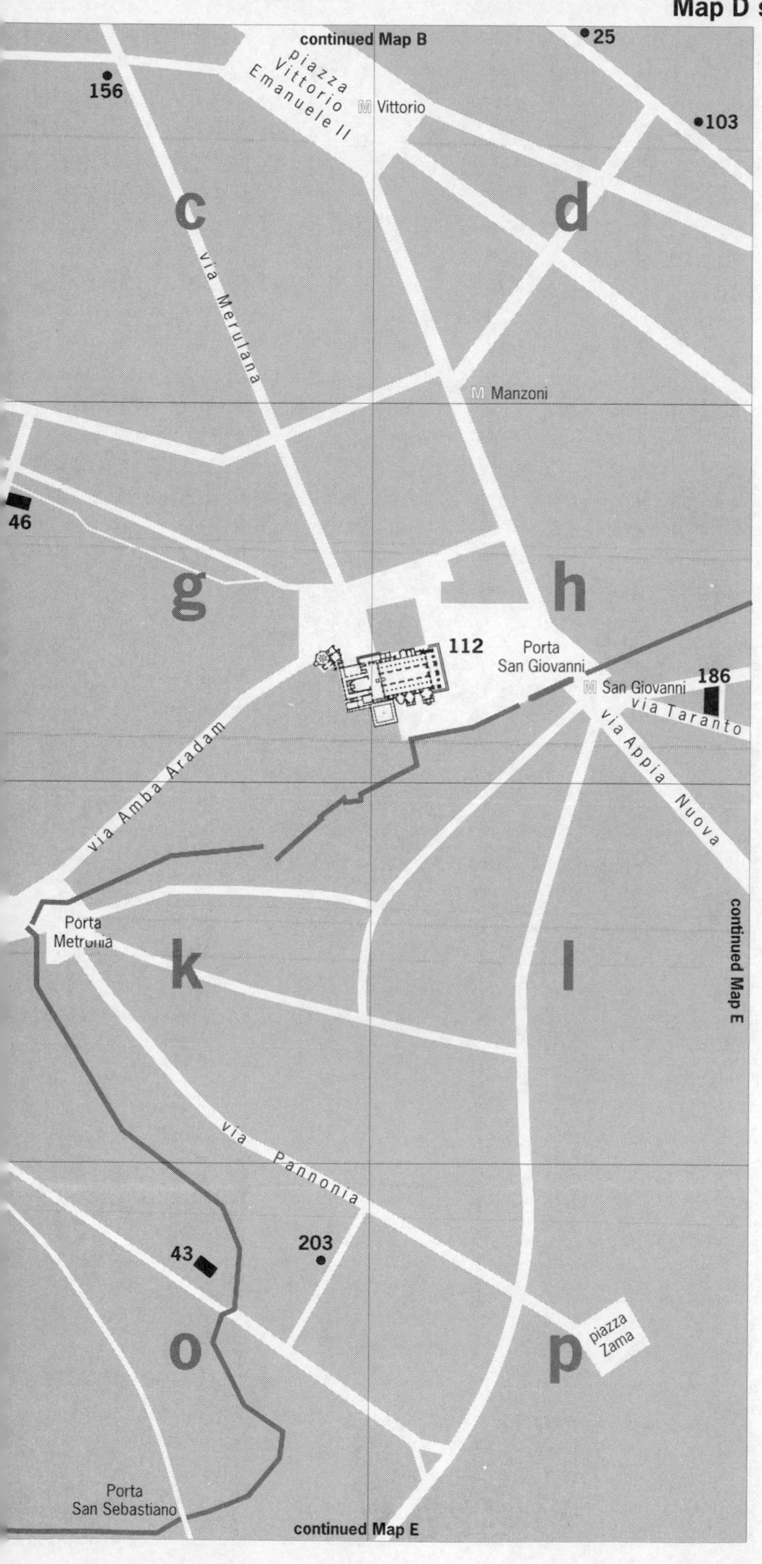
continued Map B
25
156
piazza
Vittorio
Emanuele II
M Vittorio
103
c
d
via Merulana
M Manzoni
46
g
h
112
Porta
San Giovanni
186
M San Giovanni
via Taranto
via Appia Nuova
via Amba Aradam
Porta
Metronia
k
l
continued Map E
via Pannonia
43
203
o
p
piazza
Zama
Porta
San Sebastiano
continued Map E

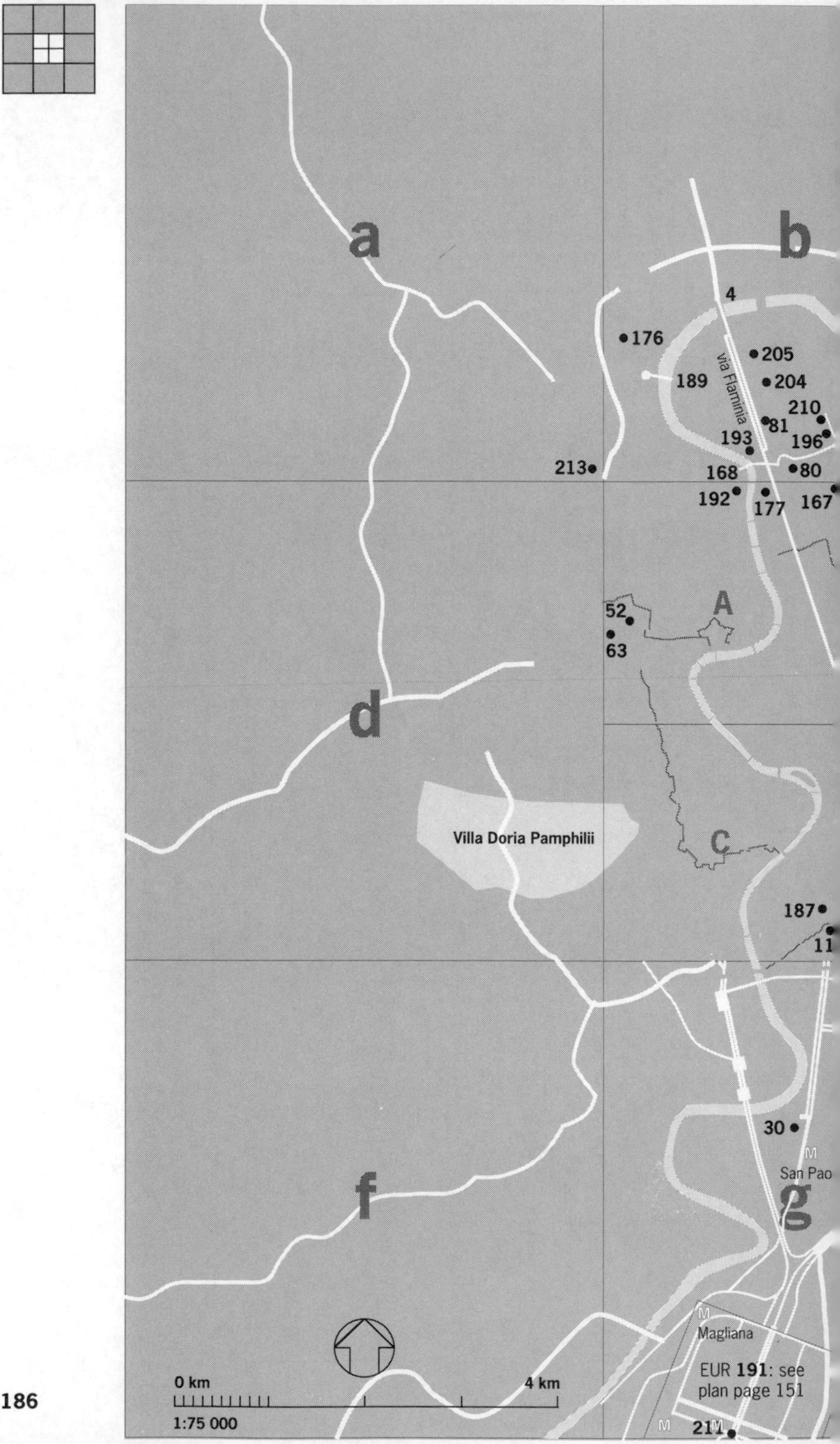

Map E outer Rome

a
b
4
176
205
189
via Flaminia
204
210
81
193
196
213
168
80
192
177
167
52
A
63
d
Villa Doria Pamphilii
c
187
11
30
M
San Pao
g
f
M
Magliana
EUR **191**: see plan page 151
0 km
4 km
1:75 000
M
211

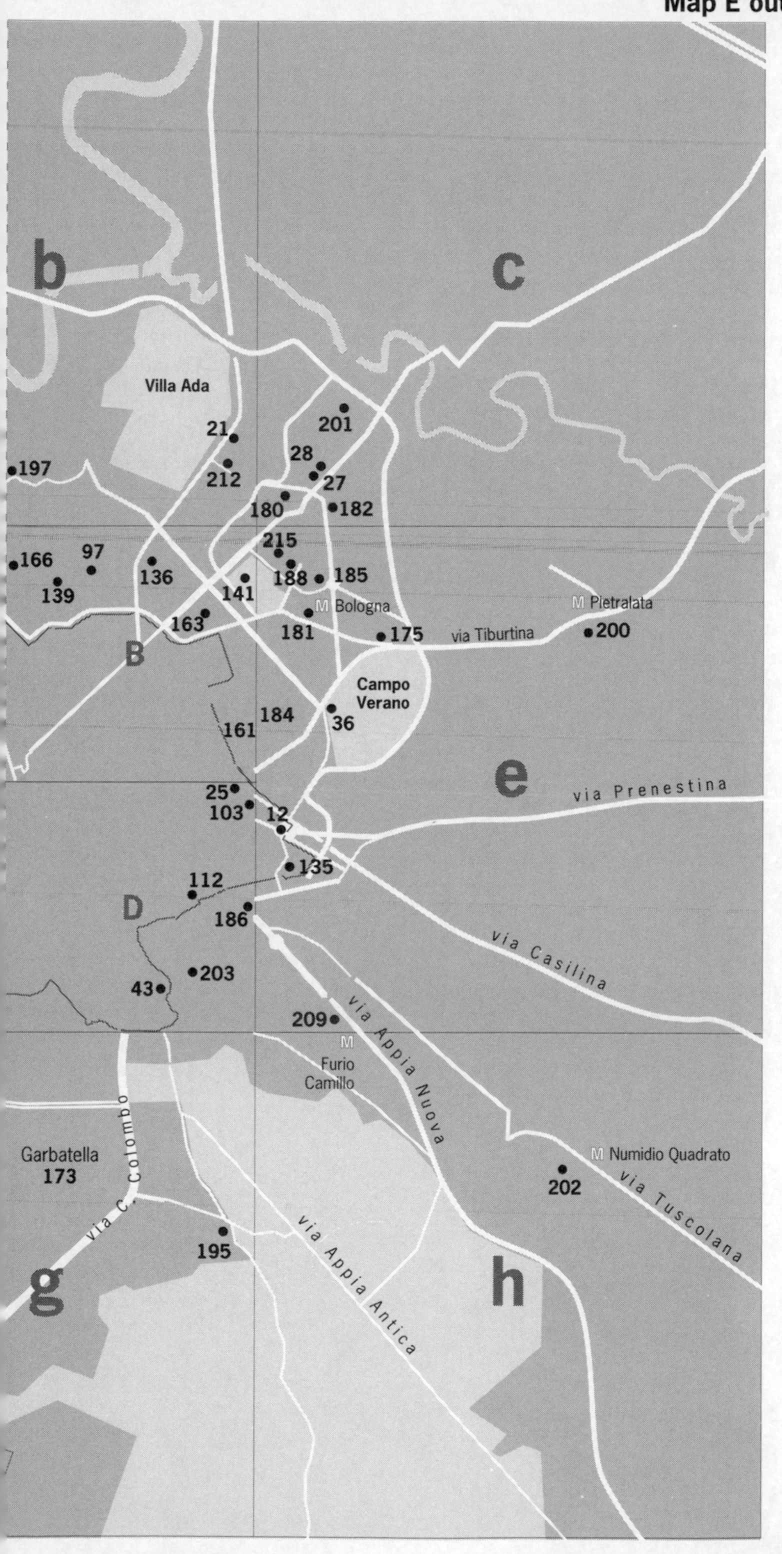
b
c
e
g
h
B
D
Villa Ada
21
212
197
201
28
27
180
182
215
188
185
166
97
139
136
141
163
Bologna
181
175
via Tiburtina
Pietralata
200
Campo Verano
184
161
36
25
103
12
135
112
186
203
43
209
via Prenestina
via Casilina
via Appia Nuova
Furio Camillo
Garbatella
173
via C. Colombo
Numidio Quadrato
202
via Tuscolana
195
via Appia Antica